Child C

Child C

Surviving a Foster Mother's
Reign of Terror

CHRISTOPHER SPRY

POCKET
BOOKS

LONDON • SYDNEY • NEW YORK • TORONTO

First published in Great Britain by Simon & Schuster UK Ltd, 2008
This edition first published by Pocket Books, 2008
An imprint of Simon & Schuster UK Ltd
A CBS COMPANY

This is a work of non-fiction as told to Andrew Holmes by Christopher Spry.
The names of some people and some details have been changed to protect the
privacy of others. The author has warranted that, except in such minor
respects not affecting the substantial detail of events, the contents
of this book are accurate.

3 5 7 9 10 8 6 4 2

Simon & Schuster UK Ltd
Africa House
64–78 Kingsway
London WC2B 6AH

www.simonsays.co.uk

Simon & Schuster Australia
Sydney

A CIP catalogue record for this book is available
from the British Library.

ISBN: 978-1-84739-189-6

Typeset in Bell by M Rules
Printed and bound in Great Britain by
CPI Cox & Wyman, Reading, RG1 8EX

I would like to dedicate this book to my Mum and Dad.
You did not give up hope of reaching us even when others did.
We've had highs and lows but you've always been there for us.
You have provided unconditional love and support.
Thank you.

Also to our family friends, Chris and Kayleigh
and their new-born son, Blake

Acknowledgements

In the last three years I've had to relearn a whole new way of living and surviving in an uncertain world. Here are just a few who have helped me in this task and to whom I would like to say thanks.

My brother, for being a good friend when I needed one. Both my foster sisters, who helped me through the worst times in my life. DC Victoria Martell – without her crazy amount of hard work, we would never have had justice. Haley, for being a good friend in and out of work, and pushing me when I needed it. My social workers of the past three years, but a huge thank you in particular to Andrew Frazer, who believed in me when others didn't. And Gordon, who in my opinion is simply a legend.

To all the foster families that tried to cope with me; without your help I would have never made it to court. Rob Reed and his partner for helping me when I was at my weakest and for being good, sound friends. Duncan and Jacky, for helping me and my brother in the early days. Erin Thomas, for being a good friend across the seas. All the Grapevine crew for their help over the years, and also a big shout out to the Gloucestershire Nightstop. Andrew Holmes for the help in making this book. And a very heartfelt thank you to Gill Kershaw – without her I would not be around to write this story

And the many others who have been a source of support, thank you to you all, the nameless and the named.

About This Book

In February 2007, Eunice Spry was sentenced at Bristol crown court to fourteen years in prison for subjecting three children in her care to horrifying physical and mental abuse over the course of two decades. The judge told the court it was the worst case of child abuse he had heard of in his long career.

What you are about to read is one child's account of what it is like to live in fear. Yet this brutality did not happen in a war zone, or in a distant past when people knew no better. These crimes occurred in Gloucestershire, in England, not far from the picturesque Cotswolds. Even in the most tranquil and ordinary of places it seems evil can find a home.

Christopher Spry is now nineteen years old. Although he lives in constant pain from the injuries inflicted on him by Spry, he is courageously rebuilding his life, looking to the future and proud to be a survivor. This is his story.

Prologue

'Do not withhold discipline from your children,' shouted Mother. 'If you beat them with a rod, they will not die.'

Facing the wall I screwed up my eyes, knowing what was to come and hearing the evil *swish* of the bamboo. Then screaming as it tore fresh agony into my back. Again the swish, again the blinding pain across my back as I stood in the gloom of the sitting room, receiving my punishment. At the window a sheet was up. Across the floor was strewn rubbish: plastic Safeway carrier bags spilling clothes onto the carpet, dog-eared boxes full of disused toys, old rugs, discarded kitchen appliances fit only for the bin . . .

'He who spares the rod hates his son,' she screamed. 'But he who loves him is careful to discipline him.'

The cane scalded my back. Once more I yelled in pain, screaming, 'No, please, no,' twisting away, feeling her pull me back, her hand steadying me at the wall. Then another stroke across the back, then another. My hands were against the wall, nails digging into the wallpaper. *Swish. Swish.*

'I'm sorry, Mother,' I screamed. 'I'm sorry.'

I was sorry because I'd left a dead hen in the yard. It was my job to move the dead hens, I knew that. If a hen died you had to move it quickly because the rats could get to it and we had enough rats without encouraging more of them. It was my fault. All my fault I was being whipped.

'Demon child,' she shouted, and still the blows came.

'I'm sorry!' I screamed in return.

Sometimes she would say nothing during beatings and would deliver them with a calm, almost serene air. Other times, like now, she would scream and shout, say that she had to drive the demons out of me ready for the apocalypse and quote passages from the Bible. Always quoting. The same quotes I would hear again and again.

'Do not withhold discipline from your children,' she reminded me. 'If you beat them with a rod, they will not die.'

I felt something warm and wet slide below the waistband of my jeans. Blood or sweat, I wasn't sure. And I sank to my knees, my shirt in tatters at my back, able to stand the pain no longer.

The whipping continued for some time, until at last she stopped, breathing heavily from the exertion, dropped the cane and left the room. In agony, tears of pain streaming down my face, I remained on my knees alone in the dark and filthy sitting room. I would remain on my knees for my entire childhood.

This is the story of how I got to my feet.

List of five advantages of being brought up by my evil foster mother Eunice Spry

1. I am well mannered and polite
2. I do not swear
3. I don't spit either
4. I know how to behave in restaurants
5. I can differentiate between brands of washing-up liquid just from their taste

List of five disadvantages of being brought up by my evil foster mother Eunice Spry

1. I can differentiate between brands of washing-up liquid just from their taste
2. I rarely sleep, and when I do I have nightmares
3. I am in constant pain from an injury in my knee, from where she disciplined me with a cricket bat
4. I do not make friends easily
5. I can never have children of my own

Chapter One

*E*unice was my mother, and I called her Mother right up to the trial. I've only just stopped. Sometimes I still catch myself thinking of her that way. It's rare these days, though.

I hated the trial. I mean, of course I hated the trial, anyone would. But I hated it so much that I went to the bridge over Golden Valley – a dual carriageway connecting Gloucester and Cheltenham – and stood at the edge a couple of times, thinking about taking the one step that would send me plummeting to the road below.

I thought about throwing myself in front of a car, too, but that particular method of suicide is too much of a gamble. You might survive – which is not much use if you're trying to kill yourself – because the car needs to be doing almost exactly 73mph. Any faster and you run the risk of being bounced straight off the bonnet. Any slower and you might simply be dragged along the road. No way do you want that kind of pain.

On the other hand, I don't know – at the time anything felt preferable to the alternative: the guilt of giving evidence against Eunice – the horror of facing her across the court.

In the event I sat behind a curtain for my appearance, so we were screened off from one another. Still, though, our eyes met just as she was being led out, one tiny second as we both turned heads at the same time and clocked each other across the courtroom. There was nothing there, in her eyes. There never really was.

She'd pleaded not guilty; she told the court that the worst

punishment she ever gave us was a smack on the bottom. In the end, the court believed us: Children A, B and C, as we were for the duration of the trial, then for the media coverage afterwards.

Child C, that's me.

Child A is my foster sister Karen, who was fostered by Eunice a year or so before I was.

Child B is Lulu, my other foster sister, who is older than me by four years, and was fostered by Eunice at the same time I was. Of the three of us, she always knew something was up, Lulu did. She's that bit older than me and Karen, so I suppose she'd seen a life outside of Eunice that we never had. Lulu was the one who tried to tell the neighbours, who tried to run away. We used to get quite angry with her; used to say pull yourself together, come on, just get on with it.

Lulu knew, though. Over the years we kept a tally of the times we cried. Cries from pain didn't count; we're talking about emotional cries. Lulu was on thirty-one of them. Karen was on twenty-something. I was on three. I'm the lowest, the best.

We weren't the only children Eunice had fostered, us three. There was another girl, Charlotte, who was the eldest and who had been fostered from birth; plus my younger brother Bradley – my real younger brother. Like Charlotte he came into Eunice's care from birth, and like Charlotte he was never touched. Well, they were touched in the sense that they were cuddled and hugged and kissed and Eunice loved them. But they were never beaten with bamboo. They were never starved, or forced to drink washing-up liquid for stealing food. Instead, what Eunice did to them was hold them back and stop them from growing, keeping them in a permanent state of very early childhood. When Charlotte died, her bedroom at the farmhouse was in the process of being transformed into a pink grotto fit for a princess, a paradise for a little girl. But Charlotte wasn't a little girl when she died. She was seventeen.

And Eunice had done the same with Bradley, keeping him back, treating him like a baby. The attic floor of the farmhouse was Bradley's playroom and you couldn't move for the toys she'd bought him. Couldn't move. He lived in that room like a spoilt little child-king, ruling over an empire of countless Thomas the Tank Engine toys and radio-controlled cars. Throwing tantrums, getting us into trouble for upsetting him.

Directly below his playroom was the room where Karen and I were locked for a starvation punishment. We spent a month in there; the spoilt little child-king in his playroom upstairs, the princess painting her grotto pink.

But that makes me sound bitter, and I'm not. Not to Charlotte, because you shouldn't speak ill of the dead and, anyway, she was a child, same as all of us. And not to Bradley, because he's Bradley – Bradley my little brother – and I taught him all he knows about cars (and I know a *lot*, so he knows a lot), and, yes, sometimes he's a little bastard, but . . . he's Bradley.

Eunice had two other daughters, natural daughters, who were the product of her second marriage. The daughters were older, grown-up. There was Judith, and again I don't like to speak ill of the dead, but she helped with the abuse – at times as the torturer's apprentice. And there was also Rebekah, who never helped, but who saw things that tripped warning buzzers in her head and considered telling social services, but never did, probably because Eunice was her mother. She gave evidence at the trial, though, Rebekah did. We all helped send our mother to jail.

Which is where she is now. She was sentenced to fourteen years for twenty-six charges including child cruelty, assault, unlawful wounding and perverting the course of justice. The judge said it was the worst case of child abuse he'd ever encountered. What made it worse, he said, was Eunice in court; her face was unmoving, set in stone for the entire trial. Like I say, there was nothing there. Nothing at all.

And then I'm on *This Morning*. If you saw it, I was the one sitting with my back to you. The moment I started talking my trouser leg began to vibrate as people tried calling me. Lucky I'd set the mobile to vibrate, come to think of it. And then I'm on Sky News. And I'm talking to newspaper reporters. And everybody wants to know what I think of her now. Do I hate her? No, I say, she was my mother. Did I ever try fighting back, they want to know. Of course not, she was my mother. Why did I stay? they ask. Why did I stay for over a decade of torture and abuse?

Because Eunice was my mother.

Chapter Two

I was born in Cheltenham in 1988. December the 20th, to be precise, although I never celebrated my birthdays because Eunice was a Jehovah's Witness and her beliefs did not extend to birthdays and Christmases. I had a night out on my eighteenth, but that was less to do with being eighteen than being alive at that point. I celebrated my fourth, too, one of my very earliest memories – one of the few times I ever saw my natural parents when I was growing up.

I have a very vague memory of being with them, my natural parents. Well, not really a memory so much as an impression. I remember some stairs in their house, and climbing up them. I was about one and a half, I reckon, probably able to walk but still at that stage where it's quicker to climb stairs on all fours. And I can recall that they had no carpet on them, and that new carpet was due to be fitted.

My next memory is of being with Eunice at George Dowty Drive in Tewkesbury. Not an outstanding house, not from the outside anyway. Neither is the street itself much to look at; it's actually a cul-de-sac, part of the Northway estate, and it's named after Sir George Herbert Dowty, who lived in Cheltenham and who invented the first internally sprung aircraft wheel, as used on the Gloster Gladiator. Lovely aircraft.

Sir George Dowty died in 1975. It was around that time the Northway estate went up and George Dowty Drive was built. Eunice Spry lived at number 24 and was a council tenant there, eventually buying it from them. She had two daughters, both grown-up, and she fostered children in her three-bedroom, semi-detached, not-very-remarkable ex-council house. She fostered me.

It had a huge kitchen, the location of my second proper memory, which finds me sitting in a high chair in the kitchen in the evening. The door's open, so it's probably summer, and I can hear a dog barking outside, which would have been ours. Meg or Jet perhaps. We had a lot of dogs over the years. A lot of pets. Eunice was obsessed with them; she used to become fixated with one pet before losing interest then moving onto another one. Our menagerie grew as a result. We had a goose in the garden, plus a duck called Queenie, who had ducklings that I remember Eunice used to drive around in the car. And we had rabbits – lots of rabbits – plus cats, of course, as well as hamsters, gerbils and a snake called Sequin. And like I say, this was just a residential cul-de-sac. All those animals in the garden – the neighbours must have hated us.

On one side of us we had a Welsh couple; on the other side a family. The Welsh couple . . . I don't know what they thought of us. I think we used to infuriate them. The way we spoke to them. One of the many things Eunice was obsessed with was manners, and we had to address everybody by their surnames. 'Hello, Mr and Mrs Smith,' along those kind of lines. For some reason I have this memory that the Welsh couple hated that. Perhaps they thought we were taking the mick.

The Welsh couple lived on the other side of our semi, so we were joined to them. They never heard anything of the abuse, though, as far as I know. One of the weird things – well, the only weird thing – about the appearance of the house is that there was space left for a garage that was never filled. It meant that although the two houses were joined, there was only one room in each property that shared a wall. What I'm saying is, they never heard anything, and I believe that. The husband, Brett Young, later told Sky that there was no sign we were being abused; that we were always well dressed and clean and tidy, and he was right, we were always clean and tidy. Always polite and on our best behaviour. We were well-brought-up children.

On the other side of us was a family, and there was a bit of rivalry there but we didn't see much of them because there was an alleyway separating our two houses, with a fence that burned down one time. Somebody thought it would be funny to creosote it, then set light to it, and I guess it was sort of funny. Suddenly the dog was barking, we looked out of the window and the garden was on fire. Someone – I think it was Charlotte – dialled 999 and the fire brigade and police came. Eunice wouldn't bring them in. The house was filthy and Lulu had a large gash on her arm that Eunice didn't want them to see. The gash was from where Eunice had attacked her with a stick that had a nail in it. Of course, Lulu had moved, so the nail had opened her arm up. Obviously, Eunice didn't want anybody seeing that. So she dealt with the police in the car and sent them on their way.

Sorry, I'm getting ahead of myself. Because before all of that – before life at George Dowty Drive and the fence burning down and the beatings, was how Eunice took me and my younger brother away from our natural parents.

Chapter Three

Good fortune is not something that ever lingered long at my natural parents' house. It's almost as though Eunice knew that; as though she exploited that fact to take away children who didn't belong to her.

It all happened when I was very young, of course – too young to remember – so to find out how I came to be in Eunice's care I have to ask them, my natural Mum and Dad. That's not a problem; I see a lot of them these days. We're making up for almost fifteen years of lost time.

Their names are Pete and Elaina. He's from Gloucester, born and bred; her family is originally from Malta, and you wouldn't miss them if you saw them in the street, they're a striking couple. Years and years ago Dad went to Glastonbury. This was in those days when it was all hippy convoys and free entry. You look at my Mum and Dad and you think, it figures, you can imagine them at Glastonbury. They dress and act like two people who grew up with idealism and watched it slowly fade. Mum with her fortune-teller clothes, her nails that she keeps painted in frankly weird colours. Dad with his long hair – at the time of writing it's jet black. No, you wouldn't miss them if you saw them in the street. They stand out and they stand for something – something a bit different.

The two of them have been through so much: illness for most of their lives, the pain of what happened to Bradley and me. But still, they carry themselves with a bearing, a pride. And they're funny, too. Dad, in particular, has never lost his sense of humour. He goes pretty serious when he talks about Eunice, though; Mum, too. When I ask her about what happened she looks down and frets with her painted fingernails, picking at her clothes. She rolls a cigarette and her hands shake. When she speaks it's with the dreamy West Country accent you get around the Cheltenham area. It's soft, comforting, the kind of voice you want to hear last thing at night, tucking you in. Dad reaches across and takes her hand.

And Mum talks.

She was abused as a child. Her own mother sold her to men from the age of nine. She spent her childhood in care and had sixteen foster mothers of her own. When I came along in 1988, the last thing she wanted for me was a lifetime of fostering and abuse. The last thing.

But fate has a way of confounding even the biggest wishes, and Mum became ill. She needed a gallstone removing, which meant she had to go into hospital, so therefore had childcare problems. My Dad, at that time, wasn't capable of helping, so the only other option for my Mum was to ask her own mother to help out. Rather than do that, she called Social Services, who found Eunice Spry.

Eunice and Gloucestershire Social Services were already old friends by then. Eunice first applied to become a childminder in 1979, but they turned her down because of 'unspecified concerns'. This was according to a paper later published, the Executive Summary, which you can probably still find on the Internet. Whatever those unspecified concerns were, they were subsequently lifted and Eunice got the green light to become a childminder. Next, she applied to become a foster carer and was at first declined 'as it was felt her lifestyle was not conducive to her being a foster parent'. Those objections were removed, though, and she became a fully fledged foster parent, able to help out mums in their hour of need.

Or, in our case, our three months of need, because that was how long Mum was originally in hospital.

Mum came out, lighter by one gallstone, and life as a family resumed. There were outings and visits to the cinema, and it was after one such trip that Mum was struck down with meningitis. And everything changed. Everything. For a start, Mum went back into hospital, and it was no short-term tenancy this time, she was in for the duration. For a long time she was in intensive care, her condition critical, and my father was told she wouldn't make it, not to hold out hope. He set up camp in the hospital so he could be at her side twenty-four hours a day. At nights he fell asleep by her hospital bed, holding her hand in his.

There was a complication. The doctors attempted a lumbar puncture, a procedure where a needle is inserted into the spine in order to collect a sample of cerebrospinal fluid – very common in cases of suspected meningitis. She describes herself as a 'bigger lady', my Mum, and as a result doctors had problems inserting the needle. In the end, they had to go in eight times, the last time so hard that the needle snapped. The resulting operation to remove the snapped part of the needle left her with severed nerves in the spine, which left her facing the rest of her life in a wheelchair, able only to walk very short distances. Mum would eventually spend eighteen months in hospital.

I was very young then, only just walking. Plus, I was – as my parents are nowadays fond of telling me – a 'boisterous' little boy. When I went to a foster family during mum's hospital stay, I was apparently so boisterous that I broke the leg of the family's pet dog, tried to ride on its back, giddy-up horsey, that kind of thing. Wherever that family is now, I'm so, so sorry. You have no idea.

And then my Mum's mother bumped into Eunice's daughter Judith in town. One of those chance meetings, just, 'Oh, hello.' It was in Tesco, or Sainsbury's – somewhere like that, somewhere mundane. My grandmother had remembered Eunice from before, when she had helped out during the gallstone operation. Mum had been wondering about her, too, what with things going so badly with our present carers, the dog incident, the fighting.

So that day in the supermarket my grandmother asked Judith whether Eunice still fostered.

Yes, said Judith, Mum still fosters. Why?

Chapter Four

Soon after that, my Mum had a visitor in hospital.

Eunice Spry, then in her mid-forties, had been married twice. The first time to a Frank Phillips, with whom she had two kids, Judith and Rebekah; the second time to Jack Spry. She was already a foster mum, having privately fostered Charlotte from birth in 1984, then two years later Karen and, recently, Lulu. Plus, of course, Mum and Dad knew her. They trusted her.

She came with gifts for the kids: for me and Mum's newborn, Bradley, who had been born in hospital. And by that I mean while Mum was in hospital still recovering from meningitis. It never rains, it pours – Mum had been five months pregnant with Bradley when the meningitis struck. She went into the delivery room five times – Bradley was ready to be delivered, then not – and each time the procedure was postponed. She was at her wits' end. Coping with that, and her illness, worrying about the kids . . .

But here comes this lady, this Eunice, this full-time foster mum. She has presents for the children. She fusses around Mum, a word or two to the nurses – she hints that she used to be a nurse, in fact – full of advice, gently chiding, taking control – almost a maternal figure to my Mum, who, more than anything, needed just that in her life. Someone to look after her, someone to tell her that things were going to turn out fine. Eunice came at exactly the right time, an absolute godsend who offered to look after us kids; who promised that we would be cared for until Mum was well enough to have us back. Mum said yes, and the beleaguered foster parents and their hobbling pets breathed a sigh of relief as I waved goodbye and left for Tewkesbury.

By early 1993, via a private fostering arrangement, Bradley and I were living with Eunice at George Dowty Drive, where we joined Charlotte, Lulu and Karen. Eunice's two natural daughters had left home by then, of course. Over the years they would be regular visitors and occasional residents, but they had to all intents and purposes flown the coop. Mostly, there was just us lot, a weird pick 'n' mix of personalities, but close in age – only two years between me and the three girls. No doubt we were all subconsciously competing for our new mother's affections; children do, don't they? There would be spoils for the winners in later years, and penalties for the losers.

Meanwhile, luck still declined to visit my real Mum and Dad. My Mum would eventually spend what amounted to years in hospital. Mostly confined to a wheelchair, she would, variously, suffer from a recurrence of the meningitis, abscesses, diabetes and, perhaps inevitably, depression.

Also, guilt. Because as she lay in hospital, her kids were flourishing in the care of another woman. I'd taken up horse riding; endearingly, I had discovered an interest in clog dancing. I was also making a special book for Mum. Eunice collected all of Mum's photographs and her videos too – all for this special present I was planning. Mum was touched beyond belief, especially as I'd never mentioned anything about the book during our weekend visits.

And there were, at first, visits. Regular visits. We used to have parties. The conflict over Eunice's religious beliefs versus my parents' . . . well, *lack* of religious beliefs had yet to surface, because I remember at least two birthday parties.

The first was one we had at my parents' house. I remember it being a good day, in fact, a great day. I remember there were fairy lights up, and we had teacakes, and Dad had an Amstrad computer for playing video games. And that was it for me – I was on that computer for the rest of the day. Apparently they were trying to take birthday pictures but they couldn't drag me away. I'd just fallen in love. That Amstrad. Wow.

Then, another party, this time for my fourth birthday – and this one was held in the grounds of a hospital where Mum was convalescing at the time. They'd hired a hot-air balloon, the idea being that I'd go up in one, but it turned out that I was too young (the old luck working its magic again). But hey, we made the best of it, and instead I was allowed to run actually into the balloon. I remember running inside as it billowed around me, feeling tiny but protected inside its huge, warm canopy. It would have been December, so I guess the weather wasn't great at the time, but in my mind, when I remember it, the sun is shining.

It's my last memory before the abuse started. The last memory of my childhood.

There were no more birthday parties after that. Eunice had begun to exert more control over my parents. Whatever word you want to use to describe my foster mother, impatient was not one of them. Over a period, not of weeks or months, but of years, she came to assume a position as the dominant personality in my family. She knew how to work my parents; she used guilt with the skill of a surgeon, wielded hope with scalpel precision. She exploited my Mum's feelings of inadequacy, of maternal anxiety, saying things like:

'Are you sure you should be using these nappies? They're bad for the children's skin. You should be using cotton nappies.'

And, 'Don't bathe the children that way.'

Don't do this, don't do that. 'Let me do it for you, dear.'

So the birthday parties stopped because, according to Eunice, celebrating one child's birthday is unfair on the other children. Instead, we would have 'party days', and we did actually have one or two, except they sort of tailed off as you'd expect when there's no fixed date to celebrate; or, as you'd expect with Eunice, who was gradually, slowly, carefully, removing us away from our natural parents. Get-together days were being kept to a minimum.

And the weekend visits began to decrease because, according to Eunice, that's when I took part in my activities. Except there were very few activities. There was certainly no book that I was apparently making as a present for Mum. Eunice had taken the photographs and videos because she wanted to cut me out of my mother's life. I wonder what happened to them.

My Mum and Dad would turn up for visits, picnics out, and Eunice wouldn't come. They'd phone and get an answering machine. What visits did take place were conducted either in neutral territory or at Eunice's parents' house; Eunice wouldn't have wanted my Mum and Dad to see the state of George Dowty Drive. When I did see them, Mum and Dad noticed a change in me. Before, I'd been loving, clingy almost. I used to hold my Dad's face with little fists, hold it still and stare into his eyes, scrunching up his cheeks at the same time – for a while they'd even worried I might be deaf because of it. Gradually though, over time, I pulled away and there was no more face-holding, no more clinginess. They noticed that I avoided him, took refuge with Eunice.

It was because she'd been telling me my father was evil.

My biological father. That was what I was told I could call Mum and Dad: my biological parents. I had a new mother now. Eunice was my mother. And she was telling me that my real parents were evil, and that they were drug addicts – *drug dealers*. She told me that we had been taken away from our real parents because they had been unclean with us. She offered to mend a black basque belonging to my mother but she never did; instead she used to flourish the basque before me: 'Look what a whore she is. Look what a whore your mother is. Only a whore would wear something like this.'

She changed my names. My given name – the name my parents wanted me to have – was Damon. But Eunice changed it to

Christopher. (She had done the same with Lulu, changing her name to Mary-Beth.)

Every time they visited, Eunice would be sitting close to me on the sofa. I would be telling Mum and Dad how happy I was, how well my language lessons were going. I was learning seven languages, according to Eunice; I would come out with words in Chinese. I was so happy, I'd say. I'd talk about the holidays I was going to go on, how I was being educated, how nice Eunice was.

But, of course, she was sitting so close so she could make sure I was saying the right thing to Mum and Dad. She was twisting my arm. Literally twisting my arm.

The visits continued to decrease. Sometimes Mum and Dad would only see us once a month. Eunice would use the same techniques on them that she'd end up using on us, techniques common to abusers. Guilt, exploiting feelings of inadequacy and the force of what a review board would later describe as her 'dominant personality'.

Mum and Dad would go to George Dowty Drive hoping to catch her out. But we weren't spending much time there because by this time Eunice had befriended George Parker, the owner of the farmhouse. We were at the farmhouse looking after Mr Parker, who, it turned out, was in the last months of his life.

When he died he left his farmhouse to Charlotte, my foster sister, the little girl he'd formed a bond with. In the will it went to Charlotte, but of course, as her legal guardian, it went to Eunice. Who effectively moved house. In fact, the first my parents would ever know of the farmhouse was years and years later, when we were reunited.

Meanwhile, Eunice was making even bigger plans. She applied for a residence order, which would effectively make her our legal guardian. Social Services had never objected to the private fostering arrangement – in fact, they'd arranged it – nor did they make any objections to the application for the residence order, despite concerns noted 'about potential long-term care of the children by

Mrs Spry, primarily because of her strong views and alternative approach to childcare'.

I love that. 'Alternative approach to childcare'.

So my Mum signed the residence order.

(At this point in her story, Mum's hands are shaking; Dad reaches over and takes her hand, squeezes it.)

Mum signed on the understanding that Eunice would have legal responsibility for the children until such time as my mother was well enough to have us back.

She did it on the understanding that it was for the best that her children stayed together, because Eunice told her that Social Services had been threatening to split us up.

She did it on the understanding that her children were receiving wonderful care and were being given opportunities we never could have had with our natural parents at that time. She was young, she was in poor health. She did what she thought was right.

She signed. And by the end of 1993, Eunice had legal responsibility for all five children – that's Charlotte, Karen, Lulu, Bradley and me – either through residence orders or adoption orders.

And the involvement of Social Services in our care simply stopped. We belonged to Eunice. She was Mother now.

Chapter Five

A fog came down the night Mother stepped over the red line. A thick, grey peasouper, it seemed to settle over the Northway estate, making houses fuzzy and indistinct, hiding us from our neighbours. When I went outside to give the hens some food, scattering seed on the patio and grass, I noticed how the mist seemed to come off my hands, as though my hands were smoking.

It was 7 October 1994. I was five years old, and it was about six or seven o'clock in the evening, the fog just coming down. The house was in turmoil, buzzing with the noise of children, all of us excited about the Mop Fair, which was that night (and that's how I know the exact date Mother crossed the red line, because it was that night), the Tewkesbury Mop Fair – one of the biggest nights of the year. It's massive, absolutely huge. It takes over the entire town centre. And they have great rides. The best rides on God's earth. A huge Ferris wheel that's lit up so you can see it for miles around, traditional carousels, merry-go-rounds and old traction engines; plus they have all the modern rides as well, everything a kid's heart desires. No wonder we were buzzing.

And then came the call:

'Christopher!'

Then, 'Christopher, Mary-Beth, Karen. Get in here. All of you!'

When Mother called we didn't hang around. There was a thundering on the stairs, a dash to the kitchen – our big, L-shaped kitchen – where we congregated in front of Mother, who stood by the table in the middle of the room.

On the table was the tin of chocolates. The lid was off. Inside it were the chocolates, gaudy wrappers twinkling at us.

The thing with these chocolates, this particular brand of them, is that there is a special red chocolate in the middle, the best chocolate, the queen of the tin. It's the one you save for a special occasion – for someone if they've been really good, for a favourite child.

'Who's taken it?'

We stood before her, wide-eyed, shrugging a collective 'not me', looking at our mother.

The press shots after the trial showed a lady in her sixties, wearing glasses and staring out of the page with a look that combined pride, self-righteousness and contempt. She looked so striking in those pictures. Almost iconic.

But it's not the Eunice I remember. Not Mother. Not the woman who stood before us in the kitchen on the day of the Tewkesbury Mop Fair. For a start, she wasn't wearing glasses that day. I remember that, clear as anything. No glasses. She was wearing jeans and her white fleece, a favourite white fleece. She wore it to death.

'Who took the chocolate?'

She has a strong West Country accent. Not soft like my real mother's, but harsh, demanding.

'Come on, who took it?' She stared at us, her eyes boring into us.

We said nothing, each of us thinking the other had taken it and now we were all going to cop for it. I was hoping it wouldn't be the slipper again. It hurt, the slipper.

'Upstairs.'

This was new. Still, we did as we were told. We trooped up the stairs and into Charlotte's room, stood in a little line in front of her bed.

The way it worked at George Dowty, and then later at the farmhouse, was that Charlotte had her own room. Mother and Bradley slept in another room – they always did right up until the end. And there was another room that was Judith's, which was empty most of the time because Judith travelled a lot with the folk music scene.

Which left a fourth bedroom, which was where Karen, Lulu and I slept – a tiny room with a single bunk bed. We always shared a room when we were with Mother, just one bunk bed in it, so one of us always had to sleep on the floor. And guess who always had to sleep on the floor?

At George Dowty, Charlotte's room was the biggest. She had a bunk bed but only used the bottom half; the top half had stuff piled on it, toys and things. And what a lot of stuff there was. She had everything in that room. Mother was always buying things for her. I remember a Panasonic radio – one of the best radios money can buy. As we lined up I looked at it, as always, coveting it.

Mother walked in holding a chair leg.

The police still have it, that chair leg. It had become detached from the chair because Meg the dog had attacked one of the kitchen chairs, and you didn't mess with Meg. Put it this way, if it was Meg versus Kitchen Chair you wouldn't want to bet on the kitchen chair. Sure enough, this particular chair had lost a leg.

It was dark brown. A big, thick thing. Mother's eyes were cold, I noticed. Downstairs, she'd been angry, getting ready to blow, but now it was like all the emotion had been drained out of her.

'Shoes and socks,' she said, indicating our feet.

We did as we were told, removing our shoes and socks, standing there barefoot in front of Charlotte's bed like three little soldiers ready for inspection. Downstairs, Charlotte was getting ready to go to the Mop Fair. She was probably sitting at the kitchen table eating chocolates.

I don't remember the exact order she hit us in, but I do recall that Karen was first. Mother brought the chair leg down on top of her feet, as hard as she could. There was a sound like a muffled slap, and Karen screamed. Then, a moment later, that same sound. And again. And again.

Then it was my turn. I'd hardly had time to register what was happening, heard the sound – that same hard *slap* – then agony. Pain like I'd never felt before. A whole new kind. To think I'd been dreading the slipper.

She did us one after the other, beating us across the tops of our feet with the chair leg. One, two, three. One, two, three.

She hit us across the feet because it's so painful, and because feet don't bruise, she said – something she'd learned during her time as a nurse. It was the kind of fact she was so proud of knowing.

We screamed, cried, we shouted and pleaded with her to stop. I went to the floor and she grabbed me by my clothes, hauling me up and holding me upright, hitting me again, all the time showing no emotion, for all the world like a lady thumping the dust from a living-room rug. One, two, three. One, two, three.

'Own up,' she said. 'Own up who did it.'

Eventually one of us did. Lulu, I think. It might even have been me. And if it was me, then I wasn't owning up because I'd taken the chocolate – I hadn't. I was owning up because I wanted the pain to stop.

Whoever it was, Mother didn't believe us. She accused us of lying. And that was something she always did, over the years. She'd beat you until you owned up and when you did she'd accuse you of lying – and then she'd beat you for lying.

All in all she hit us for around five minutes. At last we dropped to the floor and she didn't reach to drag us upright. She'd stopped.

She told us to put our shoes and socks back on and left the room.

That night we went to the Mop Fair. We still went. After the beating we got ready as before, but there was no anticipation or excitement now; the house was almost silent where before it had been alive with energy. We sniffed and snivelled quietly, our heads low, hardly able to absorb the shock and pain. I winced as I pulled shoes onto painful feet, stood gingerly and followed my family out to the Transit van. Karen was limping as she stepped onto the drive, I noticed. My own feet felt twice as big in my shoes, as though I were walking on someone else's feet. They felt wrong, swollen, tender as bruised fruit. Only, of course, without the bruises showing.

Around us were the houses of George Dowty Drive, beyond them the Northway estate, behind shrouds of fog their curtains were closed, the living-room lights on. We climbed into the van.

The fair was as we expected it to be – as we had hoped it would be when we were preparing for it earlier. Noise, lights, music, ringing bells, air-horns – and that huge Ferris wheel we'd all been looking forward to going on. All around us were kids running about, going on the rides, barely restrained by parents. The whole thing was a riot of noise, colour, life and fun.

Except not for me, Karen or Lulu.

Because being beaten wasn't enough. We would go to the Mop Fair, we were told, but only so we could see what we were missing.

We lived just around the corner from Eunice's mum and dad – or, Nanny and Granddad to us – so we dropped Bradley off with them then drove to the fair.

Arriving, we'd gravitated towards some fire-breathers in the middle of the fair, a strange unsettling sight, geysers of fire chasing away the mist which otherwise seemed undaunted by the noise and light of the famous Mop Fair.

'Come away,' snapped Mother, seeing where our attention was and pulling at my coat sleeve so hard that I almost stumbled.

She'd brought along a video camera, and she used it to record Charlotte as she went on her first ride of the evening: the waltzer. We stood by and watched, the three naughty children. Next, Charlotte was bought some candyfloss and, when she went on her second ride, I was told to hold it. She went on the magic mirrors and we stood and watched her. We trudged after her from ride to ride, Mother with her video camera, taping Charlotte and only pausing to turn and snap at us, 'Keep up, keep up.'

Keep up, keep up. That was what she said all night. Like weary, wounded soldiers we trudged after her and Charlotte, our feet burning, loaded down with her candyfloss, sweets and cuddly toys, Charlotte's booty constantly growing as she threw hoops, stuffed her hand in a prize-bucket full of sludge, and generally had the night of her life. I looked longingly at dodgems as we walked past – 'keep up, keep up' – and at a merry-go-round with small cars on tracks.

Mother saw me looking over at it – I was already obsessed with cars then; like most little boys are, I suppose. 'You could have been on that,' she said, 'if only you'd have owned up.'

When Charlotte had finished having her fun we left the fair, went back home, got out of the Transit and went inside the house. Karen, Lulu and I were told to go to bed because Charlotte was going to have Marmite on toast, so we did. Hungry, we climbed the stairs, got into our pyjamas and went to bed, Karen and Lulu in the bunk bed, me on the floor, wrapped in my quilt. (And I always had just the quilt, no mattress; I rarely slept on one while growing up, and even now I sometimes climb out of bed to sleep on the floor, through force of habit.)

There was silence in our room, just the sound of the telly from downstairs, Charlotte watching it, enjoying her Marmite on toast. I lay there, feeling . . . shock, I suppose. A feeling of awakening to a new and unpleasant reality. What had happened – the beating – was so far out of my realm of experience up until then, but it was obvious that this was the way things should be. This was all a part of getting older.

There was a song we used to sing, the Alleycat song from *The Aristocats*, called 'Ev'rybody Wants to Be a Cat', and Karen sang it now, a little voice in the darkness, breaking the silence in the room. Very quietly, so as not to be heard, she sang a couple of lines and I let the song soothe me a little, smiling in the darkness when Lulu joined in, her voice a hush, so that it was almost as if they were whispering the song. I joined in on the fourth or fifth line, and

together we sang the chorus, then the next verse, until one of us
blew a raspberry and we collapsed into hushed giggles.

There was a silence.

'I'm going to run away,' Lulu said, after a moment or so.

'Shh,' hissed Karen.

'I am,' whispered Lulu. 'I'm going to run away and meet new
people.'

'Stop it,' hissed Karen, insisting, 'You'll get us into even more
trouble.'

Perhaps she knew it was only the beginning and that there was
so much worse yet to come, that there would be many other nights
of lying together in the dark, comparing battle wounds, telling
each other, Pull yourself together, you'll get us all in trouble.

Charlotte went again, on the second night of the fair. But we
weren't made to watch that time. Instead, we had to stand out in
the garden. We could hear the fair from where we were, two or
three miles away. A warm October night, it was, not too bad really.
After that, the punishment ended – that one did at least. A couple
of days later she put me on starvation for the first time, when I
went a day without food, my stomach in outrage from about 11
a.m. onwards. The next time it was two days. After that it was
simply a regular fact of life. I would be hungry for the next five
years.

Was it a shock? Did I feel that she'd crossed some threshold? I
don't know. Before then, there had been punishments, don't get me
wrong. She never made any secret of the fact that she was a strict
disciplinarian. But it was really only the odd smack over the knee
when I'd been naughty – nothing unusual. The worst weapon she
ever used was the slipper.

But then again, I'm talking about me. Because after Eunice was
sent to jail there were reports in all the papers; there were editor-
ials of the 'How could this be allowed to happen?' and 'How could
this have gone on for so long?' variety. Going through them –
because I did, avidly – the same incidents of abuse appeared in

them all – sticks, sandpaper, bleach – plus there were reports of punishments that took place either when I wasn't around or before I can really remember. Like the note Mother pinned on Karen's back at a Jehovah's Witness meeting, a note that said: 'This child is evil. Do not look at her or talk to her. She wets the bed and is an attention seeker.'

During the post-trial fallout there were letters about that very note in the local paper. A Jehovah's Witness wrote in expressing doubt that it had ever happened. In the next edition was a reply from someone who said it did happen. She knew it had happened, she wrote, because she'd seen it, and it had happened some time in the period before the day of the Tewkesbury Mop Fair in 1994. There were reports, too, of Mother seen squeezing Karen's arm, around the same time. So perhaps she'd already crossed the red line that day – just not with me. Maybe some part of me knew it was inevitable that one day she would.

People ask me now if there was anything that changed the day she crossed the line, anything to prompt the sudden escalation in violence. Were there drugs or alcohol involved, a sudden change in personal circumstances?

But she never took drugs – not that I saw anyway – and she hardly ever drank; she was too devout for that. There were her marriages, of course, but they were ancient history by the time I came on the scene. I was just five years old so perhaps there was something I missed, something that pushed her over the line and turned her into the sadist who tortured me for the next eleven years.

I don't know – maybe she was just really looking forward to that red chocolate.

But at least we had that bond in the beginning, Karen, Lulu and I. Later, as the beatings and starvation became a regular part of our life, Mother hated it that we had that – the kind of bond you'd expect between prisoners, I suppose – and she did her best to break it. There were times, for example, when we were being starved. We were starved a lot; it was probably the most regular punishment. If you're being starved you'll try and steal food, it's the only thing you can do if you haven't eaten for days. You'll steal it, you'll see a loaf of bread on the side, slices of bread spilling out, you'll reach out and grab a slice, stuff it hungrily into your mouth. What other choice do you have?

None. So we all did it when we were being starved.

But Mother used to count the slices of bread. She was obsessive about it. And one of the things she used to do, she'd call me into a room and confront me with the fact of the missing slice.

'Mary-Beth says you stole it. She says she saw you take it. Now are you going to own up?'

'No,' I'd say. Might have been me. Might not have been. Didn't matter. Not to her anyway.

'Are you telling me Mary-Beth's a liar? Is that what you're saying? Are you saying she's a liar? *Are* you?'

That was how she'd do it. How she'd create wars between us. And it worked. We'd get angry with each other – sometimes physically. I think Mother liked that. I think she got a buzz off it. There were other things she'd do, too. Much, much worse things.

So while I'd love to say that the three of us maintained that bond we first felt, it wouldn't be the truth, not really. I guess it was there, under the surface – because I loved my foster sisters and still do – but Mother did so much to pull us apart that in the end we simply became numb to each other's hurt. We'd compare battle wounds, but only in the same way other kids compare collections of football stickers. Instead, we ended up developing our own ways of dealing with what was happening to us. We had no other choice, because nobody else cared. Most kids go to their mother when they're hurt. Who do you go to when it's your mother doing the hurting?

Well, teachers, perhaps. But it was around that time that Mother took us out of school.

*

I do remember school, vaguely. I have one quite clear memory of being in primary school and singing. In class, this was. As in, when I was supposed to be listening. And being told to be quiet, please, Chris, there was a time and a place for singing and this wasn't it.

It was a big school. I recall being dropped off there each day by Granddad in his Nissan Sunny. The main building was an old church but, like a lot of schools, most of the classrooms were mobile homes. They have such a distinct smell, such a unique sound when loads of pairs of little feet come tramping in for lessons.

I spent roughly six months in that environment before I was removed for home schooling, along with Karen, Lulu and Charlotte. And this is something that Mother had every right to do; every parent has. Parents do it in order to provide something at home they feel isn't being given by the school. Or perhaps because of a bullying situation, which was what Mother alleged.

What had actually happened was that Lulu had gone to school with a bruise on her face and it had been noted by a teacher. There had also been incidents of Lulu taking snacks from other children's lunchboxes, because, even back then, one of Mother's favourite punishments was to make us go without food. As a result we rarely took it to school and, like I say, when you're starving hungry you'll get food any way you can, even if that means breaking into a classmate's Tupperware.

So teachers were asking questions. And Lulu was saying things that made teachers wonder about her home life – how stable it was. The alarm bells would take over a decade to start ringing, but this is one of those occasions where they almost began.

And when this came to Mother's attention, when the school got in touch, she responded by withdrawing Lulu from school, saying teachers and parents were ganging up on her, that she was being bullied. Next, I followed.

And that was it. One minute I was in school, with mobile classrooms, their comforting smell and reassuring sounds – the kind of sensations my childhood should have been filled with. The next I was at home every day. The residence order of late 1993 made Mother our legal parent. By the end of the following year, she was our tutor, too. The punishment beatings became daily. We were falling further and further away from normality.

Chapter Six

The house at George Dowty Drive quickly began to resemble I don't know what. Something you might need a biohazard suit for, anyway.

Imagine. There were five of us kids living there, full time, not even going to school. Plus Mother, plus the pets. And, as I've already said, we had loads and loads of pets. Mother was obsessed with them, and she'd have sudden phases of acquiring more and more. Geese, ducks, dogs, rabbits, gerbils, hamsters, a snake, a parrot. She'd go through periods of doting on one set of animals more than the other. Some would get driven around in the car, some of them were allowed in the house, and you can guess what used to happen; it's not like they were house-trained.

Then Mother had this mad spree of buying stuff. She'd buy books by the dozen, and toys. And there simply wasn't room for all the things she brought home, so it was just dumped around the house. To us, we were young and it was just toys and Mother's books. It was just normal to us, the mess and animal filth around. If anybody else could have seen it, though, they would have thought we lived in a bomb site, a zoo, a madhouse. In a way, I suppose, we did.

Like everything else, Mother went through phases with the house. For much of the time, she was messy; she'd just drop stuff on the floor until rooms became so cluttered the doors wouldn't even open. Other times, though, she'd get suddenly house-proud, and she'd want the place cleared up. That meant she'd organize one of her clean-up parties. She'd do it when things had got particularly bad – and at George Dowty that meant things had got very, very bad indeed: animal waste, books, toys, magazines, clothes, shoes, all of it strewn about the house. Cleaning it up wasn't just a five-minute job. So we'd get the overnight detail.

She'd tell us over dinner, a meal that was usually cooked by Karen. We'd sit eating it in the kitchen.

'Clean up the playroom tonight,' she'd say, and I'd feel something inside me sink, knowing it meant another night of no sleep. Because these cleaning parties didn't happen during the day. No, we had to wait. While Mother, Charlotte and Bradley were tucked up in bed, Karen, Lulu and I were downstairs, tidying up like little puppets that only come alive at night.

Most of the time we'd get the job finished by about four or five o'clock, then we'd crawl into our bedroom to get a few hours' sleep before Bradley woke up. Bradley usually woke up at 8 a.m., and it was our job to see to him, look after him, make his breakfast and see that he was entertained.

For a while he went through this phase of throwing himself down the stairs in the middle of the night. He'd get out of his cot, crawl to the stairs and hurl himself down, laughing as he tumbled. This, for Bradley, was great fun. For the rest of us, it meant that one of us – me, Karen or Lulu – had to stay up all night, to make sure Bradley didn't break his neck chucking himself down the stairs. This wasn't a punishment to do this, nor was the cleaning. These were just our duties.

And it meant that we were tired. All of the time. And because we were tired, we didn't respond to the home schooling.

I really do believe that towards the beginning of the home schooling, Mother wanted us to do well. For about five minutes, anyway. Both of her natural daughters, Judith and Rebekah, had done well at school; excelled, in fact. Mother was constantly telling us how clever they were. The first home-school session had dissolved, though, mainly down to the fact that we hid the pencils. The whole thing literally broke up.

There was the odd formal lesson after that, but any attempt at a routine quickly fell apart. We just weren't that kind of family. We were up half the night and the house looked like a pigsty.

Pretty soon there was no formal schooling at all. I was taught to read and write by my sisters. They showed me some basic maths, although I still struggle with that one. I learned a lot by reading the *Encyclopaedia Britannica*, which Mother had a full set of.

For me there was no school, no school friends, no scary teachers or smiling dinner ladies; no sports days or concerts with Mum and Dad come to watch. There was just my duties, and the punishments. School was the *Encyclopaedia Britannica*. Everything I learned, I learned from reading that.

Chapter Seven

*O*ne morning Mother woke us up early. We'd only been asleep an hour or so and my body was crying out to stay that way. I was on the floor as usual, and I stayed still, trying to make myself invisible, curling up as though I could make myself disappear, hoping for more sleep. Why did I keep hearing the word 'London' mentioned? It didn't matter. I didn't care. All I wanted to do was get some rest . . .

But no. I felt a kick or a nudge. Mother. That word London again. Some trip we were about to make. Still rubbing sleep from my eyes, I joined the others as we performed our usual morning ritual: getting Bradley ready, picking rabbit droppings up from the floor, squabbling, feeding the animals, then pouring ourselves into Judith's Nissan Prairie and driving off, the whole ragtag lot of us.

We were on our way to London. And it was exciting. Had I ever been before? I don't think so. I'd heard a lot about it, of course, but never been. And anyway, anything that gave me a day off from cleaning out animals and looking after Bradley had to be a good thing. A really good thing.

As if that wasn't enough of a treat, we were given sweets to eat on the journey. Mother handed out pick 'n' mix. You know the kind – the ones where you help yourself with little scoops, take a bulging bag to the checkout. There were chocolate sweets, little pink shrimps, strawberry jelly lips, sour sweets coated in sugar. We had huge, bulging bags of them.

Then we stopped off at McDonald's, burgers all round and

plenty of fizzy pop. Bradley and I had a litre of it each. Back on the road and we hit the outskirts of London. We were high as kites by then. Full of sugar and caffeine, a car full of hyperactive kids.

Except for Karen, for some reason. I'm not sure if we noticed at the time, but Karen wasn't offered any sweets. She didn't have a burger, either.

But did we care at all that our sister was missing out on the treats? Probably not. As I say, Bradley, Lulu and I were all over the shop.

Which, of course, is just how Mother wanted us. We parked the car in a suburb – I can't remember where now. From there, we took the Tube into the centre of London, still gripping our super-size cups of fizzy pop from McDonald's, still munching on pick 'n' mix. First time on the Tube. Complete sensory overload to go with our sugar high.

'Act happy, act hyper,' she told us on the way.

No acting involved. We were bouncing off the walls of the doctor's surgery when we eventually got inside.

What it was, she needed a diagnosis. She needed a doctor to say we were suffering from ADHD, which is attention deficit hyperactivity disorder, so she could give us methylphenidate, which is the drug you use to treat hyperactivity, more commonly known by one of the market-leading brand names: Ritalin.

Methylphenidate is a mild stimulant that works on the central nervous system. It calms you down, stops you being impulsive and aids with concentration. In addition, it combats drowsiness and eases the symptoms of fatigue. Users say that it helps them get on with their work, helps them focus, keeps out distractions. Sounds creepy when you put it like that, as though the drug creates some sort of super-efficient robot person.

And maybe it is. Maybe it is creepy. Because some parents have said that it turned their children into zombies. Indeed, one of the side effects of the drug is a reported 'loss in awareness of self', a tendency to 'zone out', and sometimes even depression.

Mother was obsessed with control, that was her thing; she was absolutely obsessed with it. Looking at what it does, methylphenidate was her kind of drug.

She later told us that the diagnosis had cost her £2,000. And last time I looked, pick 'n' mix just isn't that pricey. As far as I know, she paid the London doctor to say we had ADHD, and with that diagnosis she was able to get regular prescriptions for methylphenidate locally. From that day on, Bradley, Lulu and I took it regularly. You're supposed to have holidays from it, so your body can recover, but we never did. I first started taking it at the age of seven; I was eighteen when I came off it, after we'd been released from Mother. And I'm not hyperactive, never was as far as I know. I don't have ADHD. Never have.

Sometimes I refused to take the pills. When that happened, she would ring other Jehovah's Witnesses who would come round to persuade me I needed my medication. I'd feel so stupid having some guy following me around saying, 'Come on, Chris, take your pill, be a good boy,' that in the end I'd just take them. It was one of her weird little tricks, getting other people involved in the medication. For virtually every other wrongdoing I'd be beaten, or starved, or worse, but for not taking the pills, she'd call in the cavalry. It was as though by doing it she could be saying to the outside world, 'Look. Just look what I have to put up with.' The Jehovah's Witnesses who came to do their bit were none the wiser. They probably thought Mother was a saint to put up with me.

We soon realized that if you take too many pills, it had an effect – one that I've since read is like cocaine. So on the tidy-up nights we'd overdose to keep us awake, downstairs at 3 a.m., tidying up and hardly even realizing we were off our little heads – just grateful not to feel like dropping dead of exhaustion.

Except for Karen, who never took it. All the same, she was prescribed it at the same appointment where Bradley, Lulu and I were diagnosed with ADHD. While we were on the ceiling, working off a Pepsi high and following Mother's commands to 'act hyper' to the letter, Karen was on a different mission. She'd been told by Mother to 'act dumb', and this she did by refusing to speak, not making eye contact and staring vacantly around the room. Again, Mother got the diagnosis she was looking for. Karen was diagnosed with Asperger's syndrome, which is a type of autism. Symptoms include poor communication skills and repetitive behaviour among other things although, unlike other forms of autism, non-social aspects of an individual's life are rarely impaired. The treatment for it includes social-skills training and Cognitive Behavioural Therapy, occupational and physical therapy and speech therapy. She never got any of this, of course. In all fairness she didn't need it. Karen has not got Asperger's syndrome and never had it.

Why was she diagnosed with that, and us with ADHD? All I can say is that carers who foster children with special needs are recompensed, and perhaps it's possible to make that system work for you if you play it, and there was never anybody better at playing the system than Eunice.

Medication for Asperger's syndrome is the same as for ADHD – methylphenidate – so Karen was prescribed that, too. She was always calmer than the rest of us, though. Lulu was the rebellious one, Bradley the little rascal, and I was . . . oh, I don't know, I was away with the fairies. But Karen was the most normal, almost the mother. So she never, to my knowledge, took a single pill for ADHD. Instead, her pills were saved, in a box that we called the Armageddon Box.

List of five things my evil foster mother Eunice Spry was obsessed with

1. Gazebos
2. Control
3. Torture
4. The Safeway cafeteria
5. The imminent Armageddon

Chapter Eight

Mother liked to think of herself as a devout Jehovah's Witness, and I suppose she was – in the sense that we attended the Kingdom Hall on a regular basis and she was able to quote huge passages from the scriptures. I'm not sure God would have approved of her parenting, though. I'm not sure He advocates forcing children to watch Freddy Krueger movies at four in the morning. I don't know – maybe He does.

Either way, she certainly considered herself devout and we did have periods when we'd go to the Kingdom Hall two, maybe three times a week. Other times we'd just go to the Sunday meetings. It all depended what mood she was in.

One thing most people know about Jehovah's Witnesses is that they come to your door, and we were supposed to do that, too – although we actually only did it once. I remember that well. It was me, Karen and a Witness who I won't name, because she's one of the few Witnesses I ever heard swear, so she wouldn't thank me for it. She did it when a lady opened a top-floor window of her house and emptied a bucket of water over our heads. Three wet Witnesses wandered home that day, one of them making her feelings known in no uncertain terms. Karen and I were unsure whether we were more shocked at being drenched, or hearing our chaperone let out a string of swear words.

The bucket-throwing lady wasn't in a minority with her dislike of Jehovah's Witnesses, though. Most people we visited closed the door in our faces. There were other times – just walking to the

Kingdom Hall, dressed in our smart clothes for meetings – that people would shout things at us in the street. 'Weirdos' was a favourite, with 'Freaks' another popular name to shout.

We didn't go preaching door to door again. Not because of the drenching, just because Mother didn't let us. She'd make excuses for us, blaming it on illness mainly.

So we didn't get to spread the word, which was always going to be a tough sell anyway. Jehovah's Witnesses have a great many ideologies that can appear at odds with the outside world, especially an outside world that's living in the 21st century. Mostly, these beliefs are very conservative. Witnesses believe homosexuality and premarital sex are sins, believe in dressing modestly, think abortion is murder and do not approve of gambling. They don't drink much and – this is a weird one – they won't clink glasses and say 'cheers', something to do with you toasting the devil. Since being released from Mother I'm no longer a Jehovah's Witness, so I can clink my glass whenever I want, and I do. Me and my Dad, when we go for a drink together, we make a point of doing it.

Another thing about Jehovah's Witnesses is that they don't celebrate birthdays or Christmases, believing them to be unchristian. And they take the word of the Bible very literally, leading to some controversial interpretations of the text, such as the ban on storing blood, which means blood transfusions are not allowed if you're a Witness.

They also believe that Armageddon is on its way. According to Witness beliefs, the 'last days' began in 1914 and the end is almost nigh. When it comes, false religion will be destroyed, governments will crumble and any who are not considered faithful in the eyes of Jehovah will be destroyed. Those who have been faithful get to survive Armageddon and will form a new society, an earthly paradise, while there will also be an unknown number of people who will be resurrected, and they'll be able to enjoy paradise too.

Mother was enthusiastic about most aspects of Witness teachings, but it was the Armageddon bit she liked the best. During the writing of this book in 2007 we were flooded in Gloucestershire, the worst floods for hundreds of years. You no doubt saw it on the news: massive tracts of land turned to flood plains. We were left without fresh water for days, Tewkesbury briefly became an island nation, the troops moved in to help distribute supplies and people squabbled over the distribution of bottled water in supermarket car parks.

As I say, I was writing this book during that period. But even if I hadn't been doing that my thoughts would still have gone to Eunice – the same way you might think of a friend when you see news of their football team on the TV, and you imagine their delight. With Mother it's not Arsenal but Armageddon that makes me think of her, and I pictured her there in prison, telling whoever would listen that the floods were the first sign of Armageddon. It was here at last. If you're reading this, Eunice, you did, didn't you?

Because that was her thing. Armageddon was on its way. Anything that happened on the news, any kind of major disaster, it was, 'Armageddon is here'. I remember the September 11th attacks not just for the devastating footage of the plane strikes on the Twin Towers, but for Mother, panicking, literally screaming at us that the Day of Judgment had arrived.

'Armageddon is here, children,' she was yelling. 'I told you it was true.'

Sometimes, when she was beating us, she'd tell us that she was disciplining us because we were possessed by demons and that beating us was the only way we'd be saved from the Armageddon. She claimed that God had a big book in which we were all judged, and that only if we behaved could we avoid being thrown into the big fire-pit of hell. (She was wrong, of course – living with her we were already in the big fire-pit of hell.)

Other times, she'd make us sit while she delivered one of her famous lectures. These would take place either in her bedroom or in the living room and they'd start without warning at about

9 p.m., finishing around three or four o'clock – up to eight hours of Mother telling us about the upcoming day of reckoning.

Bradley would be upstairs asleep, of course. It was Charlotte, Karen, Lulu and me who had to listen to the lectures. If any of us had to go to the toilet then the lecture would be put on hold until we returned. Charlotte would often nod off, but that wasn't a luxury afforded to Karen, Lulu or me. We had to stay awake for the entire talk.

Sometimes she would tell us about her dreams of Armageddon, how the dreams had told her it was on its way, how the wicked would perish and only the faithful would be saved. Who knows, maybe she kept us awake because she thought it applied more to us than Charlotte. Sometimes she'd vary the lecture a little, and she'd quote from scriptures – even ones not so concerned with the Armageddon. Or she'd tell us stories from her past. She liked to tell us about the times when she was a nurse; she enjoyed recounting stories of deaths that had occurred at the hospital. Sometimes, if we were really lucky, she'd tell us about the holiday she was planning for us. Our big holiday to Florida. She spoke about it all the time and often she'd use it as a threat: if we weren't good we wouldn't be going to Florida, that kind of thing.

Mainly, though, she lectured us about the Armageddon.

When she wasn't looking we'd pick at bits of fluff and muck from the carpet and flick them at each other. Sometimes she'd catch us doing it, stop, give us a look, a purse of the lips to let us know she wasn't happy, then carry on with the lecture. We'd hide our yawns behind hands, looking jealously across at Charlotte, who often slept with her head on Mother's lap.

We were never really clear on what form the Armageddon would take. Obviously it would change depending on current events. Nevertheless, she had a shotgun, just in case the Armageddon might take the shape of an invading ground force. In us, she had her mini army to offer a reply. We would take to the trees, she used to say. We'd have to push Granddad, who was in a wheelchair by now, to safety, hide him somewhere, then take up position out of sight, camouflaged by the landscape. She used to talk of how Jehovah's Witnesses went into hiding in 1940s Germany, and how the same thing could easily happen here, now, in 1990s Gloucestershire. If we had to go into hiding, Bradley would be the one to give us away – Bradley was incapable of remaining quiet for more than two seconds at a time. So she was making sure we had extra supplies of pills ready for the Armageddon, to subdue Bradley if necessary. Which was why all of Karen's pills went into the Armageddon Box. The box was eventually taken away by the police. Apparently the collected pills had a street value in the tens of thousands of pounds.

She had other ways of illustrating the Armageddon, too. I don't know if you've ever seen the horror film, *The Fly*. It's about a man who transforms into a housefly after an experiment goes wrong. First, his fingernails drop off. Then he has to eat by puking up his own digestive juice onto his food. Bits of his body begin to fall off and his flesh starts to mutate. At one point his jaw gets ripped off and he uses his acid digestive enzymes to dissolve the hand and foot of a guy who tries to stop him.

That, she said, was what the Armageddon would be like. She made us sit down to watch it. I was seven, maybe eight.

Mother used to watch them with us. We watched *The Fly* together, and *The Thing*. In *The Thing* a dog turns inside out, a man's chest opens, heads fly off and worse. It's a pretty sick film. In fact, it's only really family viewing if you happen to be a member of our family. We watched *The Birds*, too, the Hitchcock film, which was altogether less distressing, it being that much older. Still, like *The Fly* and *The Thing*, *The Birds* was how it was going to be when the Armageddon came. *Piranha*, that was another one, about the military experiment that breeds flesh-eating fish who escape.

'This is what it's going to be like,' she'd say, indicating the screen. Her face was always blank, stone cold, when she watched the films. 'The animals will turn on us.'

She used to add that the lions would be let out of the zoos and roam the streets, looking to eat us up – all when the Armageddon came. We'd have to protect Granddad, she'd repeat, hide his wheelchair in a hedge. *Schindler's List*, that was another one we watched. It's a film about the Holocaust, but as far as Mother was concerned it was about the Armageddon.

It wasn't so bad, watching the films with the rest of the family. It even got so we'd find *The Fly* funny (at least that's what I told myself at the time).

Worse was when she used to make me watch them by myself. It was the first Freddy Krueger film I remember most, although I think I ended up seeing virtually all of them. But the first one I remember well. This was a punishment. This wasn't to show me what the Armageddon would be like, not like the other films. This was because I'd done something wrong. And like a lot of these things – even with some of the very worst abuse – I don't remember what it was that I'd done wrong. Perhaps, sometimes, there simply was nothing, and she did what she did out of spite.

She put me in the room at about half past one in the morning and just said, 'Watch this.' Then she left and went upstairs, leaving me by myself, the lights off, the video going, Freddy Krueger on the screen. If you haven't ever seen a *Nightmare on Elm Street* film, Freddy Krueger is the serial killer who appears to kids in their dreams. He has a horribly scarred face and he wears gloves with knives as fingers.

When I eventually went to bed that night it was Freddy Krueger appearing in his victims' dreams that troubled my racing mind. I lay on the floor, watching every shadow, for a few sleepless hours before daylight.

She liked to scare us. A frightened person is a controlled person, perhaps. She used to come up to us when we were sleeping and scream into our faces.

One time, I'd fallen asleep on the landing. I was sleeping there because Karen was on the floor of our bedroom asleep. Lulu was on the bottom bunk and I couldn't reach the top bunk for some reason, probably the same reason that Karen was sleeping on the floor, that there was stuff on it.

About 3 a.m., Mother came out to go to the loo and saw me sleeping there. She bent down and growled into my face. I woke with a terrified start, the growl had got louder and it ended in a roar as she straightened up, laughing, and walked away. I watched her go and pulled the quilt back over my head.

I'm not sure if it ever occurred to me that a mum, when she's visiting the loo at three o'clock in the morning, isn't supposed to roar into her son's sleeping face. She's supposed to reach down and brush a lock of hair from his eyes, give him a kiss and say, 'Sleep tight.'

Chapter Nine

Mother had met George Parker over free-range eggs in Pershore, apparently. He sold them at market there. They'd become friendly (and I do mean just as friends, despite some of the gossip) and latterly she'd been caring for him as his health deteriorated – a result of his chain-smoking; he was on oxygen by the end.

He was a proper farmer was Mr Parker. He wore a tweed jacket to go and feed the chickens, and he put a cap on when he climbed into his yellow Ford Escort to go to market. A proper farmer, a nice man.

He lived at Eckington in Worcestershire, about twenty minutes' drive from George Dowty Drive, a tiny village. His farmhouse was on the way out of the village, in the direction of Pershore. Leaving Eckington, there was a graveyard, dark, spooky at night, then the farmhouse, then the open road, up the hill to Pershore.

The first time I ever visited the farmhouse I was dropped off there by a friend of Judith's. He was a guy from the folk scene who took us in a van that had seen far better days. I think he was trying to chat up Judith, but if he was hoping to impress her with his van, he was onto a lost cause. It was *slooooow.*

Even so, he somehow managed to sail right past the entrance to the farmhouse. The entrance turns straight off the main road that runs through Eckington. It's not like you could easily miss it, but it's kind of secluded, it comes up on you quickly. Opposite is a scout hut and a recreation ground. These days there are recycling facilities there, too, although probably not back when I'm talking about, when folk-friend-of-Judith's turned his van around and we sputtered back up the road and turned into the farmyard.

And I remember it all very well, arriving at the farmhouse for the first time. Not just because of Judith's folky friend and his prehistoric van, but because I fell in love with the house right from the moment we drove through the gates.

The gates themselves were quite something: wrought iron, proper curves, a grand, stately entranceway. Then there was the garden. It was so different from George Dowty. Our garden there was a good size and it had trees to take shelter beneath if you were locked out as a punishment. But it was nothing like this. This had a beautifully manicured lawn, a path with overhanging trees. Behind was a field. George Parker ended up selling a lot of his land in the run-up to his death, but the field he retained, a flat piece of oil-painting land that swept away and back, almost as far as the eye could see.

I was just six then, and it looked like a paradise for a little boy. There were barns to explore, a whole row of them. In the field was an outbuilding. There was a huge horse chestnut tree at one end, and later I tried to build a tree-house in it. I only got as far as doing the floor before the whole thing collapsed.

Inside, the farmhouse was old-fashioned, but cosy. A big kitchen area was dominated by a Rayburn, in front of it a big wingback armchair where Mr Parker used to like to sit. Off the kitchen was a pantry the size of most people's kitchens. He was into shooting. There was a large hallway, with a stag's head regarding you from the wall, and he said he'd shot it himself. There were leopard skins and stuffed leopards around the place. Trophies, he said, from Africa. Everywhere you looked in the house there was character. It was great – I loved it.

George Parker had taken a shine to Charlotte. He liked having her around. And he absolutely loved Meg, our snow-white mongrel with a face like a Jack Russell. He never got to find out about

Lulu, Karen and me, though, because Mother told him we were guttersnipes, that we were the scum of the earth. In return she told us that Mr Parker had warned her about us, Lulu and me in particular. She told us that Mr Parker had said we were bad news and that we'd be the ruin of her family.

But I don't believe that. I don't believe he would have said something like that, it just wasn't him. At least, that's what I think now. At the time, though, we believed Mother and we stayed away from George Parker as much as possible. He thought we were bad news; he'd told Mother so.

In the six months before his death he became so seriously ill that we took to living in the farmhouse with him as we cared for him. Us kids spent the days doing our duties and playing in the barns, and it was brilliant. Great days of fun and exploration, a good time – painfully short as it was. From the barns we'd watch Mr Parker, who was still out and about – and was right up until a week before his death. I remember him struggling to walk around the back of the farmhouse on his Zimmer frame, poking the brickwork with a walking stick to check for crumbling bricks. Any that trickled red chunks to the floor he replaced himself. A sprightly guy, but then, he was only in his mid-fifties when he died.

Shortly before he did so, he changed his will, leaving the farmhouse to Charlotte.

After that, we moved in.

Mother took down the stag's head and burned it out the back. George Parker's stuffed leopards and trophies she sold. She removed the beautiful wrought-iron gates and replaced them with a gate more suited to a yard than Mr Parker's once-prized home. And she closed the curtains.

I found something else on the Internet the other day, a report from a local newspaper in Worcester: 'I Warned People About Her, Says Vicar'.

The vicar in question was Peter Thomas, who had been the vicar of Eckington from 1992 to 2005. According to the report

Rev. Thomas became suspicious about the level of tuition we were getting at home – because Eunice was using books she'd bought at a jumble sale. He'd contacted the Local Education Authority, which turned out to be two education authorities. Because Eunice now had two homes, she flitted between Tewkesbury, which was under Gloucestershire LEA, and Eckington, which was under the then Hereford and Worcester LEA. It turned out that Eunice had been playing one off against the other – something she had a genius for doing.

Peter Thomas said he had met Eunice during the period she was looking after George Parker, but that after he had died it all changed. Eunice had been reluctant to let people in the house, he said. Sometimes she answered the door but after the first couple of months she never let anybody in, and the curtains were always closed. He added that he never saw any evidence that we were being mistreated – but that he hardly ever saw us. Almost as soon as we moved in, he said, 'The sheets went up and we couldn't see much of them.'

Chapter Ten

Things became worse when we lived in the farmhouse. I don't know why. Perhaps it was something to do with power – she now owned two houses, one of them virtually a country pile. Perhaps it was something to do with control – we were five children, a handful. Bradley, who was by then walking and talking, was a particular handful. Maybe Mother felt she was losing control of us, what with two houses to keep up and all those animals to look after, too.

How did that square with her control obsession? How did she try and take it back? Some of the books the police found when they searched the houses involved mind-control techniques, interrogation techniques, methods of torture. There were six books altogether, all of them recovered from beneath her bed. Some of them were library books, believe it or not. I sometimes wonder if they ever got returned; if they didn't, she owes some pretty hefty fines by now.

I got to see one of the books, and felt a horrible sense of sick familiarity as I turned to the page with the chair torture. Another they found described how to wire up prisoners prior to interrogations, and how to deliver electric shocks in order to disable muscles. And I can see why these books would have appealed to her. We were being beaten on the feet regularly, hit about the face – punched, usually – plus other punishments like being shut outside, made to run up and down the stairs, or jumping up and down on the spot. These would be the consequences for the usual kind of thing: leaving a mess, upsetting Bradley (you couldn't upset Bradley; if you upset Bradley you'd pay dearly), not cutting the lawn quickly enough, not raking the grass properly, leaving a door open, closing a door that was meant to be left open, not feeding the chickens, feeding the chickens too much, feeding the wrong chickens, making too much noise, bouncing on a bed.

Here's yet another thing I found on the Internet. Another story in a local newspaper. This one's from the perspective of Rebekah, Eunice's younger natural daughter. I've said before that, even though I hate to speak ill of the dead, Judith knew, and sometimes participated and could almost be described as an accomplice in the abuse, but Rebekah never did. I've remained on good terms with her and we've been cycling together since (she's a mean cyclist). After the trial, some of Eunice's family refused to believe anything had ever been wrong; they said we'd made it up. But Rebekah was always clear-eyed about it. She came out on our side, even giving evidence.

Anyway, the newspaper report. The headline is: MUM HAD NO IDEA HOW TO GET OUT OF MESS. In it, Rebekah says she recalls seeing the five-year-old me in the hallway of George Dowty Drive, jumping on the spot. I looked tired, she said, and I was stumbling around, crying and finding it hard to keep my balance.

She asked what was wrong and I told her that Mother had caught me bouncing on a bed, so she'd said I had to jump all night. Rebekah had a word with Eunice and I was allowed to stop. Another time, Rebekah walked into a room and found Karen naked, crying and facing a wall, told to stand there by Eunice because she'd been naughty.

It surprised Rebekah, this type of behaviour, because she'd never been subjected to it herself as a child. Yes, Eunice was a strict mum. She would smack your bottom if you'd been naughty and on one occasion she horsewhipped Rebekah when she was particularly bad. But there had been nothing like this, the forced jumping, the naked-in-the-corner treatment.

The paper quotes Rebekah as saying she was able to remember the first time Eunice had adopted, when she'd had a child from a woman studying to become a Jehovah's Witness who was considering having an abortion. This was Charlotte – Eunice looked after her almost from birth. The next child she had was Karen, and it was Rebekah's opinion that Eunice and Karen never really 'bonded'. Rebekah remembers Karen as being 'unresponsive' and 'slow to develop' (the kind of symptoms, of course, that Eunice would later use to have Karen diagnosed with Asperger's). She would refuse to eat and Eunice would have to force food into her. Karen's real mum and dad were sending her birthday and Christmas presents, but Rebekah recalls that they were 'kept back' by Eunice, because Jehovah's Witnesses don't celebrate either birthdays or Christmas and she didn't want to unsettle the child.

(I put 'kept back' in inverted commas there because that was how it appeared in the newspaper report and it struck me – 'kept back', as though they were somehow held in storage for another time. But they weren't. Mother used to burn birthday presents and cards that were sent to us. We were allowed a quick look at our cards, then they were thrown on the fire. It's funny, I know it happened, but I don't really remember it – it's as if it was too traumatic, or not traumatic enough.)

Rebekah had lost contact with Eunice, the newspaper report goes on to say. When she next got in touch, the children were all living at home. Eunice had told her that we'd been taken out of school because we were having problems learning, because Lulu had been bullied over her name and had stolen from another girl.

Over the years, Rebekah is quoted as saying she saw a lot of aggression. She saw Eunice shouting at the children, inches away from their faces, with 'staring eyes'. She saw the houses get messier and smellier, with too many animals until there was 'almost not enough room for the people'. But Eunice only seemed focused on how 'awful' the children were. On one occasion Rebekah had said to Eunice, 'You're in a mess,' and Eunice had agreed, adding that she had no idea how to get out of it.

So she beat us instead, and at the farmhouse it got worse, maybe because she could feel her grip slipping, maybe because the farmhouse was secluded, the curtains closed, and nobody saw much of us.

Chapter Eleven

*T*here were plenty of things that needed to be done at the farmhouse each day. We had an open fire back then, and it was my task to bring in coal from the coal shed, so the fire was constantly fed. The garden needed upkeep, too. A big thing was making sure the stinging nettles were kept down. When you've got that much land, the nettles are everywhere, so I had to see to them. Plus I'd clear the paths, as well as seeing to the animals. I had to feed the dogs and the rabbits and clean out the pigs. Karen was supposed to clean out the chickens and did so until the rat outbreak.

This was later, though, when things had got really bad. We'd torn the farmhouse apart and it had begun to rot, inside and out. Suddenly there were rats everywhere, and the rats ganged up on the chickens. Rats versus chickens, the chickens with the extra handicap of being trapped in a chicken shed – there's only ever going to be one outcome to that fight. So we had dead chickens everywhere, rats feasting on dead chickens, kids trying to keep the whole thing together. And Karen just couldn't handle that, the chickens and the rats. She never did get used to death. Lulu and I, we were in charge of all animal burials. After that, there were a lot.

Apart from these duties there was, of course, the cleaning, some of the cooking (though Karen mainly handled the cooking), and the biggie: keeping Bradley happy.

So, more things to do at the farmhouse than at George Dowty Drive. More things to be punished for doing wrong.

We had an orchard on the farm. A lovely Bramley apple orchard – those apples that are great for cooking with, delicious as apple sauce, great in pies, beautiful in crumbles. Pigs like them, too. We had pigs then, and one of them, Bessie, loved the Bramley apples. She used to bash the base of the tree, shaking it to loosen a trio of Bramleys that would *thunk-thunk* to the ground around her, and she'd get stuck in.

It was stupid, really. It was my fault. My fault for being so dumb. I shooed Bessie away from the tree, stopping her from scoffing the Bramleys. My thinking was that Mother wouldn't want Bessie bashing herself into the tree because she might hurt herself or make herself ill from eating too many apples.

But that was me being stupid, because Mother wanted to fatten up the pig. As far as she was concerned Bessie could eat as many apples as she wanted.

I received one hundred across the feet for that. And that was with bamboo, which burns.

We had two living rooms at the farm. One we called the lounge, and the other one we called the sitting room. The sitting room was where the punishments usually took place, only we wouldn't be sitting, we'd be lying down. She'd say, 'Right. A hundred. Go and lie down,' and you knew – you knew to go into the sitting room and lie on the floor, shoes and socks off, feet in the air.

A hundred strokes I got. For trying to please her.

Another day, she called me in there. A chicken had died and I'd either not seen it or seen it and not remembered to move it. Either way, it was my fault the corpse of the chicken was out there, crawling with maggots. She told me to stand in the corner. I did, staring at the wallpaper. George Parker's wallpaper. Still these last remnants of the farmhouse's previous owner about the place. He'd be turning in his grave if he could see what we were doing to his beautiful home . . .

There was a noise behind me and I still don't know what happened because it was a noise like Mother was answering the phone.

Perhaps she was reaching for the bamboo cane and her hand brushed the telephone as she did so.

It was agony. Searing pain – pain that hit me so hard that for a moment, a tiny moment in time, I thought, Oh, that's not too bad, that didn't hurt much, and then it arrived. It exploded in my back, punched through my body then immediately regrouped to a white-hot burn across the shoulders.

'Do not withhold discipline from your children,' she screamed. 'If you beat them with a rod, they will not die.'

She did it again, and again, and again. I dropped to my knees, the blows ceasing to have endings and beginnings, becoming a single block of pain slamming into my back.

I've no idea how long she whipped me for. Five minutes? Ten? I remember thinking that it wasn't right – it wasn't right to leave a dead chicken hanging around in the chicken shed – but still, Mother was going too far.

Bamboo doesn't usually draw blood. The skin blisters instantly from the heat of the hit and perhaps a tiny bead of blood will escape, but then it seals and welts. I was wearing a checked shirt at the time – the police still have it. It was torn, as though I'd been wearing it while trying to crawl through barbed wire. My back still bears the scars but, luckily, I never fancy going swimming.

And there's something inside me that still blames myself for the bamboo whipping. It wasn't right to leave a dead chicken in the yard. I shouldn't have done it. I know she was wrong to beat me for it – I do – but there's a voice inside that says, You could have helped yourself; you made it worse for yourself. I can't help hearing the voice. Like the dreams in high definition, it's one of those unwanted guests in my head I can't wait to get rid of.

We had a black shed at the bottom of the garden that was practically filled with bamboo canes, so Mother had a good supply. She used raspberry canes, too. Still, though, her favourite punishment was to beat the feet with the chair leg. She had progressed from beating the tops of the feet to the soles. She made us lie on our backs in the sitting room, our feet in the air, shoes off.

'And socks,' she'd say. 'Don't forget the socks.' (But what she never realized was that a beating on the soles of the feet hurts even more with socks on than it does off: the fabric drags on the skin, you get friction.)

Often, she used to make us wait in the washroom for our beating. She would tell us the number to expect then make us stand in the washroom, like patients in a waiting room. Sometimes she'd make us wait for hours, just standing there, shivering with dread.

If you were really, really lucky she'd forget about the beating, or pretended to – another mind game maybe. I remember one time, standing in the washroom for over three hours, when she entered the room: 'What are you doing standing here?'

Oh, nothing, I said, innocent-eyed, and I darted past her before she remembered or changed her mind.

Mostly, it would be fifty on each foot. Sometimes more. If you were lucky she'd simply get tired in the middle of a beating and stop. Mostly she didn't, though.

There were times, if we'd been particularly bad, when the same punishment could go on for days. There was a particular occasion, during the renovations; I remember we were having the electricity done at the time. Mother had stored a huge sum of money in a box in the cupboard and the girls found the box.

Mother said later there was £2,000 in the box. I'm really not sure, to be honest, but either way, the girls started taking from the box and spending it at the shop. They bought sweets, and chocolates, and pork pies. Karen, Lulu and Charlotte, this was, and they did it on several occasions, too. I wasn't involved.

I know what it sounds like – that I'm trying to rewrite history to make myself look good, but I'm not, I didn't have anything to do with it. I'd be hiding in my bedroom and they tried to tempt me by offering me chocolate from the bags. OK, I did have some chocolate. Just one time, though. Maybe two.

And then she found out. It was only a tiny village shop, just one little room. Tiny shop, tiny village, and the shopkeeper phoned Mother. He phoned to thank her for the custom: 'Your three girls have been spending an awful lot in here lately, thank you very much.' That kind of thing.

Charlotte was sent to her room. Lulu, Karen and I took up position on the living room floor, and she beat our feet.

We screamed that we were sorry, we pleaded for her to stop. But she beat them that day and then the next day. After they had blistered overnight she just beat down on the blisters. A lot of the sweets and chocolate went back to the shop; the shopkeeper accepted it back, luckily. But still Mother took the chair leg to our feet.

She'd lash out with knives, too. I've got scars crisscrossing both of my forearms to prove it, another treat under UV lights. There was never a knife far from hand, either at George Dowty Drive or the farmhouse. A Stanley knife was her favourite. She'd just grab, reach and slash, before you had the chance to pull away. We never had first-aid training, but Karen, Lulu and I all became expert at patching each other up.

We didn't sing the Alleycat song together any more, though. There wasn't that bond of old. None of us ever talked about our real parents. Somehow the topic had become out of bounds. I used to think about mine sometimes, though. I used to wonder if they really did worship the devil. If my real Dad was evil. Yes, of course they did. Of course he was.

Mother said so, didn't she?

Chapter Twelve

*T*he chair torture was horrible, one of her worst. It's what they call a stress-position torture – one that puts the victim in a position where an incredible amount of pressure is placed on just one or two muscles, so that eventually the muscles give out. It's more or less as it sounds. You adopt a position as though sitting on an invisible chair, with your back against a wall, and you have to hold the position, thighs parallel to the floor.

Almost straight away you feel pain in your legs, right above the knees, a knotting of the muscles that start complaining about this unexpected weight, then begin to tighten and flare. My hands would be on the wall – the kitchen wall, we always did it in the kitchen – my fingers digging into it, trying to get a purchase so I could use them to help take some of the weight off the tops of my legs, which would be shrieking with pain, my eyes screwed up with the effort. Gradually my legs would give out and I'd drop to the floor. About a minute and a half in that position, that's the best I could ever manage. And I held the house record.

'That's one more.' Mother would reach over to make a pencil mark on the wall. 'Go again.'

I'd pull myself back up to the chair position to start again, legs screeching disbelief. The next day, my leg muscles would be sore and I'd spend the day hobbling around like an old man.

Even so, that wasn't the punishment. The chair torture wasn't the actual punishment. It was only used to determine the amount of strokes on the feet we'd get the following morning. The marks she tallied on the wall were the number of strokes we'd get the next day. Sometimes, during a chair-torture session, we might fall up to 200 times in an evening. On those nights I'd lie awake, unable to sleep for the threat of the beating coming my way, those telltale marks on the kitchen wall. We always tallied them up before bed. She used to say that she was too tired to do the beating the same night, she needed a night's rest. It made it worse, of course; I just wanted to get it over and done with.

Then one night, I remember, she took a seat in the kitchen to watch us from the other side of the room. Either Karen or Lulu, I can't remember exactly who it was, had responsibility for making the marks on the wall. That became a regular thing. One of us would have to watch over the other and make their marks. If we didn't make a mark and Mother saw it, then we'd get a beating also. It was one of her favourite things, to make us responsible for each other's pain, by forcing us to tell tales on each other, playing one off against the other. That was the reason we never sang Alleycats any more.

Still, there would be the odd bit of comradeship. Sometimes, if we were sure she wasn't looking, the score-keeper would rub off a mark or two. One or two fewer strokes of the chair leg the following day.

And then a sleepless night and, the next day, the beatings. Which were routine now, daily, part and parcel of life at the farmhouse.

But if we ever thought things couldn't get worse, then we were wrong, because they always did.

'Christopher! Mary-Beth!'

We were both mucking out the chicken shed at the time. We looked at one another. We knew the tone in our mother's voice and it wasn't good. We'd hardly got through the back door, hurrying, fearful, when she grabbed Lulu by the ear, dragging her – Lulu almost pulled off her feet – to the kitchen, then to the side, where a loaf of bread sat on the worktop.

'Look.' Mother held Lulu by the ear, pointing at the bread. It was missing slices. Mother was counting the slices because we were on starvation, and she needed to know we weren't stealing food. It wasn't us, though; Bradley was often helping himself to food. Even so, we were going to get the blame: for stealing food *and* for breaking the starvation punishment.

Moments later we were in the living room. It was around three o'clock in the afternoon, but dark. The curtains were closed. Of course.

'Shoes and socks,' she ordered, in the gloom. I realized that she was carrying the chair leg. A chair leg is how I always thought of it, but in fact it wasn't actually a leg. It came from a chair, but I think it was a strut, so it had a fat shaft that petered off to a thinner end. A dark-brown, walnut colour, it was.

We did as we were told, took off our shoes and socks.

'Lie down.'

We did.

It began. She started beating the soles of my feet. My back arched as the first blows came down, but I caught the scream. I caught it at the point where the jawbone meets the cranium and I kept it there where it filled my ears, a silent scream heard only by me. Because I knew better than to scream. I knew what would happen if I screamed.

There were times, during the punishments, when I'd find my mind wandering. Maybe it did that because the pain was not great enough, or too great, I don't know. But I remember once when she was doing something to me – not a beating, something else, something I can't talk about in this book – a time when I really wondered if I might die, and I found myself suddenly thinking about flowers. I pictured a flower above my head and I clung on to the image.

Lulu said that Mother's eyes shook when she was beating us. She was right, Mother did take on this psycho look, but she rarely said anything, not when she was doing the beatings. The only sound she made was of the effort of raising the wood, bringing it down, raising it again . . . Given the violence and pain in the room, it was almost eerily silent.

Now, I found myself looking at the TV. It had one of those front panels. You know the kind of thing, you flip it down. But the little panel had disappeared, and I thought, Where's that gone?, wondering if Bradley was to blame and thinking, I'll get the blame for that. And below the TV was the video, the LED blinking because the time needed setting. And I watched that for a while. Watched the blinking light as Mother beat my feet.

Then I screamed. Some new and brighter pain had forced its way into the party. A splinter from the chair leg had become embedded in my foot, and I screamed out in agony, screamed, 'No, please, no, Mother!'

She shoved the wood into my mouth. I should have seen it coming, but I didn't. I had no time to reach and try to stop it and I felt it rasp against the back of my throat, then tasted blood in my mouth. Suddenly I was no longer screaming, I was choking, gagging on the chair leg which stayed rammed into my throat for a moment or so, Mother peering over it until she was sure I had stopped screaming. Then she removed it and resumed the beating.

I have scars down my throat now – from then and from other times – because the sticks down the throat became part of the routine, as daily and regular as the beatings themselves. If we screamed out in pain – and sometimes it was impossible not to – she'd force the stick into our mouths, choking us, making us bite down on wood, then remove the stick and carry on beating us. When the police took it away after all those years, it looked as though a dog had been at it. That time, after the beating was over, I went to the outside toilet where I fell to my knees, held my head over the toilet and coughed up blood.

The feet beatings were bad. You've seen it in comedies where people cool their burning feet in water – we've done that for real, except nobody was laughing. We'd limp for a while after each beating, but she was right, they never did bruise, they just stayed sore. My feet used to feel like they'd been turned into blocks of hard plastic; they went solid after a beating.

But it was always worse if there were splinters. Sometimes she'd use whatever came to hand and later, when we were repairing the roof of the farmhouse, that meant the long, thin pieces of timber we'd taken from the old roof. Some of these pieces of wood must have been a hundred years old. She'd beat us with them. When we screamed she rammed the timber into our throats and we choked and gagged around the wood. Later, Mother used tweezers to pull the hundred-year-old splinters from our feet.

She never said sorry, though; never removed a splinter then rubbed the hurty spot with her thumb, saying, 'There, there, that's better.' I don't know – maybe it would have been unbearable if she had.

Lulu had it worse. She'd had an operation when she was a baby and it had left her with a weak throat. The sticks made her bleed more than Karen and me, and she bled loads, coughing up blood everywhere – so much so that once, when it got particularly bad, Mother put her on a diet of milk only. I don't know why, she said it clears the throat; she made Lulu drink a carton of it a day.

That was another kind of torture for Lulu. She hates milk.

Chapter Thirteen

There were good times, too. There was an accident once, I remember. Not *the* accident, but a much smaller one – a little prang basically. We had a green Transit van and we used to drive around in that van all the time, us, Mother, the animals. Driving between George Dowty and the farmhouse, mainly, but all over. This van, you wouldn't believe how rusty it was. There were no seatbelts in it, so when she had this accident – something minor, she left the road, I think – we were thrown about quite badly. I remember we were all sitting by the side of the road, each of us pretty shaken up, so she bought us a huge hot dog each, from a roadside vendor. This thing was massive, like a baguette filled with sausages. We ate them by the side of the road, feeling a bit better.

Then there were the bonfires. We used to have huge bonfires, not on bonfire night but in the middle of summer. Because we ended up doing so much renovation work at the farm, we had lots of stuff that needed dumping: DIY materials, old pallets, unwanted furniture, plus tons and tons of garden waste, mountains of stingers that needed burning and so on.

Anyway, we'd have these bonfires, big bonfires, almost an annual event. And they were *big*. One year we needed a JCB just to push all the stuff up together. Half the size of a house the bonfire would have been. We'd light it and it would burn for three days straight. If it went out overnight we'd come out in the morning and get it going again. Mother wasn't part of it – perhaps that's why I remember the bonfires as such happy times. She just used to let us get on with it. She gave us permission, but she wasn't involved, so we'd mess around. We'd put petrol on the fire and watch it go whoosh. We had wire trays and cooked food on them. Loads of stuff, eggs even. We skewered pieces of bread onto bamboo sticks and made ourselves toast. We were doing this on a yearly basis I'd say, right up until the end. We must have been because I remember Karen being in a wheelchair one year. They were great; the stuff childhoods are made of.

We had a den, too. It was a secret hiding place that we didn't think she knew about. We called it a farmer's hut and it was just above the chicken shed. You could climb up there and make a little fire and just hide out for hours on end, which we sometimes used to do if a beating had been particularly bad. A period of physical and psychological recovery, I guess. She used to get angry if she couldn't find us, and it occurs to me now that she was worried, probably because we might finally have run away. When she was worried-angry she was never violent, though; there were no beatings. It was almost like a game of paper-scissors-stone, where one kind of angry beats another kind of angry. Still, it was our little den. You could build your little fire, stay up there, and be cosy and warm and off in your own little world.

And we did laugh as a family, too. There was one time . . . What it was, she used to strangle us a lot. As far as I can remember, it was chiefly to stop us screaming. This was in the early years of the abuse, mainly, when we were a lot younger, and I think both Karen and Lulu could take more of the strangulation than I could. So I began having blackouts. I had problems with asthma, breathing difficulties, and I just used to go to the floor if she put her hands around my throat, like a panic attack, really. Once, I was out for four or five minutes, just because she'd touched my face.

But on this one occasion it happened in town, in Tewkesbury. We were shopping and it must have been one of the good days because I remember things being OK, but then Mother reached to grab me. Who knows, she was probably only reaching out to pull me away from the road or get me out of somebody's way – God knows, I was in that much of a daze half the time. But I had a panic attack like I did at home and I went to the floor, sprawled on the pavement as though I'd been shot. It was a bit hairy at the time: me, half-conscious on the street in Tewkesbury, people crowding round to see if I was all right, but when we got home we were killing ourselves laughing about it.

Chapter Fourteen

*O*ne of the things I'm asked most about growing up in Eunice's care is how and when the punishments started to get worse. As though it's possible to plot their progression on a nice, orderly graph.

I can see that. I can understand why people want an answer to that question. They want to be able to say that the punishments started in one place, here, with some mild strangulation and a little beating of the feet, and ended up here, with the cricket bat or the tuna tin incident. They want to be able to chart Eunice's gradual progression from abusive foster mum to monster, because that's how we like to see our villains, as fringe elements whose actions become more and more transgressive until they eventually *have* to be caught. But, of course, that wasn't how Eunice was caught.

Still, though, it's true that sometimes I find myself attempting to rationalize events, put them into order. I tell people that things were bad once she stepped over the red line at George Dowty Drive, and that they got worse when we moved into the farmhouse, but that things became really bad – she moved into monster territory – when we started renovation work on the farmhouse. Which is one way of looking at it, and I suppose if you wanted to chart a rough graph of the abuse, then that's how it would look.

But that would be to ignore the starvation, and the month Karen and I spent locked in a room at the farmhouse.

Starvation was one of her most regular punishments. It was one of the few things Eunice admitted to in court, though she would only go so far as to say we were made to miss the odd meal, not the days and days, and sometimes weeks, of food we really did go without.

'Right, one meal, she'd say.'

This would be after I'd done something wrong. Bradley crying, some grass left on the path, stinging nettles too high in the field. Something, anything, whatever.

But it would never just be one meal I'd miss. Maybe it was part of her mind games, maybe she genuinely believed I was stealing food in defiance of the punishment, but the one-meal punishment would always, always be extended.

'Right, a day.'

But after a day without food you need to eat. Mother rarely used to cook. Mostly it was Lulu and Karen who did the cooking and, out of those two, Karen was very good at it – so good that the only time I ever knew Mother to cook was when Karen had made a meal that was so nice, she had to go one better and cook a superior one. I'm not sure she ever managed it, though, but that was what she was like. She had to show us who was boss.

Sometimes, when Karen or Lulu was cooking, they'd bung me a piece of bread. Me, skulking in the kitchen, watching them, my stomach empty and fizzy with the cooking smell. Karen would look around from the worktop, cocking an ear to make sure Mother was nowhere near, then throw me a slice of bread from the counter. Gratefully I grabbed it and shoved it into my mouth, feeling the thickness of it, the chewy crust. After a day without food, it tasted like heaven.

If Mother caught me taking or accepting food I'd be beaten.

If she even thought I'd eaten while on starvation punishment, I'd be beaten.

A vicious, vicious circle. On starvation I would *have* to eat. I would steal to eat. I would take scraps, anything. And if I was caught, I was beaten and the starvation period was extended.

There were times we could eat without her noticing, just by surreptitiously feeding each other, like we were some kind of underground resistance unit, smuggling morsels to comrades. And those were the best times; the starvation wasn't so bad then. But of course she became aware of what we were doing, and then she'd go through obsessive phases when she'd start counting food — especially slices of bread.

It got tough at times. Say, I'd be making a sandwich for Bradley and not keeping a tally of how many slices I'd used. Mother would march into the kitchen, go up to the worktop, and count the slices.

'There's one missing.'

'It's not . . . I haven't . . . Please . . .'

She would gesture in the direction of the washroom, bark out a number I didn't even hear. I'd walk through to the washroom and wait there for my beating.

It was easy to forget to count the bread. One of the first things to go when you're being starved is your concentration. Then you start to lose energy. You just have no energy at all — even getting up in the morning seems like an impossible mission.

But, of course, not getting up is never an option. Not when you still have your duties to do, the animals to look after, the mowing and strimming to do. Your temper goes, too. I remember I used to lash out when I was starving. I was so hungry I'd feel these irrational surges of anger.

During starvation punishments, all I could think about was food. Later, during the renovations, I was on starvation and we were doing work on the bathroom floor. I was measuring out floor tiles using wooden battens. I was drilling but I couldn't concentrate, had no energy, nothing, all I could think about was food. And I went through three tiles with the drill before I'd realized what I'd done.

I was beaten for that. It was a bad one, I recall. Ten minutes or more. She beat me until she was too tired to continue.

Again, Lulu suffered badly. Once, she was being starved and she began coughing up blood. That happens, apparently. With nothing to line the stomach, it literally starts to eat itself, and you begin puking bits of your insides out.

Once again, Mother forced milk into her. But even though the vomiting stopped, Lulu simply couldn't get out of bed in the mornings. In the end Mother put her back onto food. I remember that feeling well. When she put us back on food – when we were at last allowed to eat after – how long? Three days? A week? More? – our bellies would swell up and we'd walk around with swollen tummies sticking out like we were pregnant. Even so, once Lulu was strong enough to get out of bed again, Mother put her back on starvation: she needed Lulu up and about because there were still jobs to be done. But she wasn't going to forget about the punishment in a hurry.

But the worst time on starvation was that time in the room. Neither Karen nor I, try as we might, can now remember what we had done wrong that we were locked in the room, but I can remember the room, every little detail. I remember sitting in it, day after day.

Chapter Fifteen

We are in our underwear. Me in a pair of boxer shorts, Karen just in knickers. I'm eight years old. Karen is eleven.

The door is stripped, bare and white, ready for an undercoat of paint. On the walls the wallpaper has faded from a brown to a yellow, and it is peeling. If you look up into the corners of the room you can see the wallpaper coming away from the plaster, dark patches of damp or mildew beneath, like ants' nests.

The room is virtually bare. Once, there would have been a fireplace but that's been ripped out, leaving a huge black gash in the wall. By its side is a random bedside table, empty. The only other thing you might call furniture in the room is a bed frame, which is old and rusty and probably hasn't had the bother of a mattress for many moons. It's been hoisted up onto its side and leans against the wall. One day we try pulling it down (we make sure we do it very, very quietly) and try it out for comfort.

After all, the floor is just bare floorboards. We've stripped them ready for varnishing. In one corner of the room there are floorboards missing, exposing an irregular rectangle of under-floor, like a puzzle with one piece lost, removed in readiness for plumbing work that has yet to be carried out. Even so, the floor is still more comfortable than the rusty iron bed-skeleton. Very quietly we return the frame to its original position and go back to curling up on the floor, our arms wrapped around our middles.

The window has no nets or curtains. It is the middle of the summer and in the daytime it gets very hot. At night the temperature drops, and because we are in our underwear and have no bedclothes, we start to shiver, pressing into one another for warmth, receiving little comfort and not giving much in return.

During the day we talk.

List of five things Karen and I talk about during the month we were locked together in a room at the farmhouse

1. Barbie dolls
2. Ice cream
3. Fish and chips
4. Mother
5. Heaven

Chapter Sixteen

Karen likes Barbie dolls. The Barbie doll conversations come from her.

We sit with our backs against the faded wallpaper. We have our hands held over our stomachs because if you're hungry and you hold your stomach like that then it isn't so bad. Or rather, it doesn't feel so bad. Another thing we do to keep the hunger at bay is to lie on the floor and bring our knees as close to our chests as we can, making ourselves as tiny as possible, making ourselves into small people – small people who don't need much food.

But mostly, if we're awake, we sit. I talk about cars (I should really have added cars to the list, to be fair). We talk about the same things, day in, day out, over and over, sitting with our backs against the faded wallpaper. Karen talks about Barbie dolls. She tells me about heaven.

A lot of the time we sleep. As the days pass we grow weaker and weaker and we spend a lot of time asleep, both night and day. It gets so we don't know when one day has ended and another begun. All we can do is rely on hearing the others in the house; we look at them from the window.

Some days we kneel at the window and watch Lulu and Bradley in the garden outside. They're playing. While we're shut in the room Mother's treating Lulu well, so Lulu's being treated better than she ever has been before. Sometimes we tap on the window and they stop playing. Bradley looks up at us – he just sees our faces looking at him over the windowsill – and he sticks his tongue out, he's only three or four. Lulu never looks, though. When she hears the tapping at the window, she looks away. She's being treated well so she doesn't want to look at us, because doing that might break the spell. Mother might see her looking and think we've been contacting her; she might throw Lulu in with us. More than anything, Lulu doesn't want to be in the room with Karen and me.

So sometimes we sit with our backs against the faded wallpaper. Sometimes we lie on the floor with our arms wrapped around our skinny bodies. Karen talks about Barbie dolls and tells me about heaven, where the 144,000 will live.

The 144,000 is something Mother's always telling us about. It's one of the beliefs of the Jehovah's Witnesses. How there are 144,000 people who will receive eternal life in heaven as co-rulers alongside Jesus Christ. They must have been born in 1914 or before, and when they are all dead, the Armageddon will take place. Jehovah's Witnesses believe they will live a renewed life after the Armageddon, but only if they're judged worthy of it.

'What will heaven be like, then?' I ask Karen.

She rests her chin on her knees. 'There'll be flying. Everyone will have wings and they'll be flying all over the place.'

That's Karen's idea of heaven: wings with which to fly.

'I don't think so.'

'Well, what do you think?'

I tell her that heaven will be like a motorway. It will be full of dream cars and they'll be speeding along straight, open roads. That's my idea of heaven, I say, all those cars. I think about it for a moment, picturing the scene. (What I'm picturing, I realize later in my life, is an autobahn, pretty much.) Although sometimes, I say, sometimes heaven can be different. Sometimes heaven is like living, except you're dead. You live in an alternative reality, a dream world where you're a different version of the person you are in real life – only a better person, happier, more successful and more confident. Again, I sit and think about it for a moment.

We play I-spy.

'I spy, with my little eye, something beginning with B.'

'Bed.'

'Yes.'

'OK. I spy, with my little eye, something beginning with W.'

'Window.'

'Yes.'

There are bits of insulation in the room, titchy little balls of it. We play games with them, flicking them around the room. We have a contest to see whose ball will hit the wall first.

One day, we make a plan. This plan is called The Great Escape and it goes like this. We'll pick the lock of the room and sneak to the room next door, where there is a huge pile of clothes. Next, we'll sneak as many clothes as we can back into our prison-room, and we'll close the door behind us. Phase One complete.

Phase Two: we'll tie the clothes together to make a rope. Then we'll open the window as wide as it will go and toss the rope out, then both climb down and make for the car.

It's a Ford Escort estate, custard colour. It does 70mph in reverse. I know that because one day the forward gears on it failed and we had to reverse it all the way home. Mother was driving. She got it up to 70mph.

But I'm not planning on reversing it. Instead, I'm planning on . . .

Phase Three.

I dive into the driver's seat of the Escort. Karen scrambles in beside me on the passenger side. I reach down and snatch wires from the dashboard, hot-wiring the car, which starts with a roar. We look at one another and smile. I floor it. The Ford Escort leaps forward, tears out of the gate and we escape, laying down rubber as we go, escaping the room, the farmhouse. Escaping the hunger and cold and pain. Escaping Mother.

But there's no lock on the door. Not one that can be picked, anyway. Instead there's a bolt on the outside. Neither will the window open. Well, it does open, and we have to have it open because it has begun to smell in the room – smell like a kennel – but it doesn't open very far. It's a sash window and Mother has hammered nails into the frame so it will only rise up by about three or four inches. That's phases one and two of The Great Escape rendered unworkable. As for Phase Three, I'm eight. I don't know how to hot-wire a car, beyond once seeing someone on TV grab a batch of wires from beneath the dashboard of a car they were stealing. But then what? I can't drive either.

Instead, we sit with our backs against the faded wallpaper. Karen talks about Barbie dolls; I talk about cars. We play I-spy, flick bits of insulation, and watch the others from the window.

Chapter Seventeen

One day, she comes to us holding clothes.

'Put these on,' she says, tossing them into the room, 'you're coming out today. Nanny and Granddad are coming.' She leaves, closing the door behind her.

We do. We fall on the garments, instantly sorting the pile into Yours and Mine, slipping on jeans and a T-shirt each, feeling instantly so much better, clothed and ready to come out of the room, both of us thinking of food and freedom. My clothes feel loose. I feel as though I'm wearing somebody else's things.

We wait.

And wait.

The aroma of Sunday cooking rises to taunt our stomachs. We sit and clutch our arms around ourselves, tortured by the smell of the dinner. Roast beef. Roast potatoes. Gravy. In vain we try to ignore our bellies, which clamour for food, gnawing at us, acid splashing our insides.

Then the door opens.

Mother is standing in the doorway.

She's holding two plates of roast dinner. Suddenly the scent of roast dinner is overpowering in the room. As one we scramble on to our haunches.

She towers over us, the plates held. She's wearing her glasses, the ones with round lenses. She has her work boots on, and a pair of jeans. Her mouth is set straight apart from a slight downturn at the corners, her lips thin. She stares at us. Behind her glasses her eyes are cold and hard.

'I've told Nanny and Granddad you're in here for the day,' says Mother, 'and that you'll be eating your Sunday dinner in here.'

Bending, she places the plates to the floor. We stare at them and I realize I am leaning forward as though led by my nose, the posture of a starving, tethered dog. I look at Karen and she's doing the same. Both of us are waiting for the moment when she turns her back and closes the door. The moment when we can at last eat.

There is no cutlery. Doesn't matter. Who cares?

She studies us a moment. 'I know what you're thinking,' she says, 'but if you touch one morsel of food on that plate your lives won't be worth living. Am I clear?'

We look at her. Neither of us says anything. Neither of us can believe what we're being told.

'Remember what I've just said,' she says, and she turns and closes the door behind her. There is a *chunk* as the bolt slides into place.

We stare at the two plates of roast dinner.

For the next three hours – we think it is three hours – we stare at the two plates of roast dinner on the floor of our prison-room, watch as the warm food goes cold, the gravy coagulates and the food takes on a pasty, shiny tinge.

Then the door opens and Mother reappears.

'It stinks in here,' she says, adding, 'You stink.'

She's right, we do. We look at her.

'They've gone, anyway. Take the clothes off,' she says.

We stare.

'Take them off,' she repeats.

We do.

She places two glasses of water on the floor, reaches and picks up the clothes, which she takes from the room with the two plates of food. I think: The dogs will get our food.

Wordlessly, she turns and leaves. We drink our glasses of water. Karen starts to cry.

Chapter Eighteen

We have been in the room for two weeks. We're often given water to drink. Very occasionally we are let out and allowed to use the toilet, but then we must go straight back into the room again. Sometimes she brings us some bread to eat, too. She has to, I suppose. If she didn't feed us at all, we would probably die.

Every now and then, Judith opens the door and looks in on us. She never says a word. It's as though she's checking on us to make sure we're still alive. She wrinkles her nose at the smell, looks us over, glances around the room, looks at the window to check it's open and letting in air. We watch her. Presumably she must do it sometimes when we're sleeping, too. How are we to know? We, who are prisoners of her mother.

There are meatballs. On two separate occasions there are meatballs. This is because Mother has had a phase of buying them, one of her little fads; she gets them from Pershore market, where they're cheap. I don't like meatballs. Or, *usually* I don't like meatballs. Now, though, I love meatballs, I'm a connoisseur of meatballs, I'm meatball crazy. When we have finished our meatballs, she takes away the empty plates. She gives us more water to drink.

Mostly, we wee in the room. I have become skilled at shooting my wee into the gap where the floorboards have been taken up ready for the plumber.

The bread and meatballs have to come out, too, though. Sometimes we need to shit.

One day, we go by the bed in the corner, first one, then the other.

The room starts to fill up with the stench. We crab over to the window, sitting with our backs to the wall and twisting our heads to suck fresh air through the gap she's left for us. We cast shameful looks at our shit in the corner of the room. Neither of us knows what to do about it.

I don't know how long it's been there when the door opens.

It's Mother; she recoils at the smell. She looks over to the corner and sees the shit there – then comes further into the room until she's standing over us, miles above us. She looks from us to the shit in the corner, then back to us.

Her lips are tight, her eyebrows knit together. She's not happy.

'You're going to eat it,' she says.

I push myself back into the wall, trying to make myself a part of it; trying to push myself right through the wall and out the other side, where I can tumble into the yard, run to the custard-coloured car, hot-wire it, floor it, lay down some rubber.

'Eat it,' she repeats, her mouth pursed. She's staring at Karen.

Neither of us moves. For a moment or so Karen and Mother stare at one another, Mother's eyes burning into Karen. Then, quickly, Mother reaches and grabs Karen by the hair.

I am eight, Karen is eleven. Neither of us are large children. We have been kept without food in the room for a fortnight or more and we are desperately weak.

She drags Karen to the shit and rubs her face in it. Karen has time to let out one sound, like a gasp, before her face is shoved into her own foul-smelling waste.

Mother releases Karen's hair and Karen falls back to the floor. There is shit on her face, I can see, and I don't want that – I want more than anything *not* to have my face rubbed into it, so when Mother looks at me and says, 'Eat it,' I do. I walk over, pick up my excrement and eat it.

Before I do, I think, Let's get this over with. Let's get this over with so I can sit back down because I can feel my legs weak beneath me. I'm not thinking about what I've got to do, I'm just thinking about my legs. Even as I bend, scoop a handful and put it into my mouth.

I swallow and gag. The taste is like gone-off cake, but I keep it down. I can keep shit down because of the other things Mother makes me drink. She stares at me as I eat my own shit, satisfied I'm being punished for dirtying the room.

She doesn't make us eat it all. She gives us a bag and we pick the rest up with our hands. We're not permitted to clean up properly. Mother gives Karen a piece of kitchen paper to wipe her face but we're not allowed to wash. The next time Karen can wash is in a couple of days.

She leaves. Karen is crying. I move over to her and we hug, but we don't say anything. I don't say anything because I imagine Mother is outside the door listening to us right now, even though she may not be. Later, I find out that Karen thinks the same thing. Karen cries, we hug.

The punishment of being forced to eat shit happens twice during the month we're in the room. The second time isn't so bad.

Chapter Nineteen

*O*ne day the door opens and she enters. We have adapted to the smell in the room; we don't smell anything untoward now. But visitors cover their noses at the stench. Mother tosses some clothes into the room.

'Get dressed,' she says.

We do, but I'm thinking, Not again. The memory of last time is horribly fresh, when she made us dress the day Nanny and Granddad came over for lunch. She'd only given us clothes in case Nanny or Granddad looked in on us. That's what's happening again, I think, as I dress.

But I'm wrong. We leave the room and go downstairs to the kitchen, where a meal is laid out. The rest of the family is there: Lulu, Charlotte, Bradley and Judith. We are all about to tuck into a spaghetti Bolognese. My stomach does a flip.

Karen and I sit down.

'Where you been?' says Bradley, innocently, but nobody answers, or laughs, or even acknowledges that he's just spoken.

In fact, nobody really says much. I realize that I can't look at Lulu, my sister. But neither can she look at me. For a second or so our eyes meet across the table and I'm not sure if the moment means anything, but hers drop away quickly. There is an atmosphere in the room. For a long time there is just silence, and we eat. I begin to wolf down my spaghetti and once I've started I can't stop. I'm stuffing it into my mouth and nothing on God's earth ever tasted so delicious. Strands of spaghetti hang out of my mouth, sauce is on my chin but I don't care. I don't care that the rest of the family is watching me, probably with a mixture of contempt and revulsion. I don't care because all I want to do is eat.

Nobody speaks. The only sound is the sound of eating, most of which, I realize, comes from me.

Then Judith says to Mother, 'You should have left them in there.'

I stop eating and look at her, then start eating again. I don't care. I don't care that she thinks we should have stayed in the room, and I don't care if the family are appalled by my table manners. I just want to eat this spaghetti Bolognese.

Moments later, I'm in the downstairs toilet, on my knees, and once again I've got spaghetti hanging off my chin – only this time it's on the way out. After a month on starvation punishment, just bread and two servings of meatballs, my stomach has decided it won't tolerate Bolognese. No, Chris, sorry. My delicious, lovely, hard-earned food splashes into the toilet bowl. I close my eyes and want to cry – but don't. In my head I hear the echo of Judith's words from the dinner table. *You should have left them in there.*

She might as well have done.

I discover that a plumber had visited the house while we were locked away. He'd been called out to investigate a leak that I realize came from me shooting my wee into the floorboards. I keep that bit of information to myself, but offered a silent apology to the poor plumber who had to investigate. Not long later, Mother tells Karen and me to go and clean up the starvation room, and we enter. A few days have passed since we were last in it and we've had time to readjust to the outside world, so the smell and atmosphere of the room hits us like a breeze block. It smells worse than the animal sheds. We get to work clearing it up. The building work on the farmhouse is soon to start.

Chapter Twenty

If you'd lived in George Dowty Drive in the mid-90s you would have seen the street's most dysfunctional family engage in a strange morning ritual: our daily journey to the farmhouse.

I don't know exactly what Mother's long-term plans were, but despite Charlotte inheriting George Parker's place, she retained her house at 24 George Dowty Drive. Even so, for some time after George died, we all lived in the farmhouse. After a while, though, it was virtually uninhabitable thanks to all the building work, so we ended up spending our days there, and our nights at George Dowty.

Which is why, every day, we used to pile into the old Transit van and make the eight-mile drive from the Northway estate in Tewkesbury to Eckington.

There was Mother in the driver's seat. She would drive, a mad driver she was. At the same time she'd be shouting over her shoulder, usually preaching about the upcoming Armageddon or talking about Florida, straining to make herself heard over the roar of the engine and the noises of the animals.

Beside her on the passenger seat was her paperwork: her books and 'important documents'. Piles and piles of the stuff. Who knows exactly what it all was, but she used to take it everywhere with her. Back and forth between George Dowty and the farmhouse it went, every day. The piles of documents never left the van, just stayed in there, growing and growing like something out of the horror films

she made us watch, threatening to take over the whole van:
Armageddon via paperwork.

Bradley and I sat in the seat behind Mother and there were
seats on the wheel arches for the girls. In the middle of us all were
our animals. Although we had animals that needed tending to at
the farmhouse, there were other animals we kept at George Dowty
Drive that couldn't be left behind, so we used to drive them
between the two houses. Almost everything came with us, apart
from the rabbits and hamsters. That meant there was always at
least one dog – usually two dogs – plus cats, chickens, a duck and
geese. At one point we were carrying a fish around in a plastic container. Mother insisted upon it – the fish must have been her
favoured animal at the time. The fish was ill, she said. For a time
we even had a peacock in the van.

Also, we had our supplies for the day. Food for all of us, in a
green plastic container that had fallen off the back of a supermarket – the sort you see with fruit and veg in it. That used to go on
the floor, full of bread and food and stuff.

And that was us, every day. Mother preaching at top volume, us
kids in the back listening, riding out the bumps of the van, trying
to stop the animals from killing each other. We were like a mini-
army, noisy and ragtag, battered and bruised mostly, too. Each day
we began a fresh assault on our mission to renovate the farmhouse.
And every day that mission seemed more and more impossible.

Because that was always her big project. Whenever I think
about the things she did to us, I wonder: why? And, the truth is, I
don't know why. I don't want to sound cheesy but I sometimes
wonder if writing this book is me trying to answer that question,
and I'm fairly sure that by the time I get to the end I still won't be
able to answer it. Only she can do that, and according to her, she
never punished us worse than giving us a smack on the bottom or
making us miss a meal or two, so it's not like I can expect much
help there. In the end it's up to me, and my best guess – the thing
I keep coming back to – is control. With Mother, she had to have

total control, and her response to losing that control was to strike out. In a way, the farmhouse represented the ultimate loss of control for her. It beat us, that farmhouse did. It beat her. The idea was to renovate it, modernize it, live in there as a family; instead, as we pulled things apart and slowly filled it with our stuff, it became more like a slum. We should have improved the farmhouse. We ended up all but destroying it.

But we tried. I, personally, tried. From the age of about seven to sixteen I did little else but work on the farmhouse, day in, day out. We started on the gardens. With Mr Parker's health failing they'd fallen into disrepair, and it was up to me to first bring them up to scratch, then to maintain them. That was my main job every day. The second major task was refitting the upstairs bathroom. We started by pulling out the old bathroom bit by bit and chucking the stuff in the yard, making it ready to fit a new one. After that we moved on to the loft, which involved stripping out the old insulation, which was easy for me to do because I was nice and small and could fit under the beams. Next, we fitted flood pumps under the sitting room and lounge – that was hard – and then, of course, we started on the plumbing, and I say 'started' because it's not like we ever completely finished it. It was a job that went on for years and years. Not just the plumbing, of course, but the electrics. They needed modernizing, too. Plus, we started work on the staircase. Plus, we wanted to replaster and redecorate everywhere, put new doors in, fit a new fireplace . . .

It was almost a complete renovation and I think, in the end, it was simply beyond us. And Mother started to lose control.

List of the five worst things my evil foster mother Eunice Spry forced me to eat while growing up

1. Bleach
2. Washing-up liquid
3. Shit
4. TCP
5. Lard

Chapter Twenty-one

*M*ost days there was at least one beating. It would be for something I'd done wrong around the house or garden, or something I'd done to upset Bradley. It could be because she thought I'd defied a starvation punishment and stolen food. If there wasn't a beating, there might be another punishment, a knife slash, strangulation, a punch or a slap around the face.

One of her favourites, if she thought I'd neglected my duties and not kept the stinging nettles cut down, was to push me into them. She'd shove me in, then walk away, usually shouting something, probably about the Armageddon or how I had demons inside me. I learned that you don't thrash about when you've been pushed into a whole load of stingers. You stay as motionless as you can, draw yourself slowly up, holding yourself still like something rising from the grave. I learned I had to keep the stinging nettles shorn as low as possible, too.

Sometimes it would be worse than just a beating or a push into the nettles, though. One day, she called me into the kitchen. I was on starvation. This was because . . . oh, like so many of these punishments, I can't remember what it was I'd done in the first place. I was exhausted, probably hungry, the farmhouse seemed to be falling down around our ears, our daily chores doing nothing to control it. There were a million things I could have done wrong.

But on this occasion, stealing food was not one of them.

'You've had two slices of bread.'

The bread. Almost always bread, it seemed. She'd been counting slices again, of course – and I knew she'd been counting the slices; she always did, so why would I take one? Why would I take a slice of bread knowing it meant an extra two days added to the starvation punishment, or a beating on the soles of my feet? It had to be Bradley, or one of the others. Or perhaps there never was a slice missing. Perhaps she needed to remind me who was in charge.

I shook my head. I denied it. No, not me, I didn't take the bread, I told her. She insisted. She demanded that I own up but I refused to do it. How could I? How could I own up to something I hadn't done?

'In the washroom. Now.'

Her eyes blazed and she motioned to the room we all knew so well. The washroom where we were made to stand and await our beatings. It had recently had new tiles put in. In it was the washing machine, and it was where we did the washing-up after meals, so there were all the cleaning products in there, all the bottles of bleach and the washing-up liquid.

She grabbed a bottle of washing-up liquid from beside the sink and held it out to me. I stared at it, looking at the label.

'Drink it,' she ordered.

She'd made me drink things before. TCP was one of her favourites. There was a time at George Dowty when she'd entered the bathroom while I was using it. We had a toothglass – a little glass where we kept our toothbrushes – and she emptied the contents into the sink, toothbrushes clattering to the porcelain. She poured TCP into the glass and gave it to me, demanding I drink it. I did, because it barely occurred to me to refuse. Fear, respect, I really don't know. Because she was my mother.

She watched me do it, then left, chuckling to herself as I gagged and spluttered, hands on my knees, eyes streaming. I hadn't done anything wrong that time. I think it was her idea of a joke.

And I hadn't done anything wrong this time, either, but this wasn't a joke. I took the proffered bottle of washing-up liquid and brought it to my lips, for all the world like a little boy with a bottle of fizzy pop.

I was a little boy, but it wasn't pop Mother had given me. I tasted just the tiniest trace of washing-up liquid on the nozzle, and instantly my senses were in rebellion. The feel of it was oily and wrong on my lips and my mouth seemed to fill with the taste of chemicals, sour, burning at the back of my mouth.

I thought: Maybe I can get away without drinking it. Maybe I can pretend to drink it and she'll never know. Maybe . . .

She reached and squeezed the bottle, squeezing washing-up liquid into my mouth. I gagged, some of it escaped my mouth and I was coughing, about to spit it out when she demanded I swallow it, shouting, 'Drink it!'

I really didn't want to drink it. I had one hand on the worktop, with the other at my mouth. My fearful eyes watched Mother, who had her warning face on. Her face that said, Do as I say. Or else.

I swallowed. And it's pure chemicals, washing-up liquid. It's oil and chemicals, and not only is the taste and the texture of it the worst thing on God's earth, but it does things to your insides. It burns away at them. It does its job; it washes.

I went to my knees, retching, then vomited on Mother's nice new, clean tiles, a rancid mixture of washing-up liquid and the meagre contents of my stomach, more gastric juice than anything else. My hands went to the floor. I was coughing and retching, my stomach still heaving and trying to rid itself of the washing-up liquid, as she grabbed the back of my neck, bringing her full weight to bear onto me, and pushed. She pushed my head into the pool of sick.

'Now eat *that*,' she snapped, her voice like a whip crack in the room.

Unable to resist, my head went to the floor, my face into the puddle of vomit, suddenly inhaling it, smelling it, gasping at the acrid stench.

'Eat it,' she repeated. 'Eat it.'

I lapped at it, forced to the floor like a dog, lapping at my own sick like one.

(Thinking back now – the dogs – she never used to hurt the animals. I never saw her raise more than a hand to give a dog a slap.)

Then what I thought about was the grouting on the tiles. One of those mental escape mechanisms. Lulu once told me that when she was forced to the floor that way, she used to stare at Mother's feet, and she had noticed, she said, that she had quite ugly feet, Mother did. With me, that time at least, it was flooring. Forced to eat my own sick and what I did was admire the grouting on the tiles.

She let go. I remained on the floor, pulling myself up slightly, my head lowered over the vomit, my back to her as I heard her leave the room. She didn't need to tell me to clean up the mess. I reached for a cloth and began to sponge the floor. It's not an easy mixture to remove from kitchen tiles.

She wouldn't always make us swallow the washing-up liquid. Many times she made us do a punishment where we had to hold it in our mouths, then walk around the lawn, circuits of the lawn with a mouthful of foul-tasting detergent. And not just one circuit, either, but however many circuits she decided, anything from ten upwards. The object – because it probably was a game to her – was to finish your circuits without vomiting. If you sicked up you had to hold it in your mouth. Punishment for finishing your circuits without either a mouthful of washing-up liquid or a mouthful of sick was to do it again.

I spent so much time on my knees by the back door, gagging and retching. Sometimes when I puked she made me take another mouthful and swallow. Again: instant sick – the kind of violent, acid vomit that brings your stomach lining with it. I wouldn't wish drinking washing-up liquid on my worst enemy, and she'd make me do the game for hours. Make me do it until I was unable to get off my knees, or until she became bored – whichever was first.

During her trial there was a nervous titter around the court when it came out that I had been force-fed so much washing-up liquid that I could differentiate between brands. It's true, though, I could. By their smell, too. And probably still can. The cheaper own-brands are worse – far worse. There's more octane, the chemicals in them are harsher. They burn in the mouth, then attack the stomach. As I say, just doing their job, really. The more expensive-name brands aren't so bad – they're bad, but not so bad – they're easier to swallow, easier to keep down if you have to. And you can, I could. Keeping washing-up liquid down, not puking it up, was a skill I acquired from necessity, a case of survival. Swallowing it and keeping it down was never quite as bad as bringing it up again, then having either to eat up the vomit or take another swig. No, it was always better to keep it down if I could.

Mother had the cheap brands, mostly. One day, she called me into the washroom and once again, I don't remember what I'd done to deserve it, but in I went. In there, she'd cut the top off a bottle of washing-up liquid, the cheap kind, a white bottle with a red nozzle, only she'd cut the whole of the top off, the way I've since learned mums are supposed to do when their children have seen something on TV they'd like to make. Except my mother had left the washing-up liquid in the bottle. And it shimmered green and oily and evil in its plastic container.

She used a quote that I think was from the Bible: 'I'll wash your mouth out with soap, get rid of all the dirty false-god names.'

Did I refuse? Did I struggle? At what point was Judith in the room, or was she always there? It almost seemed that one moment I'd walked into the washroom to see the cut-off bottle, feeling a kind of dread realization, thinking, No, she can't want me to . . . And the next I was on the floor, Judith holding me down, my legs kicking, Judith actually holding my mouth open, pinching my nose perhaps, prising my jaws apart. And Mother was pouring the bottle of washing-up liquid into my mouth.

I couldn't breathe. My mouth filled with poisonous green gloop. I choked, snorted and sucked the detergent up my nostrils, panicking, thrashing about as Mother kept pouring the bottle, holding it over my mouth, so that as little as possible could escape. She poured the entire bottle into my mouth. Perhaps she thought it was so cheap she could afford the waste. Or perhaps she just wanted to see how far she could go, how much of it I could take. Judith released me and I twisted, vomiting again and again, fighting for breath at the same time, convulsing as I puked my entire stomach onto the washroom floor.

That would need clearing up. But first she made me take another mouthful of washing-up liquid, plus I had to do some laps of the lawn.

Some of the time we were allowed to spit out the washing-up liquid and vomit at the end of the circuits, but a lot of the time she'd make us swallow. I'd learned to predict when she'd do that – and I thought that this was one of those times. So about halfway through a lap, I spat out the liquid. When my circuits were done I approached the back door, keeping my cheeks slightly puffed.

She told me to swallow and I swallowed air, making a face as I did so. All too easy to fake. I looked at her and she was satisfied the punishment was over. It was a tiny, tiny victory. Perhaps the first.

Chapter Twenty-two

*T*hese are the kind of things I learned while growing up. Not English and maths and how Spider-Man got his powers, but that the cheapest brands of washing-up liquid are the worst to swallow; that being made to drink TCP gives you diarrhoea the following day; that bleach, when it's forced into your mouth, actually tastes a little bit like mouthwash, and that it won't stay down. Ever. Not like washing-up liquid, where I'd learned to keep it in my stomach. Bleach is simply too toxic.

Most of the time when she beat us she would be hard, cold, stony-faced. She would hardly make a sound, except perhaps with the exertion of wielding the chair leg. Other times, though, she would be in a rage. There was no rhyme or reason to it. It wasn't like she'd stay calm if beating us for stealing food, or get angry if beating us for making Bradley cry. We'd never know. Never know what to expect. She had phases, times when she seemed to retreat inside herself and beat us as though on autopilot, eyes almost glazed over. Then there were other times when she'd go psycho, shouting things.

'You're the scum of the earth.'

I heard that a lot, that particular phrase. If only I had a pound for every time she'd called me the scum of the earth. She used to tell me that she was disciplining the demons out of me, to save me for the Armageddon. She'd either tell me before a beating, or after, breathless and red-faced, looming over me on the floor, still shouting at me.

They were the worst, when she was shouting, because she might not have finished. She might go on to do worse things. One day she gave me a beating with the chair leg. It was the same agonizing drill as always: I was given a number, told to wait in the washroom, an hour or so I think it was, before I was called into the sitting room for my beating, fifty on each foot. She was shouting as she did it, worked up, still shouting when she finished as I lay on the floor with blocks of pain for feet.

Then she picked up a bottle of bleach.

Not many families have bottles of bleach hanging around in their sitting rooms, just ours. She rammed the bottle into my mouth and squeezed it. Bleach squirted into my mouth and suddenly I was gulping for air, mouth full of wrong, swallowing some, the smell of it thick, toxic gas that was suddenly everywhere, in my nose and mouth, scalding my mouth with chemical burn.

Instantly I was sick. Bleach is worse going down than it is coming back up. It's different to washing-up liquid like that. Another useful life-fact I've learned. Not which felt-tip pens are the best for colouring in sky. Not which park is best for swings and slides. But which household cleaner is worse going down than it is coming up.

And up it came. It didn't burn, not in the corrosive way you might expect. Maybe it didn't stay in long enough. I hardly had time to taste it, save for a fleeting sense that it tasted like mouthwash. And then I was writhing on the sitting room floor, hands at my face, wiping bleach from it, then vomiting again, and again, bleach-vomit splashing on the carpet, on the sofa.

That would need clearing up.

She left the room as I thrashed on the floor. Self-preservation sent me darting to a sink where I splashed water on my face, gulped it down, praying for it to soothe my tortured insides. When I'd finished I set to work cleaning up the bleach from the sitting room. It was impossible, of course. The marks are still there now.

She didn't use bleach as often as she did washing-up liquid, but it happened on more than one other occasion, always with the same effect. Her favourite thing – if she was in control of herself – was to hand me the bottle, eyes like two round stones, hardly needing to say, 'Drink it.' And I would.

And what I used to think afterwards, when I was on my knees scrubbing the carpet in the gloom of the sitting room, or lying nursing wounded feet, was, Why? Why had she done that? What had I done to make her do that, and how can I make sure it doesn't happen again? Because I always used to think things through. What had I done? How can I stop it? More and more I was choosing a position of retreat inside my own head.

Mother liked to make the punishment fit the crime. I was caught stealing food once and, as we were already in the kitchen, she took a block of lard, a whole block, and placed it between two slices of bread. She pushed down hard on the top slice, squishing it so it oozed out of the sides.

'You want to eat,' she said. 'Eat that.'

I remember looking at her as if she might be joking. Looking at the block of lard between two bits of bread, like it was a comedy sandwich. She couldn't be serious. But she was, of course, and I had to eat the lard sandwich. I sat at the big table in the middle of our kitchen farmhouse. I was a little boy sitting at the kitchen table of a farmhouse, eating a sandwich. Only the farmhouse had been corrupted; it was having its insides torn out and was gradually filling with our mess. And the little boy's sandwich had lard as a filling.

She made me eat the whole thing. I sat gagging, but kept it down.

There were other times I had to eat lard, too, mainly when I was on starvation punishment. The thing with these starvation punishments was that they could go on for weeks and weeks. I think my longest-ever starvation punishment went on for six weeks.

The problem for her was that I'd get dangerously thin, look ill and emaciated. I'm sure her biggest worry was that I'd simply stop working. So she gave me lard to eat. More lard sandwiches. She used to heat up the lard, mix it up, put it between bread and make me eat that. During starvation periods I even used to welcome them. Occasionally, Mother used to make me eat a horseradish sandwich, too, an idea she'd got from a practical joke Lulu played on me.

What it was, Lulu used to make the most beautiful peanut butter sandwiches. She'd make one and leave it on the side while making another. If I saw it there I'd nick it and she'd shout at me. But hey, I'd just had a great peanut butter sandwich, what did I care? So she decided to play a joke on me and made, not a delicious peanut butter sandwich, but an evil one filled with horseradish sauce, and left it on the side, from where it tempted me, calling out to me. Sure enough, I grabbed the sandwich and ran away laughing. Until I took a bite. Next thing you know I'm at the kitchen sink trying to sluice out my burning mouth with water and Lulu is killing herself laughing at me. Killing herself. It was, I have to admit, a good joke.

But Mother stole the idea. She wasn't above doing that, as we'd later find out when the police raided the house and found the torture books under her bed. Or when I discovered a copy of the abuse memoir *A Child Called "It"* in her room and read it, feeling a horrible chill of recognition at some of the punishment meted out to its author, Dave Pelzer. They were the same. Most people read *A Child Called "It"* as a book about the triumph of human spirit. Mother read it for research.

So she nicked Lulu's practical-joke idea. She loved to turn us against one another, and that was a perfect opportunity, too good to pass up.

'You like horseradish sandwiches,' she said one day, 'then eat a whole one.'

Of course, nobody was laughing any more. And no doubt Lulu wished she'd never played the trick on me. But of everything Mother made me eat, horseradish sandwiches were the best – or the least bad, I should say. Still, I don't eat horseradish now. Just like I shy away from the smell of TCP, and the scent of bleach absolutely turns my stomach. I can't be near the stuff. I don't much like washing-up liquid these days, either. Or that's what I tell people – to get out of doing the dishes.

And at the end of each day at the farmhouse, we'd pack up our stuff into the van, our now-empty box of supplies, our animals and us, and we drove.

Most days we drove to Safeway.

Remember how I said Mother was obsessed by the Safeway cafeteria? It was the Tewkesbury branch. Like all other Safeway branches in the country, it's since been taken over by Morrisons, and when I go past now I often wonder whether or not Mother would approve of Safeway's new look. I couldn't hazard a guess, mainly because I was never quite sure what she liked so much about it in the first place. Perhaps it was just a convenient shop to meet her friend, who she met there almost every night, the two of them in the Safeway cafeteria, spending up to four hours at a time just sitting, chatting, eating, Mother enjoying the end of a hard day at the farmhouse.

While she was in there, we stayed outside in the Transit. She used to park it as close to the cafeteria window as she could, so that most evenings we could watch her inside, drinking what seemed like endless cups of coffee – cappuccino was her favourite – and chatting to her friend. She could keep an eye on us too, of course, all of us kids and the animals in the Transit.

Sometimes we were allowed to go into the shop with her; mainly we stayed out in the van. For hours it was. Hours and hours that we whiled away by bickering, reading, trying to keep Bradley happy, playing I-spy, or working out how many hours that week we'd spent sitting in the car park at Safeway. It was usually about twenty. If we needed the loo we had to nip out and use the toilets in the shop, but we were under strict instructions to return immediately to the Transit. Even so, it got so that we came to recognize regular customers at the shop and we'd wave to them. I'm not sure if they ever waved back, and I wonder what they saw when they looked in the van, us five kids in it. Happy kids, probably. Kids doing what kids do, which is mess about mostly. I remember once we decided to see how far we could rock the van before it toppled over. We weren't parked near the cafeteria window that day – we would have been properly punished if she'd seen us rocking the van like that, attracting attention to ourselves.

I was looking on the Internet recently and found a report from a local paper. (Yes, another report, and if you think I spend my whole time Googling myself, well, no, I don't any more, but yes, I once did. Nothing to do with vanity, I promise you; all these things I found, they were like pieces in the puzzle of my lost childhood.)

The report was a newspaper story about Eunice's jail sentence: 'MOTHER FROM HELL GETS 14 YEARS' was the headline. It's one of those that allow readers to leave their own comments about the story. I've scrolled through my fair share, and they're usually from fanatics arguing about the religious connection or complaining that Eunice's sentence was too light. (They say things like, 'She got fourteen years, but she'll be out in seven knowing the lenient jail system in this country!!' and I have to think about that. It makes me realize that I'll more than likely still be in my twenties when the woman who took my childhood gets out of prison.)

The set of comments on the 'Mother From Hell' story is no different from any others, the usual parade of people putting their oar in and, looking at them now, they have a point about her sentence being too lenient. Except that about halfway down the column of comments is one from a Safeway security guard, who worked at the Tewkesbury branch and saw us there, day in, day out. He thought he knew Eunice well, he says, as he saw her two or three times a day. She was always in and out with the children shopping, and she ate in there a lot.

He's right. Mother would often have her evening meal in the cafeteria, leaving the girls to prepare beans on toast when we got home. Some days she'd pack us all up in the Transit and we'd drive over to Tewkesbury Safeway for a lunchtime session. Mother would have her lunch; we'd wait in the van. Sometimes, even, the Safeway tractor beam was so strong that she'd drag us all there for a Sunday lunch. If we were really lucky we'd get to eat it with her. So, yes, she spent a lot of time in Safeway. (No doubt profits took a dip when they put her in jail.) And there she saw the security guard, who goes on to say in his comment that he never suspected anything, even though she did seem a little strange and was quite strict with the children. We seemed 'cute', he says. We were polite.

When she was charged she approached him and asked if he'd be a character witness. Initially he agreed – he'd always thought of himself as a good judge of character – but then a sixth sense kicked in and he decided against the idea. Now, he's glad he did. 'With the benefit of hindsight,' he says, 'she showed no emotion when she told me what the kids had accused her of. She could have been talking about the weather. I am still totally shocked.'

It's funny. I'm not sure I ever knew who this security guard was. After all, it was Mother who spent most of her time in the store, not us. Still, though, I'm glad. I'm glad he believed us.

There were days when we'd spend the entire day in the car park at Safeway while Mother sat in the café. We'd pack up as if going to the farmhouse, but then just sit in the car park, animals and kids, staring at her through the window. Mostly, though, it was after a day at the farmhouse, and she'd come out, say goodbye to her friend and we'd leave. Then we'd make the short drive back to George Dowty Drive, where we unloaded our stuff – Mother's pile of important documents staying just where it was, ready to expand and take over the world – and went indoors. Karen and Lulu would cook a meal and I'd go upstairs to our bedroom, where I had a stash.

A secret stash.

What it was, I'd become interested in cars. I'd always been keen on cars, but the interest had grown and become something bordering on obsession. I don't know how, exactly. The way any little boy gets into anything, I suppose. With some it's tractors or trains. With me it was cars. My car obsession had peaked; Bradley was getting interested, too. They were all I thought about and talked of. Cars, heaven as an autobahn. They were, quite literally, my escape.

Feeding the obsession was tough, though. We didn't get to see much television apart from the horror films we were made to watch, and maybe the odd soap opera that Mother used to love. We didn't really go anywhere so I didn't get much opportunity to go and look at cars in real life, in showrooms and stuff, and we weren't really allowed magazines.

Except I'd had a brainwave. I'd found one of those insert cards where you send off for more information. It had fallen out of one of Mother's magazines. For Volvo it was. I knew she'd punish me if she found out I'd sent off for it, so I'd filled it in with the right address, but a false name. For days and weeks I watched the post like a hawk, and when it eventually came I was pleased I'd used the false name because Mother got there first. She'd taken one look at the name and address, seen that it was a Volvo brochure and thrown it in the kitchen bin. That night we were on a cleaning detail, and when nobody was looking – I couldn't take the chance of anybody seeing me – I went into the kitchen bin and retrieved the brochure. Hiding it wasn't really a problem, our room was such a mess. But I pushed it underneath the bunk to be on the safe side. And then, in those moments when I found myself alone, I'd read my Volvo brochure.

Since that success I'd done it again, this time with a brochure for BMW, so now I had two, and after a day's work at the farmhouse that's what I'd do – I'd read my car brochures.

Then we'd eat, unless we were on starvation, in which case we'd take Charlotte's and Bradley's meals to them in the living room, maybe some for Mother, too, if she was still hungry. Then we'd clear away the dinner. If there was no tidy-up or preaching session, or film-of-the-Armageddon to watch, we'd go to bed. Karen and Lulu on the bunk, me on the floor.

Next day, it would start all over again. And that was my life. Seven, eight, nine years old. My childhood measured in strokes of the feet, circuits of the lawn, hours spent in the Safeway car park and number of days on starvation.

Chapter Twenty-three

I woke up, excited. Every year the Witnesses have a convention in Cardiff, and we were going. Not for the first time – we'd been the previous year and it was great. Yes, there was a lot of sitting around in our best clothes listening to people preach for what felt like hours, but it was also a chance to get away from the farmhouse and meet new people. Even better than that, a convention meant a break from starvation punishment. We used to get really scrawny when we were on starvation and Witnesses would have asked questions, so for at least a week leading up to the convention Mother allowed us all to eat properly.

As a result I woke up that morning without the gnawing hunger at the pit of my stomach. That, more than anything else, was a reason to be happy. That and the fact that my punishments were lighter than usual too. Usually, when I was being beaten on the feet, mother would use the chair leg on other parts of my body. A flailing arm would get a whack. She'd get my legs if they were kicking, or she'd simply miss my feet and catch me across the cheek, or on the side of the body. She wasn't fussy when she was giving a beating, she didn't really care.

But with Cardiff coming up she had to be more careful. She had to restrain herself to the feet or risk giving us a bruise people might notice. So that same week we were being fed properly, the punishments lacked her normal ferocity, too. She never rammed sticks down our throat during that period, either, for the same reason.

Perhaps that's why I decided to do what I did that day, because any punishment would be lighter than usual. Maybe. More likely I just did it because I could, because I had the key and I wanted to prove to myself that I could go against her if I wanted to. Looking back, God, what a stupid thing to do. I wasn't hungry, I didn't need food. The chances of getting caught were high. So why? Why steal the gateau?

Because I could. Because I had the key. Actually, Karen had the key.

'Look,' she had said one day, checking Mother wasn't around and drawing me in close. She opened her hand to show me the key.

'What is it?'

'Duh, it's a key.'

'Duh, yes, but what's it for?'

'The freezer.'

The freezer. The outside chest freezer that was full of frozen desserts, choc ices, lollies and ice cream. The freezer full of the stuff that Charlotte and Bradley loved and that might as well have existed in another dimension for all the access Lulu, Karen and I had to its treasures.

But not now. Now we had a key.

How Karen came by it is one of those mysteries lost in time. It might have been Charlotte's, because she had her own key so she could help herself to any goodies from the freezer whenever she wanted. Only her, though. Otherwise it was kept locked so Karen, Lulu and I couldn't steal from it when we were on starvation.

'Let's have the key,' I said to Karen later that day. We were all inside the house, packing for the trip. It was a three-day convention so there was a lot we needed. We had a B&B near the Cardiff City stadium where the convention was held each year (until the Millennium Stadium was built, anyway; now they hold it there). The idea was we were going to leave Eckington at about 7 p.m., pick up Nanny and Granddad, then drive to Cardiff in the night, book in and be ready for the convention the next day.

But for some reason I had the freezer on my mind. I wanted something out of the freezer. So when Karen surrendered the key I crept to the freezer, which was kept in one of the sheds, opened it up and looked in. There it was, just the treasure trove I'd been expecting. Boxes of ice-lollies, frozen desserts, frozen meat, bags of veg. I shifted more stuff around to check what was in the bottom, looking for goodies, and there, about halfway down, was a frozen gateau. A Black Forest gateau. I slid it out, closed the freezer and left the room.

We had an outside toilet at the farmhouse, a tiny brick room, and I hid the gateau inside, under a bag, where it would defrost. It was 5 p.m. My plan was to have a bit before we left at 7 p.m. and keep it stored in the outside toilet while we were away, then have some more when we got back. (I was seven then. Looking back now as an eighteen-year-old I can see that there were a couple of flaws in my scheme.)

'What did you get?' whispered Karen as I returned the key.

'A gateau.'

'Can I have some?'

'Yeah, but it's defrosting.'

An hour later and we were beginning to pack the Transit, carrying stuff to it from the farmhouse across the yard and over to where it was parked outside the barns. I moved to the toilet, over on the other side of the yard, let myself in, quelled excitement as I retrieved the gateau box from the bag and prepared to get stuck in.

Only it was still frozen. Frozen solid. Heart sinking, I replaced it in the bag, then let myself out to rejoin the others packing.

Then Mother went to the freezer. I watched her go across the yard. Would she miss it? No, surely not. It was just one gateau. The freezer was full of stuff.

She was wearing her jeans, work boots and favourite fleece. The next day at the convention she'd be smart, prim and proper, leading us around, me and Bradley in our suits, the girls in their dresses. She always made sure to stay close to us at conventions, we were never allowed off by ourselves – to the toilet and that was about it. She liked us to speak only when spoken to by other Witnesses and then behave with almost supernatural politeness. She also liked us to show off our knowledge of the Bible, and that went for normal meetings, too. In the week she'd make us stay up late before meetings studying the *Watchtower* so that when questions were asked we could give the right answers. She wanted other Witnesses to see us as perfect Jehovah's Witness children: well behaved, devout, a credit to their Mother.

'*Who* has stolen from the freezer?'

She came roaring out of the freezer shed. She'd gone in there to pick out some supplies for the trip, looked in the freezer and seen it disturbed. I didn't think I'd made a mess or anything, but maybe she monitored it the way she counted slices of bread. Who knows, maybe I *had* made a mess. Maybe it was blindingly obvious that one of us had been rooting about in it – someone other than her or Charlotte.

Her eyes roamed the yard, where we all stood, me holding a box of something to take to the car. She seemed to pick on Karen, who flinched as Mother descended on her, ready for a slap, a punch, a shove to the dirt. But Mother knew better than to punch Karen, not with the convention the next day, so instead she stood and screamed at her. Screaming at her that she'd stolen from the freezer, until Karen cracked and pointed at me.

'It was Chris,' she said. 'Chris did it. He took a gateau. It's in the outside toilet.'

I didn't blame Karen for that. I would have done the same in her position. I would have done the same if it was Lulu. No Alleycats.

Mother turned her attention to me.

'Get it,' she said.

I was about to protest. 'Just get it,' she snapped, and I put the box down, jogged over to the outside toilet and retrieved the gateau, holding it out to her. She took it, inspecting the ripped-open box, bringing the still-frozen gateau out of the cardboard, which had taken on that soggy look that defrosting cardboard gets, like all the gloss and colour and fun has been leeched out of it and it's left looking like what it is — which is a damp bit of cardboard.

I saw into Mother's eyes and they were tiny black holes of fury.

'You will eat this,' she said. 'Here,' and she grabbed me by the arm, dragging me over to the back door where she shoved me to the ground so that I was kneeling.

'Eat it.' She shoved the frozen gateau at me. 'Eat it all, every last bit.' The gateau fell to my lap. A couple of hours ago it had been a tasty Black Forest Gateau. Now it was shoved into my T-shirt and I was crouching by the drainhole near the back door. And suddenly it didn't look quite so delicious.

She told the others to keep packing, and they did, passing by Mother and me as they made trips into the house for more stuff, giving me looks that were idle curiosity mixed with the relief of 'thank God it's not me' that I knew so well. I watched Karen go past. She must have been wondering, as I was, why Mother hadn't asked about the key (but she never did — I still can't believe it, but she didn't even ask how I got access to the freezer; I think she must have assumed she'd left it unlocked, or that Charlotte had). Suddenly I wasn't wondering about the key any more, though, because Mother had taken hold of my head and was forcing it into the gateau.

'Eat,' she ordered me. 'Every last bit.' She gave me until we left; she told me my life wouldn't be worth living if I didn't have the gateau finished by the time we left for Cardiff. She released my head and walked away.

I tried picking bits off to eat it. At first I could, as the outside had defrosted a bit. In the end, though, I was simply raising the whole gateau to my face and biting into it, fighting the brain freeze. My head rushed with the cold, my teeth were numb and shards of rock-solid gateau caught in my throat like broken glass. My stomach lurched as more unfriendly gateau went into it and I looked around for somewhere I might surreptitiously get rid of the gateau, but Mother saw me doing it and stopped me with a warning look. In the end, the girls and Bradley got into the Sherpa minibus we had at the time, Judith in the driving seat, all of them staring out of the Transit and at the back door of the farmhouse as Mother locked up then stood over me, making sure I finished every last bit of the gateau. At last I looked up at her, the gateau gone, chocolate around my face and an ice-cold nausea in my stomach. She grabbed hold of my arm, and dragged me to the minibus.

We hadn't been on the road long – we'd just got on the M5 – when I started throwing up. The first time was in the minibus and everybody scrabbled away holding their noses, fighting sick themselves as my vomit splashed to the floor. Mother yanked a window open with one hand, grabbed my head with the other, and pushed my head out of the window so I looked like one of those dogs you see. I vomited again and a streak of half-digested gateau pebble-dashed the side of the van. And again. And again.

Further down the motorway we stopped at a service station to try to clean up the inside as best we could. I was still heaving, but dry-heaving by now. One side of the Transit was green – the colour it was supposed to be. The other side, well, you don't even want to know.

I would have got a beating for that, if Nanny and Granddad hadn't been there. The whole thing, disgusting and painful as it was – I'd proved something to myself. That I could go against her if I wanted to.

Even if it had got off to a bad start, the rest of the convention passed by without incident. We did as we were told. We spoke when we were spoken to and when we did speak we were the epitome of good manners. Collectively, we were her children, and in public she never showed any of the cruelty we endured at home. The only thing to really set Karen, Lulu and me apart was the way Mother favoured Charlotte and Bradley with other people – Charlotte in particular. When it came to Charlotte, we were all the perfect Jehovah's Witnesses but some of us were more perfect than others. One time, when we were being beaten, Mother had screamed a quote from the scriptures at us: 'A truthful witness does not deceive, but a false witness pours out lies.' It's from Proverbs. The truthful witness was Charlotte, she told us. We were the false witnesses, and she took the rod to us.

Chapter Twenty-four

*T*hen, one day, Lulu escaped.

Lulu was always the one of us who never accepted the way we were treated. For me, Eunice was my Mother, I knew no different, while Karen had a more obedient temperament. Lulu, though, she never truly went under Mother's spell, not like me and Karen. She would always be the most vocal of us, and at night when we lay in our room, she'd often call Mother names.

'Shh,' we used to say back, 'if she hears you'll get us in even more trouble.'

We were always bickering that one or the other was making things worse for all three of us. Mother, had she heard us, would have been satisfied, no doubt. And more often than not, it was Lulu doing the making-things-worse.

Perhaps it was because she'd seen a little bit more of life before she came into Mother's care. Not enough to have memories but enough to instinctively know: this is not how mothers treat their children. This is not right. We used to tell her to behave. I think, though, that she did the things she did to prove a point, the point being that she could tell someone if she chose to; that she could leave if she wanted to. A point that she had to prove to herself more than anybody else.

The first signs of rebellion she'd shown were years and years ago. Something that came out at the trial, but I was too young to really know about, was that she threw her diaries over the Welsh neighbours' wall at George Dowty Drive. The trouble was, her handwriting was so bad that even if the neighbours had tried to read them, they wouldn't have been able to understand them. More than likely, they never even tried. Mr Young handed them back to Mother, who took them, smiled and thanked him. She made Lulu throw them on the fire, then Lulu was beaten.

She'd also said the occasional thing when we were at school, alerting teachers who contacted Mother, who in turn accused the teachers of victimizing Lulu. Again, though, it's not something I was ever aware of at the time. It's come out since, either by talking to Lulu or at the trial or in the newspaper reports. (Which is one of the weird, unsettling things about living in the aftermath of a case like this – so much of your life is suddenly in the public eye, even things you yourself don't recall. It's as though they didn't happen to me, they happened to him, Child C. Only it's me who's left with the scars, the limp and the insomnia.)

Anyway. Back to Lulu and the day she escaped. She'd backchatted Mother, that was the original offence.

Backchatting was Mother's main non-crime. By which I mean that we rarely, and when we were young *never*, actually did give her any backchat. Not unless you count backchat as answering questions with a No, Yes or I will. So instead she used it as an excuse when she simply wanted to hit out, or teach us a lesson, or remind us who was boss. She'd snap, 'Don't backchat me,' and lash out. Sometimes a slap around the face, sometimes a punch or just a painful thwack with whatever she was holding at the time. I soon learned that a punch from Mother wasn't as painful as a slap. A punch, it's just blunt trauma. But the slap stings and it's humiliating. Somehow it's worse.

I don't know what Lulu said or was supposed to have said. Maybe she genuinely had given Mother some lip (of all of us, she was the one most likely to) and that was why she was told to go into the washroom and wait for a beating. Perhaps it was Judith who had been the butt of her backchat. Either way she was ordered into the washroom.

There, no doubt, she had a Lulu moment, standing in the tiny room with the white goods, waiting to be beaten on the feet. Something inside her snapped, and she took off.

The first I knew of it was hearing a general kerfuffle. Mother and Judith were banging around the place, shouting, and I walked into the kitchen to see what all the fuss was about, finding Mother there in a full-blown panic.

This was a surprise; it wasn't an everyday occurrence for her to be like that. She had her moments – her rages during beatings, mostly – but on the whole she remained composed. Now, though, she seemed to be in genuine danger of losing it. I didn't wonder then, but I've wondered since: Why? Why was she in such a flap? She can't have been genuinely concerned for Lulu's wellbeing, surely? I might more realistically have expected her to feel a sense of satisfaction that Lulu had braved a freezing, black and unfriendly night rather than endure a beating. But no. Mother was worried; she was panicking. Perhaps it was because Lulu running away meant Mother no longer had control of her; that Lulu might tell someone she met exactly why she had run away. As Mother busied around the kitchen, calling us all in and giving us our instructions, her mind must have been racing.

It was very cold. And it may have been light when Lulu first entered the washroom but by the time her escape was discovered, darkness had fallen. Eckington – at least our bit of it – wasn't blessed with streetlamps. Behind us we had the field, now a blanket of gloom, darkness and trees outlined against a grey sky. In one direction the road led out of the village, the road Judith's folk-friend had been trundling along the day I first clapped eyes on the farm, with nothing there apart from wilderness and the next settlement along. In the other direction was Eckington, but we were on the very outskirts, hardly any houses within eyesight let alone earshot. Next to our house, about fifty yards away, was the graveyard.

Mother and Judith were already wrapping up. They had torches, which they handed out to me, Karen, Charlotte and Bradley. We grabbed what insulation we could, hefted our torches and stepped out into the cold, our breath billowing ahead of us.

'Mary-Beth!' we called, spreading out.

Judith hunched herself into her coat, feeling the cold more than the rest of us. She suffered from asthma.

'Mary-Beth, come home!'

Our torch beams search-lit the lawn. I peeked into the sheds, opened the door of the caravan parked there and shone a torch inside.

'You'll catch your death,' called Mother. I could hear the concern in her voice.

Lulu told us later that she'd legged it over the field. She'd had the Lulu moment in the washroom and, instead of waiting to be thrashed, had darted out of the back door, thumping over the lawn into the field, feeling the exhilaration of freedom. There, she'd crouched down, looking at the lights of the farmhouse. Then she'd turned her back on it and made her way to the graveyard. A short time later she heard the shouting.

'Mary-Beth!'

And . . .

'Mary-Beth, come home!'

And . . .

'You'll catch your death.'

She crouched in the graveyard, behind a gravestone, listening to our voices and watching the torch beams. All was silent, then she heard someone approaching, saw the torchlight strafing the rear of the graveyard.

A voice called, 'Mary-Beth.' It was Judith. Lulu could hear the threat and warning in her voice. She stayed still as Judith came further into the graveyard, Judith playing the torch over the stones, giving them the look of an eerie skyline.

Lulu caught her breath and stayed still, Judith passing close behind her, so close that she thought she'd been spotted. Must have been spotted. So she made a run for it.

Judith heard her. She snapped, 'Mary-Beth,' and for a second the torchlight swung crazily around the graveyard as Judith tried to locate the source of the noise. But Lulu had gone. She told us later that she'd run from the graveyard and hidden beneath a car. She couldn't tell me the make. Typical. If it were me, I would have known the make of the car I was hiding underneath.

We were still in the field when Judith came back with the news. She'd heard Mary-Beth, she thought, but she'd got away.

So Mother phoned the police.

It's not something I questioned at the time. (Did I, you're probably wondering, question anything? Maybe not.) But looking back she must have called them in, not because she was seriously concerned about Lulu being out at night – an eight-year-old girl roaming the dimly lit fields of Eckington – but because phoning the police was the kind of thing a concerned mum *should* do. To not phone them, and for Lulu to turn up somewhere saying she'd run away from home to escape a beating on the soles of her feet, would have been disastrous for her.

I've got to hand it to them, the police. They didn't mess about. I didn't hear the call Mother made, but perhaps the operator picked up on the panic in her voice, or maybe she put on a great performance as a worried mum, or maybe that's just how they always respond to eight-year-old runaways in the dead of night in Gloucestershire. But they turned up in force, and quickly, too.

We stood at the back of the house, Charlotte, Karen, Bradley and I, having given up the search, waiting now for the police to arrive and giggling to ourselves. Little kids thrilled by the novelty of our runaway sister.

'I'll deal with you later,' said Mother, seeing us laughing, and we stopped, although she meant only Karen and me, and she never did deal with us later. Not that night.

The police cars drew into the farmhouse, through the gates, and suddenly the yard was full of uniformed men, their radios crackling. They looked huge to us. They stepped out of their cars (a Vauxhall Omega and two Vauxhall Astras), adjusted their belts, and put on caps and helmets. One of them strode towards Mother, who walked forward to meet him and tell him what she knew.

Pretty soon, the policemen were out there, too, shining their torchlights, calling for Mary-Beth. A couple of them stayed behind, co-ordinating the search, drinking coffee brought to them by Mother. She did invite them inside, but only as far as the washroom. She wouldn't have wanted them to see the rest of the house – they might have spotted things, started asking more probing questions about Lulu's disappearance.

I was like, Wow. All these policemen, the cars, the gadgets they had inside them. Lulu almost forgotten, I got talking to one of the policemen, who let me sit in the car and showed me the radio.

Hours went by; the police even launched a helicopter. As if the cars themselves weren't exciting enough, suddenly the air was filled with the *whup-whup* of chopper blades, hovering over us, going one way, banking then returning, a searchlight playing over the fields behind us. It was the kind of thing a kid's fantasies are full of.

And then the call came through, about 4 a.m. Mary-Beth had been found. (I was probably disappointed at the time, shame on me.) And moments later, Lulu returned with a policeman, who brought her through the gates of the farmhouse into the yard, where we all waited for her, all of us kids, our attention instinctively going to Mother, waiting to receive her daughter.

What had happened, Lulu told us later, was that she'd stayed under the car for what seemed like hours, before crawling out from beneath it and looking for somewhere to shelter, hiding whenever she heard someone call her name. She was aware of the police, she said, and heard the helicopter, too. She'd found a donkey shed and gone inside, but one of the donkeys hadn't taken kindly to sharing his dorm with Lulu, so he'd walked out. A policeman saw the donkey, put two and two together and found Lulu, who had, unbelievably, fallen asleep. He'd woken her, called in the find and brought her back to the farmhouse.

There was a moment, a breath-holding moment, when the policeman stopped, allowing Lulu to come forward and meet Mother, who approached her. Lulu looked tired, bedraggled, hangdog. Mother's face betrayed no emotion as she walked forward, took hold of Lulu and gave her a hug.

It was probably the first time I saw her hug anybody but Bradley or Charlotte, and Lulu came into the hug, letting herself relax and be drawn in.

How would I have felt if I'd been Lulu at that moment? I know exactly. I would have felt forgiven. I would have felt healed. I would have thought, from now on, everything will be all right. From now on, Mother will love me. I am no longer the scum of the earth.

Wistfully I realized that the chopper had gone, and two of the police cars pulled out of the gate, leaving behind one, who checked that we were going to be all right, said something stern to Lulu and then he, too, left. I didn't want him to go. I so didn't want him to go. Not because I was planning on suddenly blurting out the truth to him – *motherbeatsusandshestarvesusandshemakesusdrinkbleach* – that never even occurred to me. But because, with the policeman there, Mother wouldn't hurt Lulu. She would be waiting until the policeman had left, and then the beating would start. We trooped back into the house. I was coiling inside, I could feel it, as we filed into the kitchen and Mother closed the back door behind her. Second nature made me glance around the room to see what weapons might be at hand. I was waiting for her to call out a number, or go into a rage, with some screaming about the demons inside Lulu. I was wondering whether the punishment for Lulu would mean punishment for Karen and me as well. I was thinking, Please not me this time, I didn't run away, I didn't force you to call the police.

And then, the shock. Nothing happened. Mother said nothing. Perhaps the night had given her a scare – it had got too big for her. Whatever her reasons, she didn't beat us – hardly even raised her voice – for almost a week afterwards.

Chapter Twenty-five

'Children.'

The driver's door of the Transit van clunked open and Mother's head appeared. At the same time the passenger door opened and Judith climbed in, taking her seat and twisting to look at us in the back.

It was 1998. I was nine. I had been beaten and starved for three years by then. I had been on methylphenidate for two years straight. Every day I had to do backbreaking work at the farmhouse and sit for hours in Safeway car park, and at nights I was forced to stay awake for lectures about the Armageddon, or to watch horror films, or to tidy up. I had nothing in my life to look forward to.

Judith regarded us from the front seat. She was living with us at home then. She'd often spend short periods with us before zooming off on a jaunt with her folk friends or going where the work took her. Work, for Judith, was carpentry, and she was very, very good at it. At George Dowty Drive she'd built the bookcase at the top of the stairs, the one that housed the *Encyclopaedia Britannica*. She'd done carpentry work for celebrities, too – people you would have heard of. She did a lot around the farmhouse and would have done more, had she lived.

Anyway, this was one of the periods she was staying with us, and she'd often accompany Mother on shopping trips. Once again we'd been sitting in the van waiting, but not in Safeway's car park for a change. This time we were in the car park of the Cascades

Leisure Centre in Tewkesbury, where we'd been arguing about who-knows-what when Mother and Judith returned, and we fell silent. Mother got in, turning like Judith to face us.

'Children.'

She always called us that when we were all together. At home, it was what she called when she wanted our attention, which she always got. She called you and you ran. You didn't keep her waiting. Keeping Mother Waiting meant a punch in the face, a sudden rage. If there was bamboo or the chair leg to hand – and there usually was – she'd use that, too.

Now, though . . . Now she was smiling. Mother was not a woman who smiled much. She always seemed preoccupied, and probably was, with all her thoughts of Armageddon. If you look at pictures of her, her mouth has a natural downturn, as though used to frowning. So, no, it wasn't an everyday occurrence for her to smile like that.

'We've got some good news,' she announced. Judith was smiling too, I noticed.

We waited, breath held.

'We've booked the tickets for Florida.'

People often ask where she got her money from. After all, in the whole time I knew her, she never had a job yet she was able to pay for what would be a long, long holiday in America – and not just her and us, either, but for her parents and her ex-husband as well, she paid for us all. There would be other holidays, too; plus, later, she bought a narrow boat, a Chevrolet van, spent what must have been tens of thousands of pounds spoiling Bradley rotten and paid for countless, ultimately fruitless, renovations to the farmhouse. The simple answer is, we never knew. You don't, growing up, query where your mum gets her money, it's just *there*. Neither can I really speculate. All I know is that it's one more mysterious thing about her. Like her two marriages, like whatever she used to do before we came into her life, the source of her money would forever remain a mystery.

And like I say, I wasn't thinking about that then. I'd just heard the words: 'We've booked the tickets for Florida.'

I gasped. We all did, all of us kids. We didn't have Christmas; Jehovah's Witnesses didn't celebrate it. So this, for us, was our Christmas. This was us hearing that Santa had been and left us a big sack of presents. For years, Mother had been telling us about our holiday to Florida. *Years*. It was right up there with the Armageddon for topics of conversation, one of those things that was discussed so much I had given up hope of it ever actually happening. But now, apparently, it was. We were going in just over a month's time, and we were going for *six whole weeks*. Judith was going to come (she beamed happily by Mother's side – again, she wasn't one who smiled easily, but this was one of those rare, rare moments when we were all happy), so was Mother's first husband, Frank, who was Judith's dad. So were Nanny and Granddad. We were going to hire a villa in Orlando, drive down to the Keys, cruise the Caribbean. We were going to Disney World. The Transit was bouncing up and down we were so excited.

Now, I had something to look forward to.

Even so, it didn't take long for things to get back to normal after the night of Lulu's escape.

We had a snooker room at the farmhouse. I say 'snooker room' and that makes it sound grand, as though it had portraits decorating the walls and bottles of brandy on side tables. In fact, it was one of the outhouses, just to the left as you came into the farmyard, the first one along.

In it, Charlotte had made herself a little outside den, so it housed mainly her stuff. She'd personalized it with pop posters on the walls, pictures of boy bands from magazines that she changed as they fell in and out of fashion. If you were to go to the farmhouse now they'd probably still be there – posters of boy bands who don't exist any more and only had two hits anyway; they're up on the wall, slowly aging the place.

The snooker room. It was one of Charlotte's favourite places. She didn't do chores around the house so she spent a lot of time there. The table – not quite professional standard, but a good one – reached almost to the four corners of the room, and she'd spend endless days moving around it, cue in hand, selecting another cue from the rack, chalking it up, knocking snooker balls around the table – maybe pausing every now and then to moon over one of the boys in her posters.

And she got good at snooker this way. Really good. We used to say she was so good at snooker she should be on TV, and we meant it. One of her specialities was the trick shot. It had to be, really. Lulu, Karen and I were always off doing duties, helping with the building work, and Bradley would have just run off with the balls anyway. So she had little opportunity to practise her competitive play. It was out of necessity that she mastered trick shots instead.

It was a trick shot she was showing me one day. I was skiving off my duties because Mother had gone out, as she regularly did, to the market in Pershore. It's the same market where she met George Parker all those years ago, and it's locally famous, not just for the beauty of the town and the surrounding area, but for the quality of the produce, something to do with it being in the Vale of Evesham and on the banks of the River Avon. It's a beautiful town. It's got a famous abbey, it's popular with Morris dancers and the singer Toyah Wilcox lives there – or she certainly used to, anyway – but I didn't get to go there very much. I went just a handful of times. Mainly it was Mother who visited: to fetch provisions, pick up bargains, give herself a break from the chaos of the farm.

It was a boiling-hot day, so I was grateful to get out of the heat and into the relative cool of the snooker room, where Charlotte was practising her shots. She looked up to see me, then demanded I sit down. She had a shot she wanted to show me. I sat, away with the fairies as always, but happy to let Charlotte demonstrate the trick.

She put three red balls widthways in the middle of the table, leaned over the table, cue poised, and – tap – the balls were gliding apart, the two outside balls sinking into snug pockets, the inside ball remaining exactly where it was on the table, except spinning. The whole thing had a perfect symmetry – it was a very cool trick indeed.

I asked her to show me again. She reached to set the balls up.

What Mother used to do was toot her horn as she came up the hill from Pershore. Hearing that horn was our sign to move. The yard might have been empty and silent but when the Transit's horn sounded it was suddenly filled with running children. Or, me, Karen and Lulu at least – dashing to open the gate for her like we were letting her into some kind of secret military compound.

Maybe I didn't hear the beep. Unlikely, because the Transit van had the loudest horn you've ever heard. Mother used to say that the neighbours had moaned about the beeping and we barely even *had* neighbours, so, no, I would have heard the beep.

Perhaps I heard it but thought Lulu and Karen would get the gate. That they were at that very moment rushing into the yard, opening the gate for the Transit, which would crunch into the yard, Mother's hard, staring face regarding them from the window.

But they hadn't done that.

Or maybe I heard it but for some reason it simply didn't register. Too much in a daze, too tired, too rapt in watching Charlotte set up her trick for the second time. It was, after all, a very cool trick indeed.

(But how stupid. Later, I'd kick myself, again and again. How stupid could I have been? She always gets in a rage if the gate isn't opened in time. Always. Even now, weird as it is, there's a bit of me where I still think it was partly my fault. After all, if I'd opened the gate, it wouldn't have happened.)

Mother must have let herself in. She must have been getting out of the Transit as I sat in the snooker room, oblivious.

Charlotte set up the balls on the table, stood back to check they were correctly aligned, took up position at the foot of the table, squinting down her cue, ready to play.

And everything went black.

Mother had come into the snooker room. She would have been angry that she'd beeped and I hadn't opened the gate. She'd taken a cue from the rack and swung it at the back of my head.

The thick end, it was.

I saw it coming, at the last second, just out of the corner of my eye. Somewhere, a survival sense must have kicked in and recognized that danger had entered the room and it made me turn just in time to see the cue swing at me, and I ducked. Too late. She knocked me out cold.

I went to the floor, unconscious. The next thing I knew I was hearing the sound of a TV – a TV that hasn't been tuned properly, that's trying to find a channel on the channel-search facility. Only it wasn't a real TV, it was the sound in my head, this buzzing, humming, static sound. There was a white light, flashing before my eyes, all the kinds of things you read about. And then some sound, and then I distinctly heard Mother say, 'Quick, lay him on his back,' and her and Charlotte doing just that.

I couldn't see. For a moment or so I thought I might be blind, and I was struggling to my feet, a dim kind of vision returning, before I dropped back to the floor. Apparently I mentioned the name of a local farmer, a man who rented some land from us. I mentioned his name while I was unconscious. Weird.

Mother's face floated into view above me, Charlotte peering in as well. Mother in particular looked concerned. Concerned for me – not an emotion I was familiar with. They set up a chair outside the snooker room and Mother sent Charlotte to fetch an ice-lolly from the freezer, insisting I sit on the chair and eat it. I was still groggy, my head lolling as I rode waves of faintness. She stayed with me, waiting until I was sufficiently recovered to take hold of my ice-lolly.

I sat there, in the sun, eating it, feeling dizzy.

And there was something about the dizziness, something about the way it had rearranged my head at that moment. I felt happy. Sitting there with my ice-lolly, I was almost euphoric. It was just the dizziness, of course, nothing to do with Mother's act of kindness. Nothing to do with the fact that she had been worried, and that maybe, just maybe, I actually *mattered* to her. I mean, I'm sure it was just the dizziness, because even back then I must have realized that she didn't care; that all she was concerned about was that she might have done something so bad the outside world would need to intervene. So why is it that I suddenly knew how Lulu felt that chilly early morning when the police brought her back from the donkey shed, when Mother hugged her? A little bit of me thought, She's gone too far now, she's gone too far, so she'll stop. Everything will be all right. I am no longer the scum of the earth.

But, of course, I was. I always was the scum of the earth.

Chapter Twenty-six

*T*hat summer, 1998, was hot, really hot. Occasionally, we would have bottles of Coca-Cola in the garden. And bottles it was. Mother always said that Coke tasted better from proper glass bottles, so she made sure to get those rather than the plastic sort and we'd sit drinking from them in the garden. Not long after the day she hit me with the cue, we were doing just that, all us kids, when Bradley and I started to argue.

About what? I'm not sure. One of a million things it could have been. We were brothers. Brothers argue. And once they've done a bit of arguing, chances are they'll start a bit of fighting. Which is just what Bradley and I started to do, tussling on the garden, Bradley squealing as I pinned him down, him wriggling away, squealing again as I pinned him down once more.

Suddenly, she was there. She'd come darting from the back door and I looked up to see just a blur of her jeans and boots. I was already rising from Bradley because I knew I was in trouble.

She'd picked up one of the Coca-Cola bottles. In that moment I knew. She swung. I ducked. Too late. The bottle shattered around my head and I dropped back to the floor, onto my knees, broken glass falling to the grass around me. I felt blood on my neck, reached to touch the spot then looked at my fingers. Not blood but Coke. Drips of it, the last dregs in the bottle making their sticky way around my neck. I shook my head and more bits of broken bottle fell to the floor. I moved my fingers to my scalp, feeling for blood there, too. There was none, just a ringing in my head, a feeling of fuzziness and disorientation. I looked to my side and Mother was kneeling by Bradley, putting an arm round his shoulder.

'Are you all right?' she asked him. 'Come on.' She led him away, back into the house. I studied my fingers, amazed to see no blood there. It had bruised, though. I had a lump the size of a golf ball for days, with a matching headache, too.

She must have seen us fighting, or heard us. Seen us, most likely. Mother was obsessed with keeping tabs on us, and she'd always be staring out of a window to check what we were doing. I'd be in the middle of a chore in the garden, a rake in my hand, and I'd glance up to the house. There, in an upstairs window, would be Mother, staring down at me. Just staring. Sometimes I'd hold her gaze for a moment or so – a titchy little rebellion – but then go back to work, knowing that if she disapproved of anything she'd seen she'd be out in a flash. If she noticed I'd missed a bit, say, then she'd come running out into the back garden, often for a punch, sometimes with a knife. I suppose it was just a spur of the moment thing. She'd be doing something with a knife, look out of the window and catch me doing unsatisfactory work, then come running, still holding the knife, which she hid from me until she was close enough to use it.

I never used to see the knife until the last second, that was the thing. It would come flashing from somewhere, then open up my arm, and she'd turn and leave. Don't think me vain, but I wear make-up these days, on my arms at least. Without it they're ugly reminders of my past – a road map of angry scars. I don't bother with the make-up elsewhere, of course. Not on my stomach, for example, another place she liked to cut me. Both of my sides bear scars, too. My left side she opened up with a kitchen knife one afternoon in the farmhouse kitchen, around the same time she attacked me with the bottle.

I don't remember what I'd done wrong – I don't even remember the attack, funnily enough. What I remember is the aftermath. She walked away – she always did after something like that. I stood there with blood leaking from the wound in my side, down my trousers onto the floor, and I thought, that'll need clearing up. I wadded some kitchen towel, pressed it to the wound, then got down to wipe away the blood with some more kitchen towel.

As I did so, I thought about Florida.

Because it was happening, it really was. The holiday we'd heard so much about was *actually going to take place*.

Or was it? The threats had begun. During midnight preaching sessions. While we were sitting in the back of the van. Even during beatings. With blows raining down on us she'd be threatening to leave us at home during the Florida holiday, because demon children don't get to go to Florida. There are no demon children allowed at Disney World, no demon children there. It was the stick she used to beat us with, literally. Before it had been some kind of vague, far-off threat, hardly worth a thought during a punishment. Now, though, now it was real, and it was real because the tickets were booked and it was real because Charlotte had made Bradley a calendar so he could count down the days.

Really, it was a Mickey Mouse poster, but Charlotte was fairly arty so she'd customized it. In her version, Mickey Mouse was on a cruise ship, and she'd made little doors for Bradley to open, one for each day. Behind each door was a chocolate, a little square of Dairy Milk, and in the last door was a special final prize, a big fizzy sweet, cherry flavour. Yum.

The calendar hung on the wall in Bradley and Mother's bedroom at George Dowty Drive. In the evening, when we'd returned from a day's work at the farmhouse, I'd go upstairs, silently slip into the bedroom and stare at it. Everybody else would be helping to make dinner but that hour or so before the meal was the one time during the day I had to myself and I used to cherish it. Mostly I'd go to my bedroom and read my car brochures, sitting with my back against the wall, mess strewn all around me, flicking through the well-thumbed brochures and dreaming. Always dreaming. I knew every inch of those magazines, every word, every picture, I even used to pore over the advertisements. These days I know a lot about cars, but I got my education on the floor of my bedroom, exhausted but happy to grab some moments by myself.

And sometimes, when the calendar was up, I used to go into Bradley and Mother's bedroom and look at it.

The room smelt beddy – of bedclothes and sleepy people. The covers were always skew-whiff on the big double bed that Mother had for her and Bradley.

Standing in there, I used to get this weird feeling of needing to go to the toilet. I guess that was because I was somewhere I shouldn't really have been, the danger and excitement of being there. And what I did when I was there was look at the calendar. I'm not sure why. Perhaps because it represented escape. Because we would be going away from George Dowty and away from the farmhouse with its sticks and washing-up liquid. And maybe also because there was chocolate and sweets in the calendar, and I was very, very hungry, and if I just went a few steps nearer and opened one of those little doors, there would be a chocolate there. And, yes, Bradley would make a fuss but if I closed the door again perhaps they'd think that Charlotte had forgotten to put a chocolate in that particular door, or that it had fallen out and one of the animals had got it. So tempting just to . . .

No. I'd be suspected. Hunger or not, I gave the Florida calendar one last look, turned and went back to my bedroom and the well-thumbed mags, sat down to read, dreaming of cars and America. Just under a month to go.

But God, I was hungry. The starvation seemed to go on forever.

During those days it felt like every day was a starvation day, and every day on starvation the punishment – however many days it was I'd been sentenced to go without food – would be increased, until the days ran into weeks, and then months. Mother was a massive fan of the soap operas, and it was my job to make sure they were always taped, so she never missed an episode. *Emmerdale*,

EastEnders, Coronation Street. She didn't have a particular favourite – she enjoyed them all, avidly. I'd try and make sure I was taping the right ones but things would go wrong sometimes and she'd get furious, and when she got furious she'd either lash out with whatever was at hand or add days to the starvation punishment.

It seemed like the whole of my childhood, I was hungry. The whole time. Sometimes I'd steal food and sometimes I'd be too scared to steal food, but in the end it wouldn't matter because she'd blame me for any missing food anyway, and I'd lie or tell the truth, but in the end it wouldn't matter because she'd accuse me of lying and I'd be punished anyway.

One day I was in the kitchen and Mother was cooking. She was standing at the cooker in our big farmhouse kitchen – a Goldstar cooker it was; it's in one of the barns now – and she was using the hob. She was cooking bacon, a bit of bacon for lunch, for her, Bradley and the girls, but not for me, and oh my God but my stomach was growling, the smell was like nothing else on God's earth. To me it smelled like a heaven I would never, ever reach.

I lurked in the kitchen, skulking. I circled the table and cast looks at Lulu and Karen, who were helping Mother to prepare dinner. They shot me quick glances then looked at Mother, who stood with her back to us. She was using a fork to turn the bacon in the frying pan, the sound of it frying almost the only noise in the room.

Nothing was said. There was a loaf of bread on the worktop and I caught the eye of either Lulu or Karen who looked at me, then again at Mother. The room was embraced by the smell of frying bacon and the girls must have known how I felt to be in there – what torture it was for me to smell that smell.

But I hung around, despite the gnawing feeling at my insides. Everyone knew I was hanging around hoping to get food, my hunger was the elephant in the room that nobody talked about. The girls hardly needed to look into my pleading eyes to see that

I was desperate for one of them to surreptitiously pass me a slice of bread or toss me a piece of ham.

Her back was to me, flicking slices over with the fork. I looked at Karen, who looked at me and, keeping her eyes on Mother's back, reached for a slice of bread.

I moved forward to take it . . .

Mother turned, snapped, 'What are you doing?' and the room froze.

I stared at her with what I knew were guilty eyes. Close by, Karen resumed buttering bread. She was buttering the slice she'd been about to toss my way, I realized, with my heart sinking.

'I said, "What are you doing?"' repeated Mother.

Still I was mute. I stood staring at her. The girls busied themselves preparing the dinner, their heads down. The bacon still sizzled in its pan.

'Did you take a slice of bread?'

I shook my head.

'I said, "Did you take a slice of bread?"' Her voice had risen, though her mouth had narrowed. I knew the signs and tried not to flinch away from her, but she had the fork in her hand and I found my eyes drawn to it; I knew from experience that the fork could jab. I wondered if it would have traces of bacon on it and whether the mark it left on me would taste of bacon.

She'd moved away from the cooker and was bearing down on me.

'No,' I said, finding my voice at last, shaking my head at the same time. 'No, I didn't take any bread.'

'You were going to, though.' She looked from me to Karen, who was busily buttering away, as though nothing was going on.

No, I tried to say, thinking the lie must be showing on my face.

'You were going to though, weren't you? Admit it.'

She was shouting now.

And what I did – what I always did – I tried to decide what she wanted to hear. I tried to think: which answer will enrage her the least? Do I admit it and be punished for trying to break the starvation? Or do I deny it and be punished for lying?

Think: which answer will enrage her the least?

I chose the wrong one.

'No,' I said, 'No, I wasn't.'

'Liar!' she roared, and the room filled with venom. I saw the fork move and I tensed, but she wasn't using the fork, which went flying. Instead, she was reaching, grabbing me by the arm, almost pulling me over as she dragged me towards the cooker. With her free hand she swept the frying pan from the hob – and pressed my hand onto the ring.

She did things to me that caused me more psychological harm, but nothing – nothing – she did was as painful as that.

The funny thing is, for a split second I felt nothing. A delayed reaction perhaps.

And then it was indescribable, white hot, searing. She must have only held my hand on the hob for a second or so, but it felt like longer, every nerve in my body demanding I yank the burning hand away, but unable to do so as she held it there and shouted, 'Liar!'

I screamed. I screamed more loudly and with more agony than I've ever screamed before or since and I think it was that scream that made her let go. At last, she let go.

I went to the floor, banging down to the kitchen tiles, my back against the oven door, shoes kicking on the floor, my hand held out in front of me.

It was somebody else's hand; it belonged to another person – a burns victim, not me. It was already blistering – a red, gooey mess of traumatized skin and shrieking nerve endings. Somebody in the room was screaming and I realized that it was me, and then I was gasping for breath, unable to breathe, and Mother looked down at me as though regarding me from the other side of the glass in a zoo, her face implacable, all that anger suddenly gone and replaced by a calmness that even through my pain I found eerie, and she studied my hand, her lips pursing slightly. She looked from my hand to my face. I was screaming, gasping for air. Then she straightened, as though her curiosity had been satisfied, turned and left the room.

I pulled myself to my feet, still fighting for breath, holding out my wounded hand. It had started to bleed down one side. It was smoking, I saw. Actual tendrils of smoke were coming from my hand. Later, the girls told me that the smell of bacon in the room was gone, replaced by the smell of my flesh burning. You don't smell it yourself, though, something to do with the injury and the way your senses cope with it, but the girls said it was a horrible smell – the worst smell in the world. The palm of my hand and fingers had blistered and sealed, already ballooning, even as I regained my breath and grabbed some kitchen towel to wrap up my hand.

Which was the wrong thing to do. The kitchen towel stuck to it like it was raw meat. I should have used clingfilm, I found out later. Apparently, if a burn is bleeding you should lay (not wrap) clingfilm on it, so it protects the wound, but also so you can see the progress of the injury, because a burn wound will blister for a long time afterwards. You should put it under water, too, of course. But I didn't do that either, because I was too busy wrapping it in kitchen towel and shouting at Lulu, who was insisting I put honey on the injury. She was already opening cupboard doors to look for it.

Honey. I hate honey. Besides, did we even have any at the farmhouse? We tended to bring just the food we needed for the day.

She was right, though, Lulu was. Honey is good for treating a burn, I've looked it up since. I'm not sure how she knew, but over the years we all learned quite a lot about first aid. We were always patching each other up, we learned it as we went along, so the next time Mother burned me I knew to use cold water. She never burned me so badly that I needed the clingfilm dressing, though. Not since that burn, nor before.

Because it might have been the worst burn she gave me that day, but it wasn't the first. The first, I remember that one – it happened at George Dowty Drive, one day not long after she'd stepped over the red line. We were both in the kitchen and I think we may have been alone in there, no sisters for once. I was a lot younger then, just five years old, and I was doing some cooking with Mother, she was teaching me how to cook an omelette. I stood next to her at the cooker while she showed me how to break an egg by cracking it gently on the side of the pan then opening the shell to let the yolk and the white slide out into the milky mixture in the pan, being very careful, of course, not to get any of the shell into the omelette mixture.

Except I wasn't careful enough, and some of the shell went into the omelette mixture, and instantly she was furious, grabbing my clumsy hand, pressing it onto the hob. I sent myself flying as I yanked it away, holding it to myself, as much in shock as in pain. The omelette-making lesson was over. I'd learned another one instead.

After the bacon day I kept away from mother when she was using the cooker. Still, later – after Charlotte and Judith had died, this was, when Mother's punishments went from organized and harsh to terrifyingly random and brutal – she got me again.

Once again, it was in the farmhouse kitchen, only now we had the big Rayburn cooker working again. It tended to go in and out of commission, but when it was working it used to heat the whole house, the water and everything. One of my jobs was to take the ashes out each morning and put new coal in, and it was a job I didn't mind doing. We formed a bond, me and that Rayburn, we were mates. I loved it. It kept us warm and in return I made sure it was always hot.

She grabbed my hand one day, though, and put it onto the Rayburn hob, held it down. I jerked and pulled my hand away, expecting the excruciating pain of the burn.

But it never came. What she knew that I didn't was that the

Rayburn was off, the hob had cooled. Mother walked off laughing. It was one of her jokes.

The day of the bacon, though, that was the worst burn. And I still didn't get to eat any bacon (she never softened – she never relaxed a punishment no matter how harsh she'd been; she would only ever feed me if I was simply too weak to continue). Instead, I tended to my wounded hand, which Lulu had patched up with a bandage from the first-aid box. That evening, we got back into the Transit and drove back to George Dowty and I sat in the back, bumping along the back roads, holding my bandaged hand. When we arrived at the house, the girls went to make dinner and I disappeared upstairs, crept into Mother and Bradley's room and stared at the Florida calendar on the wall.

Chapter Twenty-seven

The skin on the burn healed, the doors on the calendar opened and every day Florida got that tiny bit closer.

The beatings continued, of course, and so did the threats. 'You won't be going to Florida' had so much weight now the holiday was actually booked. Now, when she screamed that children with demons inside them couldn't go to Disney World, I froze inside. More than any pain on the feet. More than a slap, or a punch, or a knife slash, the threat of not going to Florida really scared me. It didn't feel like an idle threat either. She'd say, 'Right, you'll be staying with Judy while the rest of us go to Florida,' and Judy was Nanny and Granddad's next-door neighbour, so it could happen. What's more, Karen had told me that before Lulu, Bradley and I had arrived to live with Mother – when it was just Mother, Karen and Charlotte – there had been a holiday where Mother and Charlotte had gone by themselves, leaving her behind with Nanny and Granddad. So Mother would and could do it. She could leave me behind.

I was on my best behaviour. I made sure I did my jobs as well as I could. I never stole food. I kept Bradley happy. I made sure all Mother's soap operas were taped ready for her to watch and I kept my lip buttoned. I was the perfect little soldier in those days and weeks. The fear of being left behind kept me like that. I was still punished, of course. I'd still be accused of things I hadn't done, or get a punch for not coming quickly enough, or there would be some problem with work I'd done that I hadn't anticipated. And when I was punished I made sure not to scream or shout or make a fuss. I desperately tried not to do anything that would enrage her further because I was terrified she'd come good on her threat.

Lulu, though, the littlest rebel, didn't seem so worried. One morning at the farmhouse, with just a few nail-biting days to go, Mother was screaming at her. It was something about Lulu being a liar, that she had demons inside her, and Mother ended it by saying that she wouldn't be going to Florida.

'Oh, yeah? Let's see you cancel the tickets then,' shot back Lulu.

Not many families have piles of sticks stacked in corners of rooms – just ours. We had chair legs, bits of bamboo, lengths of wood for the renovation work, timber from the loft – all kinds of stuff. We'd occasionally use it for work we were doing around the farmhouse, but mainly Mother used them for beatings, and she grabbed one now, a chair leg.

They were vicious things. She swung it and connected with Lulu's jaw. I swear she almost broke it. Lulu went to the floor, screaming. She had a bruise there afterwards, right across the side of her face. She didn't give Mother any more backchat about the holiday, though. Not even Lulu.

As the days wore on, Mother's mood changed a little. She became brighter, more cheerful. Even better, she seemed to be less strict and the beatings became more infrequent. It was one of those times, like the run-up to a Jehovah's Witness convention, when I had a taste of what things were like for a normal family.

There was another glimmer of light on the horizon about that time, too. Bradley, then five or six, had started to take an interest in cars, just like his older brother. Because Bradley was Bradley, he could ask for things and Mother would buy them, so I persuaded him to ask for car mags. I knew every single word in the brochures I'd sent off for, so I was desperate for something fresh to read. Soon there were new car magazines lying around the house. Strictly speaking they were out of bounds to me, of course. They were

Bradley's, they were bought for him, and scum of the earth don't get to look at car magazines. But Bradley insisted on having somebody read the magazines to him, so guess who got the job? Pretty soon, any spare minutes I had I was reading the mags to him. We learned all the nought-to-sixty times of the cars, and we used to test each other on the times. I always won, which used to annoy Mother. There can't be that many mothers who are car nuts, but she was one of them. She knew tons about them herself, and she was always buying them. She was always buying vehicles full stop, and over the years we had three Ford Transit vans all told, plus a Sherpa minibus. We had two Volvos (a 265 V6 with an automatic gearbox, and a green Volvo estate), plus a Nissan Prairie and later, of course, the Chevy.

So, yes, a lot of cars. A car-mad family. And Mother hated it that I knew the nought-to-sixty times better than her. There was that competitive streak of hers again. She resented it, I think, that I was able to beat her. Another tiny little victory for me.

And the doors on the calendar kept opening, the cherry sweet getting nearer, until there were just six days left, and we were in even more turmoil than usual. Mother ordered us to start packing, to get our clothes together. We needed a lot for six weeks – in the end I think we had three suitcases each, as well as a pushchair for Bradley, now five, but still Eunice's little baby, and a wheelchair for Granddad.

Just a few days before, and we'd piled stuff up in the hallway of George Dowty Drive. We'd organized people – friends who were Jehovah's Witnesses – to look after Meg and Jet. We were so nearly ready . . .

And I had to go and backchat her, didn't I?

It wasn't really backchat. Once again we were in the kitchen at the farmhouse. She'd accused me of something – something to do with the chicken coops, I think it was – and I denied it, got told not to answer back, and I said something, barely audible, under my breath.

It was something like, 'But it wasn't me,' then I was recoiling as she bore down on me, grabbed me. I saw the bamboo stick in her other hand as she spun me round, heard the swish in the air, then felt the searing pain of it on my back. The agony of it knocked the breath out of me and for a moment my body tautened as though a current was passing through me.

Then, *crack*. Again. And again.

'Right,' she snapped, 'you won't be coming to Florida.' And my heart sank.

But I did. I did go.

We had a friend of the family, Ken the mechanic, who was going to look after the animals while we were away. What would happen was we were going to take all the animals over to the farmhouse and he'd visit the farmhouse to make sure they were fed. On the day of the holiday Mother paid him to drive us to Gatwick Airport. And it was lucky she hired a mechanic for the job. We all piled into the van, and we could only just squeeze in, the lot of us. Including the driver there were six adults, five children and enough gear to emigrate in the vehicle. (Which was a Leyland Sherpa, by the way. We took that one because it had been converted for Granddad's wheelchair and already it felt like a holiday: no more Transit van for six weeks.) Once inside we sat expectantly as Nigel turned the engine over.

It wouldn't start. Moments later he was out of the door and had the bonnet open, moments after that he was underneath it. That van always had a bad coolant system and I think he had to make an adjustment to the radiator underneath. He got back in, beaming, rubbing oily hands together, started it up and off we went. Florida, here we come.

Thinking about it now, it might not have been a complete disaster if the van had broken down. Mother had left us plenty of time. Our flight was due to leave at 11 a.m., but she had us arrive at Gatwick on the afternoon of the previous day. She hadn't booked a hotel either; we spent the night in the airport.

Like the day of our trip to London, this was all new territory for us, and we didn't sleep a wink. Karen, Lulu, Bradley and I spent the night exploring. At three or four in the morning airports are quiet, but there's still enough going on to keep four kids entertained. We spent a lot of the night with Bradley on a luggage trolley, whizzing him around a near-deserted part of the airport we found. The odd security guard would give us a glare but let us get on with it. We gazed in the shop windows. One had a Cadbury's chocolate fountain in its display, and even though the shop was shut the fountain continued to work. We stared at that fountain a long time, almost silent, just watching the liquid chocolate move, our tummies growling.

Chapter Twenty-eight

*T*he flight over was fantastic. Long, but fantastic. On the way over we watched cartoons, a Bob Hope film called *Cancel My Reservation*, and we charted the plane's global position on an in-flight GPS thing they had – I loved that. Everything was new to us; it all seemed so high-tech. I don't want to give the impression that we were completely backward or anything – we weren't – but even so, it all seemed so bright and modern. I often wonder if that was when my love of gadgets was born.

The thunder and lightning kicked in when we were almost there – around midnight – and it was the first taste of the weather that was to have a huge impact on our holiday. The plane rocked slightly and passengers either pushed themselves into the seat smiling and laughing nervously, or pressed themselves up against the windows, staring out into the black then recoiling as sharp tendrils of lightning lit up the sky. The sky was pitch black and then, *boom*, thunder followed the whip crack of lightning.

I gripped at the armrests as we began our descent, coming in to land. It was a pretty dramatic entrance to the United States of America, and things didn't run any more smoothly from there. By the time we got though baggage reclaim it was 1.30 a.m. and we stood like lemons on the main concourse of Orlando Airport looking for the man who was supposed to be taking Nanny and Granddad to our villa. A half-awake maintenance man with a buffing machine lazily guided it around our feet as we waited uncertainly.

After a while we became aware of a bloke in a suit, sitting vacantly in a seat, holding a piece of card to his chest. He looked at us, saw us looking at him, looked down at his card, then realized he'd been holding it the wrong way round. He flipped it over. On it was written, 'Spry'.

We let out a collective laugh of relief. Then off went Nanny and Granddad, while the rest of us went to pick up our rental car – actually a minibus.

Which wasn't ready. Three hours we were waiting in that rental office before Mother eventually got the problem sorted. But at least we got an upgrade. And then – at last – we piled into our Dodge Ram minibus for the drive to what would be our home for the next month and a half: the villa at Kissimmee Drive, Poinciana, Florida.

I was in car heaven. America was the first time (in real life, anyway) I ever heard the sound of a V8 engine – an engine I've read so much about. Because of fuel prices the V6 is the more popular engine in America these days, but back then most passenger vehicles had them – even the relatively small runarounds – and I was surrounded by them. Bradley and I had eyes on stalks, pointing out Chevrolets and Corvettes. We'd seen them on television and in the pages of the magazines, but rarely, if ever, in real life. It really was – it was heaven.

By the time we reached the villa it was late and I had fallen asleep in the back of the Dodge. I was woken up by a kiss on the cheek and, when I opened my eyes, I saw it was Mother who had kissed me.

For a second I was in shock. My first thought was, 'Weird.' I'm not sure I'd ever been kissed by her before, certainly not that I remembered anyway. And then she reached for me in the back of the Dodge, and she gave me a hug.

I fell into the hug. I felt sleepy. I felt small and warm and comforted. In that moment, I felt loved.

Why, I wonder now? Why the kiss and the hug?

Perhaps because she was happy. She was happy – after years of talking about it – to finally be on holiday in Florida, which she loved. She was happy to be in such a great villa on Kissimmee Drive.

And it was great. A bungalow with five bedrooms and a pool to die for. I shared a bedroom with Frank Philips, Judith's dad, and we had a single bed each. For the first time in I don't know how long, I had a whole bed to myself, and I could sleep at nights. There was no tidying up, or lectures, or Freddy Krueger. And nobody screamed into my face for a joke. I slept, in almost total comfort, for a whole six weeks. And it was great. There was a TV, too, a bigger TV than I'd ever seen. Forty-two-inches big, to be exact. Granddad liked that, I remember. Any time we were in the villa he set himself up in front of the massive TV and went channel surfing. And there were a lot of channels to surf – I doubt he ever saw the same one twice. Even so, he wasn't happy. Granddad liked to have a moan. By then he'd been in a wheelchair for two years with first, severe arthritis, then the onset of Parkinson's.

'Hey, little man,' he'd say to me, 'there's nothing on the bloody TV.'

'There are hundred of channels, Granddad.'

'I'm telling you, little man, there's nothing on the bloody telly.'

'Right, Granddad, right.'

It was always too hot for him, too. He had this obsession with the air conditioning. It was always too high or too low. Either it wasn't reaching him in the back of the Dodge or it was blowing cold air right into his face.

He didn't have much time for Frank Philips, either. Frank was quiet, except when he was complaining about the heat. There he thought he had an ally in Granddad and he'd sit with him to watch TV – at which point Granddad would feign sleep rather than have to talk to him.

Not that he talked much, Frank. He wasn't the most talkative guy. We didn't really know that much about him. How had he come to be married to Mother, for example? Why had they split up? During her night-time lectures she never spoke about either of her marriages, but not only was there Frank, there had been another, Jack. And apart from his name we knew absolutely nothing about him. It was difficult to imagine Mother in a wedding dress, smiling and cutting cake, tossing a bouquet for her bridesmaids. Not just difficult, but impossible, so I never did. That part of her life belonged to a Mother I not only never met, but never even had a glimpse of.

Nanny, meanwhile, buzzed around the villa. She never stopped. She was old-school like that. She couldn't sit down if there was something that needed doing, and if there wasn't anything that needed doing then she'd find something to do anyway. She was the kind of person who sits down, exhales, then gets straight back up again – 'Oh, I've just remembered' – and finds something else that needs doing.

I used to wonder, looking at Nanny and Granddad, what happened? What happened to make Mother the way she was – so hard? I liked them, they were nice. Granddad could moan a lot, but then I guess that was his prerogative, being a granddad. Both were stubborn and could be sharp and irritable, and I saw a lot of that in Mother; plus Granddad believed in discipline, I knew that from Mother's late-night lectures. Also that he was ex-army and one of the first Jehovah's Witnesses in Gloucestershire. He would make them all cycle to the Kingdom Hall in Gloucester from Cinderford, which is about fifteen miles away. Every Sunday, Tuesday and Thursday they would make the journey, Mother on the handlebars of Granddad's bike and her brother on Nanny's handlebars. If the weather was too bad – say if it was snowing or something – then they'd walk the distance, trudging through thigh-deep snowdrifts if needs be. So, hard, yes. Mother always made that clear. But she never mentioned anything about discipline. If there were beatings in her childhood she kept quiet about them. Looking back, I wonder: did Nanny and Granddad make her the way she was?

Could it be there was childhood abuse that was as well camouflaged as my own was? I don't know, not for sure. But put it this way, the cruellest thing I ever saw Granddad do was kill a snail. True, both he and Nanny had sharp tongues, but I never saw anything more than the occasional harsh word towards Mother, when Granddad would have a go at her about her 'lifestyle', the fact that she was always buying cars and was doing up an old house. Exactly what it was he didn't like about the house and cars I never really found out – it was as though it didn't need saying by either of them; as though it was written into the DNA of their family. There was something, though. Granddad disapproved of something.

We didn't stay in the villa all that much, certainly not during the days. We were out, exploring Disney World, mostly. And wow, did we explore that place.

It's huge, Disney World, or Walt Disney World if I want to give it a fuller title, or the Walt Disney World Resort if I want to go all the way and give it its proper title. It's the biggest and most-visited resort in the world; size-wise it's 30,000 acres, which is vast. I've checked and that's about twice the size of Guernsey. In it are four theme parks: the Magic Kingdom, the Epcot Centre, the MGM Studios and Disney's Animal Kingdom, as well as loads of water parks, six golf courses and a sports complex. It's also got its own race track, its own fire department, more than twenty hotels, absolutely tons of shops and restaurants and arcades, plus its own transport system of buses, boats and monorails. It is, in a word, awesome, and we spent weeks in there. We went to Animal Kingdom eleven times in total. We spent a whole week in Disney's Magic Kingdom, and a week in Epcot, which was probably my favourite out of the lot.

Because, wow, the Epcot Centre. It's like the technology area of Disney and everywhere you look there's something incredible to see. Even the paving slabs are high tech. They have a sort of fibre-optic effect, so at nights the lights seem to wave beneath your feet as you walk around. I loved that place. They had a massive lake and around it each area represented a country with areas where all the staff is, say, Chinese, and you can see a Chinese show and eat Chinese food. Then you wander across the lake and bingo, you're in Great Britain, where all the people there are British and you can get – and what a treat this was – proper fish and chips. Then, every night at Epcot, they have a fireworks show, like something you'd expect to get on New Year's Eve in London over here, except Epcot had it every single night. It was awesome, the best fireworks show on God's earth.

Then there are the water parks. We spent loads of time at the water parks. Disney World has the world's biggest water slides. I was only nine so I couldn't really go on the one that actually is the World's Biggest Water Slide, but I went on a couple of others, and they were superb, going down them was one of the best experiences of my life because they were so fast.

I would have got faster speeds on the water slides but I wasn't allowed to take my T-shirt off. Mother told Nanny and Granddad it was because of the sun, but really it was because I still had welts from where she'd whipped me with the bamboo, plus I had other scars on my back as well, so she made me leave my T-shirt on. Even so – even with that extra friction – those slides were *fast*.

Our favourite water park was a place called the Typhoon Lagoon. They have a wave pool there called Mount Mayday, and it's huge. Every half an hour or so, sirens will sound and not-so-good swimmers have to get out of the way sharpish, because they launch what they call the Tsunami Wave. We were there one day, the whole lot of us, and Granddad was in the Mount Mayday pool. His wheelchair was by the side of the pool and he was bobbing about in an inflatable chair, when, *whoooh*, the sirens started to sound, and before he knew it, the tidal wave had started up. They're as big as houses these tidal waves, and poor old Granddad was completely submerged. The wave rose and fell and all us kids rode it, screaming, and when the water had settled, Granddad was still sitting in his inflatable chair, only he'd been thrown out of the pool and was sitting by the side. It was the funniest thing to happen the whole holiday. I swear, we were killing ourselves for hours on end about that.

All this stuff we did, we did as a family. We were together almost all of the time. In fact, the only time I remember us getting split up was when us kids went to play crazy golf. The rest of the time, we were just one big, happy family, and there was no mistaking that we were all together because Mother had developed this obsession with us wearing matching clothes. She'd been to Woolworths and bought us all clothes in bright colours, so we all had a set of shorts, pants and tops in lime green, another in bright blue, and another in red. We all had matching green plimsolls, too. From somewhere else she'd bought the girls matching dresses for night-time, while Bradley and I had night-time suits that were lined with the same fabric as the girls' dresses, so that we still matched. The day-time stuff was the most eye-catching, though, and we had to get used to heads turning as we walked through the parks, the five of us kids in matching lime green, pushing Granddad in his wheelchair. Mad. Absolutely mad.

I liked pushing Granddad around. I was too short to see over the wheelchair but I could push it and look round the side. We looked after Bradley, but Bradley was in his element – all those V8s for a start – so he wasn't really much trouble. We enjoyed ourselves together, as a family, and we looked like a family. We were, after all these years, actually behaving like a proper family. There was the odd slap, just to keep us in line, but for the whole of the six weeks we were out there, Mother never hurt us, not properly – she hardly even raised her voice. There was the fact that her parents and ex-husband were with us, of course, and that was bound to have an effect on her behaviour; she was never violent towards us when Nanny and Granddad were around, nor did she ever let on to Frank how she treated us. Even so, on holiday she seemed relaxed, happier. And it wasn't just that there were no beatings, and that she rarely even raised her voice during that period – I remember on occasions, she gave me the odd peck on the cheek and even the occasional hug.

I think it was because she absolutely loved Florida. I think she would have moved there if she could; indeed, one of the recurring topics of conversation when we got back was a forthcoming move to Florida; she even told my real parents that's what she was going to do at one point.

Myself, I loved it too, but only for a holiday. It was a bit too busy for me to live there, and too hot. There was really weird stuff as well, like this strange multicoloured bread you could buy. It came in blue, pink or yellow and it tasted like marshmallow. So wrong, that bread. There was an orange shop there, too, and I don't mean a shop that was coloured orange – although it was – but it sold oranges. That was all it sold. This place was about the size of a supermarket and it was filled with oranges. You wouldn't believe how busy it was either. And Mother just loved all that stuff. Why, I wonder. What was it about America that appealed to her so much that she seemed so happy?

She liked the Kingdom Hall out there – that was a major thing. Our night-time dresses and suits were so we could go to Jehovah's Witness meetings, and we went to loads while we were there. The Florida Kingdom Hall, like just about everything else in Florida, is big and strange-looking, and inside we did our normal bit of standing, smiling and being very polite to any Witnesses who spoke to us. They were good meetings, I remember enjoying them.

One evening, we all arrived back from the Kingdom Hall and Frank went to stand by the pool at our villa. He was just standing there, hands in the pockets of his suit trousers, taking in the view, when Bradley came up behind him. I saw what Bradley was up to, and maybe I had time to warn Frank but, evilly, I didn't, and Bradley pushed him into the pool.

Frank couldn't swim but it wasn't that deep and he found his feet, just standing in the pool, soaking wet, in shock almost. I don't think he actually realized he'd been pushed in – he thought he'd slipped, probably still does (unless he reads this, of course). Bradley legged it, while I was standing there laughing, almost uncontrollably. After the Tsunami-wave-meets-Granddad-on-an-inflatable incident, it had to be the funniest thing that happened all holiday.

And then Mother came out to investigate the noise. Saw us there. Frank, in the pool, me doubled over laughing, Bradley long gone.

I stopped laughing and looked at her. I thought: Oh, no.

'Frank,' she said, 'what on earth are you doing in the pool?'

He shrugged his wet shoulders. 'I fancied a swim,' he said.

And Mother burst out laughing.

At that moment, I allowed myself to believe it was all over, the hurting; that things were going to change.

Chapter Twenty-nine

The centrepiece of our holiday in Florida was supposed to be the cruise. I say, 'supposed to be'. Hurricane Georges put a stop to that.

Hurricane Georges was a part of the 1998 Atlantic hurricane season. Trust us to go to that part of the world when they had a big Hurricane Season on – and not just any old Hurricane Season, either, but one of the very worst on record. Hurricane Georges was a bad one, it claimed 603 lives. Another one in the same season, Hurricane Mitch, killed 11,000 people, making it the worst hurricane ever. Georges affected more countries, though. He touched down in Antigua and Barbuda, St Kitts and Nevis, Haiti, the Dominican Republic and, of course, in the United States, where he laid waste to Florida Keys. In total, Hurricane Georges caused six billion dollars' worth of damages.

Not only was there the thunder and lightning of the day of our arrival in Florida, but we'd been hearing about the hurricane season ever since we arrived in the States – and the fact that it might kick off was always hanging over the holiday. It never really touched Orlando, certainly not the bit where we were staying, but it did hit the Keys. We would have been all right, then – had we not journeyed down there.

The third week of the holiday, this was. We took the Dodge down to Key Largo where we had an apartment booked at a Holiday Inn. We were to spend a week in the Keys, three days of which was a cruise in the Caribbean. The weather was getting up almost from the moment we arrived. In the end our cruise was the last to leave before they were all cancelled because of the weather, and even then it was cut short by a day. By the time we got back, the weather was really stroppy. It was hot – incredibly hot – but stormy. I'd go swimming and the waves would be awesome. Fish were being thrown out of the sea. On one occasion I emerged with a fish hanging off my trunks, tangled up in the drawstring. There was no doubt about it, something was definitely up with the weather. Still, we carried on, and the talk was that Hurricane Georges was weakening, having been disrupted by mountainous terrain in the Dominican Republic. Maybe it wouldn't hit the Keys after all . . .

Then, one night, the police came. They were going around holiday apartments advising holidaymakers to leave. Bradley and I stood gaping as a policeman came into our apartment all smiles (and he had a *gun*) and shook hands with Granddad, for some reason. When he left, Mother overruled the police advice to leave the apartment there and then. Hurricane Georges or not, we had a trip booked the following day to swim with dolphins, and we were going to keep that appointment with the dolphins no matter what. I think she enjoyed that – even over there I think she liked the idea of going against advice given by anyone in authority. She never was the biggest fan of people in authority.

We did the dolphin swim. The weather was worse. The police came again in the early hours of the following morning, and this time they weren't advising people to leave. This time it was an evacuation. The first I became aware of anything was hearing a general commotion. I had a moment of disappointment when I realized that I'd missed another police visit (oh no, and he would have had one of those massive torches they carry), but that was soon replaced by something else: a mixture of fear and excitement.

'Children.'

We came running.

'We've got to evacuate,' said Mother. She was already hurrying.

'The police have just been round door to door. They say the hurricane will be here within two days. We need to be four hundred kilometres away.'

Home, as in Kissimmee Drive, was Orlando, approximately six hundred kilometres away. We all packed, quickly. I was passing Karen and Lulu as we made dashes out to the van, taking hastily thrown-together suitcases with clothes hanging from them where we hadn't packed properly. As I looked down the row of apartments I could see other residents doing the same. It was late at night – actually, early in the morning, about 1 a.m. or so – but the place was suddenly alive, families shouting to one another, doors slamming, headlights illuminating the front of our apartment as cars pulled away.

Mother, I noticed, wasn't panicking; she didn't even seem perturbed. She was nothing like she was the night Lulu ran away. No, there was something calm about her, content almost. She seemed . . . *satisfied*, somehow.

'This is what it will be like, children,' she announced. 'This is what the Armageddon will be like.'

Of course.

Soon we were packed and, with Mother driving, we pulled out of the Holiday Inn and into absolute chaos.

Everywhere there were people. Most, like us, were in cars, heading upstate. Others were at work boarding up houses, while still more were trying to pull yachts out of the water. There were shouting matches when people got in each other's way, and car horns were sounding as drivers became frustrated with the slow going – the highways were absolutely packed. It was pandemonium. It was like something out of a film, *The Birds*, maybe. Mother was right (and she sat driving with a strange, almost serene expression), it was like Armageddon. Perhaps this was it.

I settled back into my seat. The seatbelt was digging into me. It was exactly the wrong height for me. I wanted to take the seatbelt off but that was a no-no, because Mother was obsessive about seatbelts; she made us keep them on at all times in the car.

We drove all night, the freeways packed but moving. On the radio we heard how Hurricane Georges had hit Florida Keys and we said what a lucky escape we'd had. We arrived back at Kissimmee Drive at around eleven o'clock the next morning, shattered, switching on the TV to discover that damage in the Keys was estimated at two hundred million dollars – thousands of houses had been damaged, almost two hundred were destroyed. Boats were overturned in the harbour. Palm trees and power lines were uprooted. We looked at one another. What a lucky escape!

Chapter Thirty

*B*ut that wasn't the end of our brush with Hurricane Georges. It did strike Orlando, or, rather, the very outskirts of it did, and we saw a storm like I've never seen before or since.

We'd gone to play crazy golf. This was the day after our overnight escape from the Keys, and we'd had a chance to rest. We all piled into the Dodge and took Highway 192, on our way back to Kissimmee Drive, when one of us, I think it was Lulu, said, 'Look at the skies. The skies are going dark.'

She was right. We craned to look out of the windows, and it was as though night was falling in double-quick time before our very eyes. Black clouds were moving across the sky, blocking out the light. We were right by the sea – we could see it from the minibus – and I saw that the waves were slapping against the land, rising bigger and bigger. Titanic waves.

Then it began to rain. Rain like bullets on the minibus, thumping into the roof. Brake lights flared ahead of us. Headlights behind us. The traffic slowed and suddenly I couldn't see the road for water, the rain and traffic throwing up a spray that made it look as though the cars were gliding on mist. The sky was black, and I mean *black*. Next, there was a flash of lightning, then a crack of thunder, which was deafening. Then again the lightning.

And we'd seen Florida storms before. They strike at about 3 or 4 p.m. every day and you can set your watch by them, near enough. All the theme parks, all the tourist attractions – they all shut down for the storms, just in case of a lightning strike.

But this – this was a new kind of storm. A biblical storm. This was like God venting anger and shouting thunder at the world. God angry and spitting fury.

The lightning, when it happened, took our breath away. The whole car gasped. Up ahead the brake lights flared through the rain as the traffic stopped. Then there was another crack of thunder, another explosion of light as lightning struck, stark and white and jagged against the black sky, like skeletal fingers reaching out for sinners on earth.

We had ground to a halt. The rain battered against our car, the whole highway at a standstill.

Again, the lightning, traffic almost seeming to cower, when, three or four cars ahead, something happened. Lightning struck again, and it hit the car with a secondary explosion. For a half-second the car was lit up, then it was sparking, sparks jumping off this thing, seeming to dance around the body of the car. Next thing we saw the car doors open and three people – I think it was three – came running out, running for safety to God only knows where. To be honest, I wasn't looking at them. I was looking at their car, which had burst into flames. Right there in front of our eyes, just three cars ahead, burning bright despite the downpour. As a sight, as something to behold, it was nothing short of awesome.

Mother smiled. I looked at her. She was sitting in the driver's seat with her hands on the steering wheel, literally calm in the centre of the storm.

'You see, children,' she said. 'You see this? This is what Armageddon will be like.'

Chapter Thirty-one

*F*rank Philips departed the day after the storm. He was only able to get four weeks away, so he left us for the final fortnight. Up until then, Mother had been sleeping in the lounge with Bradley, but with Frank gone there was a spare bed, so Mother and Bradley moved into my room. They stayed in one single bed together, though; I still had my blissful bed to myself.

And then the holiday was over and we were packing up ready to go home. When the day finally came I wasn't as upset as I expected to be. It was the end of the holiday – of our time in Florida – but it also felt like the beginning of something else, perhaps a time when we would be a proper family. Even the absence of Frank hadn't affected Mother's mood. There were still no punishments, barely even a harsh word. Yes, Nanny and Granddad were still there, but with her and Bradley moving into my bedroom, Mother had plenty of opportunity to revert to her former ways, yet never did. There were times, on that holiday, when we all had hugs and kisses from Mother, not just Charlotte and Bradley, but all of us – like a proper mum. I really thought that the hurting had stopped, that she was going to change from now on.

So I didn't mind going home. I guess I was homesick in a way – homesick for a new life that hadn't yet begun. We all agreed that we missed the animals, too. Florida's great, it's crazy and colourful and full of life and we'd seen things we'd only ever dreamed of before, but now we wanted to get back home.

The journey back was fairly uneventful. Ken was there to pick us up from Gatwick Airport and, true to form, the Leyland Sherpa broke down on the way back. He'd arrived to pick us up with a cloth jammed in the dashboard to stop an oil leak. The repair didn't hold, though, and we still broke down. Mother was chiding Ken, claiming he must have been hammering the throttle on the way up. He looked up at us and winked.

We went back to Nanny and Granddad's first, dropped them off, then went to pick up the dogs from the Jehovah's Witnesses. Then, tired and desperate to be home, we went to George Dowty Drive, where we arrived to find boiling water dripping through the ceiling.

What had happened was that we'd timed the immersion heater to come on a day earlier and it had boiled over. It meant there was boiling water coming through the ceiling of the hall and the kitchen, and I thought, uh-oh, if anything's going to get Mother angry it'll be this. But no, she was cool. She arranged us into a tidying detail and we did the best we could, and then we went to bed.

The next day, we all got up and piled into the Transit. The farmhouse was just as we'd left it, except with six weeks' worth of nettles to cut down and six weeks' worth of grass to mow, as well as a whole ton of other stuff that needed doing. There were no beatings, though. At the end of the day we all piled back into the Transit and Mother went to have her dinner at the Safeway cafeteria.

In the Transit we played with our new toys: Tamagotchi. This was another excellent new development: Mother had started giving us pocket money. All of us, not just the other two. Out in America the big craze had been Tamagotchi and they were pretty cheap over there, too, so we'd stocked up. The idea was you had a little electronic pet and you had to feed it, and play with it and pick up its poo. If you didn't give your electronic pet enough love and playtime, it died. It died and went up to heaven, and you had to grow another one.

It was fun, and we all agreed that after looking after Bradley, keeping a Tamagotchi was a breeze. By the time we got back to the UK they were a massive craze over here, too. I saw a piece about them on the news saying some schools had banned them because the kids were taking them into classrooms. It was weird to watch. It was like the one time growing up I was actually 'in' on what was going on in the wider world.

As well as Tamagotchi, I'd bought a Mickey Mouse with my pocket money. That and the Tamagotchi were virtually the only toys I'd ever had to myself since going to live with Mother. But Jet got the Mickey Mouse for some reason. I came home to George Dowty one night and found that he had mauled Mickey. There was just a pile of plastic on one of the beds and Mickey's half-eaten lower torso. I didn't mind too much. I didn't even mind that I had given up my nice cosy bed-to-myself in Florida for the floor at George Dowty Drive.

I didn't mind because things had changed, hadn't they?

List of the five questions I'm most often asked about being abused by my evil foster mother Eunice Spry

1. Why didn't I fight back?
2. Why didn't I run away?
3. Why didn't I tell anyone?
4. How could it go on for so long without anybody getting suspicious?
5. How did I cope?

Chapter Thirty-two

I looked at the pig food in my hand, decided I had no choice, and ate a handful.

Pig food. It's cereal, really. Biscuits. It tastes like you would expect animal feed to taste, of cold leftovers gone hard. In this case, like cold leftovers gone hard and coated in syrup, for some reason.

It was winter, and I was starving, absolutely starving. I'd gone without food now for – what was it? – two, maybe three weeks, and I was skulking around the grounds of the farmhouse weak with hunger, hardly able to think with hunger, trying to do my jobs but failing with hunger. I was tired, too. Bone tired. I'd been on tidy-up two nights in a row and the only way I could keep myself awake was to take more pills than I should. I felt like they rattled around inside me, fizzing in my stomach. They kept me awake, but they made my mind wander. Even more than usual I was off in my own little world, and it made me sloppy doing jobs. I'd drift off, and if I drifted off I could make mistakes and mistakes meant beatings or – worse, much worse – extra starvation. I forced myself to focus as I made my way around the fields and garden, even though my peripheral vision seemed to have greyed out, as though my eyes, responding to the lack of sleep, had decided not to function properly. Every now and then I twitched, too, as if an electric shock was passing through my body.

I was terrified that if she saw me like this she'd beat me. Whenever I was in view of the house I desperately tried to stand up straighter, walk with more purpose. I didn't dare to look up at the windows in case I saw her there and our eyes met and somehow she would know – she would know that I was out here slacking and she'd come outside with a punch, or a knife, or send me running to the washroom with a number for beatings to the feet, or with extra days on starvation.

So, feeding the pigs, I felt what can only be described as jealousy. Why were the pigs allowed to eat when I wasn't? How come the pigs got food and I didn't? And as they stared at me expectantly, anticipating another scoop of feed to come flying their way, instead they watched me regard the food then shove it into my own mouth.

I chewed, swallowed and kept it down. Just. It was disgusting. Dry, regurgitated, recycled biscuit with a revolting sugary aftertaste from the syrup coating. But at least it was food, and the fact that I could eat it and keep it down meant at least I had somewhere I knew I could find food if I absolutely had to. And that wouldn't be the last time I'd eat pig food, either.

Looking around the garden, I could see Bradley. He was sitting in one of the cars, playing. Charlotte was in the snooker room, and I wasn't sure where Lulu or Karen were. I cast a longing look at the shed where the freezer was kept. Since the day I'd been forced to eat the frozen gateau at the farmhouse I hadn't seen the freezer key, and I supposed Karen had replaced it wherever she'd found it, rather than risk a repeat of an episode like that.

How had it got so bad, when it had seemed like all the hurting had stopped? Why had it started again? Maybe because things had got on top of us. We'd hadn't caught up after Florida, that was the problem. It was like we'd never quite unpacked before starting other jobs. Each one seemed to remain unfinished when we started another. We were ripping out fireplaces, tearing off wallpaper, tearing out a staircase even. Charlotte's room was a priority; she was turning it into her pink Cinderella palace. She was fourteen by now but she had the interests and behaviour of a nine-year-old; she'd been kept that way by Mother, who never let either her or Bradley grow, stunting their childhoods by extending them, as though she was taking the years from Karen, Lulu and me and giving them to Bradley and Charlotte. It was why Charlotte lived in a world of fairy princesses and grottos; why we'd taken a pushchair with us to Florida, so Bradley, then six, could be pushed around like a three-year-old. And the work on her fairy grotto started, even as the work on the kitchen and bathroom continued.

So, too, did work on Bradley's playroom. The staircase we tore out was the one to the loft conversion, which was now going to be his personal playroom. We fitted the new staircase ourselves. Me, Karen, Lulu, Bradley, Charlotte and Mother – all of us guided by Judith, carpenter extraordinaire, and her boss, who came to help out for a couple of days (a couple of blissful, hurt-free days).

And we did a good job. Now Bradley had his playroom, reached via brand-new steps, the kind you climbed up to poke your head into the room, before climbing through.

That room, long and with low ceilings, with boxes higgledy-piggledy in an out-of-bounds area at one end, was like the inside of a little boy's head. It was full of toys – so full you couldn't see the floor apart from the area where Bradley would sit, randomly selecting toy cars to push around the tiny bit of space he'd left himself. He had every toy car known to man, from those tiny little metal Corgi cars, to huge radio-controlled jeeps. He had what must have been a complete set of Thomas the Tank Engine toys. He had toy guns, remote-controlled robots, boxes and boxes of games. He had everything his little heart desired, and naturally all that gear spilled out into the rest of the house, where it joined dusty packing-boxes full of junk on the landing, the floorboards stripped and clogged with dirt and dust that billowed up and choked your lungs if you disturbed it; suitcases full of clothes, most of them old and fit only for chucking away; more boxes, things brought from George Dowty Drive; random bits of furniture, an upturned chair. There were building materials everywhere: pieces of timber laid out in the hall where the floorboards were dirty and rotting, piles of tools on oilcloths, parts of bathroom suites. Another room overflowed with the remnants of George Parker's stuff – things we'd never got round to throwing away in our rush to fill the farmhouse with our own things – while the main stairs were piled high with boxes of games. As you climbed them the stacked boxes seemed to tower above you, like walking into the stockroom of a toyshop.

Everywhere in the farmhouse seemed to be another project that had been started then either abandoned or put on hold. From bits of art that Charlotte was doing to ripped-out fireplaces. Apart from the sitting room there wasn't one room of the house that hadn't been attacked, or wasn't in some terminal state of disrepair. George Dowty Drive was messy – so messy you could hardly open the doors most of the time – but this was something else. Imagine a building site into which somebody has emptied the contents of a hundred jumble sales. It was like that.

Outside wasn't much better. So much junk, so much mess. The once-beautiful garden had been filled with things thrown out of the farmhouse, and despite our annual bonfires the stuff piled up. The weeds and grass were growing knee-high; down by the barns, cars had been left to rust and rot, slowly being swallowed by vegetation.

There were two caravans in the yard. One was a mobile home, really. Mother's brother bought it from some gypsies and was originally going to live in it, in the field at the farmhouse. He never did, though, and the mobile home filled up with our stuff. The other vehicle was our touring caravan, which had come with us from George Dowty Drive – we used it for a couple of Jehovah's Witness conventions in Cardiff. We hadn't used it for a couple of years, though, and that, too, was full of our things. On both, the windows and doors had all been left open and the moisture had got to the clothes, so the caravans smelled fusty. If you went in, the next thing you'd notice after the clothes strewn around and the smell was the rat droppings; you could hear the rats moving about inside. Then there were the outhouses, of course. Again, they were becoming overgrown, full of junk.

Bradley and Charlotte played all day. I was supposed to deal with all this stuff. I was nine, going on ten. I couldn't. And when Mother spotted me slacking, or getting something wrong, she'd beat me. She'd see me from a window, come out into the yard or the garden, pick up whatever was to hand and beat me with it.

One of her favourite weapons was a gazebo pole, which were like tent poles, aluminium, usually. They swished through the air and they hurt. They really were the rods she used to beat the children. We had piles of them lying around in the yard so she was never short of one. She'd stoop, pick it up and bring it down on me. Across the back of the legs was a favourite spot – she liked to see me crumple to the ground – but she wasn't too fussy where she struck. Mostly she'd just stoop and swipe, and I'd get it across the back, or around the neck or on the arm. They hurt. They stung.

Bradley and I used to play with them, the gazebo poles. We had sword fights with them and we used them like spears, too, throwing them into the grass in the field. It didn't matter if they got lost; we had absolutely millions of them, because Mother was totally obsessed by gazebos. We're talking the tent-like gazebos you buy from camping shops. Every summer Mother would buy three or four of them and she'd put them up in the garden. She, Judith and Charlotte would often sit under one on summer evenings, usually with one of those tin-foil barbecues to make some food. They were only cheap things; they'd break or go rusty, so the next summer Mother would buy three or four more gazebos, and meanwhile disused poles would pile up in the yard and in the garden, adding to the air of general neglect, and presenting themselves as handy weapons. Over the years I was probably hit more with them than any other weapon – even the chair leg. My back is a mass of scars.

Lulu coped by rebelling. Karen coped by seeming to withdraw from the world (which was how Mother was able to convince the world she had Asperger's). Me, I retreated further and further into my own head.

Chapter Thirty-three

*O*ne night, we had a visitor to George Dowty Drive. It was late; we were all asleep in bed, the whole family.

Silently, the visitor let himself in and stood at the bottom of the stairs, listening to us sleep. He wore a long, black leather trench coat, black trousers, a black shirt and, even though it was the dead of night, dark sunglasses. Satisfied he had disturbed nobody with his entrance, he swept his coat aside and reached inside, removing from a shoulder holster his Glock 20.

(He liked the Glock 20. It had a magazine capacity of fifteen 10mm Auto, which was an accurate round with good stopping power that in most small arms gave the user a demanding, powerful recoil, reducing close-combat efficiency. Not in the Glock, though. Recoil-damping high-tech polymer used in the frame kept kickback minimal, so high-performance rounds weren't a problem. Plus, like most Glocks, it was light, reliable and benefited from the same sleek design that was their hallmark. It never jammed, it never snagged, it never let him down.)

He'd had the Glock barrel threaded, and now he reached into the pocket of his trench coat and took out a silencer – a suppressor, actually – that he screwed into the barrel, keeping the weapon pointed at our carpet. The silencer wouldn't actually silence the gun, not the way Hollywood showed it. But it would take the edge off the blast. The noise it made would be like a section of the *Encyclopaedia Britannica* being dropped to a concrete floor. Hopefully not loud enough to frighten the children. With the silencer fitted, he raised the weapon, holding it in a two-handed grip at shoulder level, about to ascend the stairs. He caught sight of himself in a mirror in the hallway. He looked an awful lot like me – like an older version of me.

Noiselessly, he ascended the stairs. He knew which ones creaked. He knew where to step in order to prevent the floorboards squeaking. He looked in on Charlotte's room, where she lay, snoring in the bottom half of her bunk bed. He looked in on our room, where Karen and Lulu slept in the bunk bed and I slept on the floor. Then he went into Mother's room.

Standing in the doorway, he raised the weapon. Then paused. Bradley lay next to Mother, so, despite the fact that his accuracy was perfect, the assassin moved closer to the bed, for safety, holding the weapon two-handed, placing the silencer almost to Mother's forehead. He brought his left hand from the butt of the pistol, holding it in front of his face and splaying the fingers to prevent spray-back. He didn't want Mother's blood on his face.

He applied five and a half pounds of pressure to the trigger of the Glock 20, which travelled backwards a distance of 12.5mm.

There was a sound in the room like an *Encyclopaedia Britannica* being dropped to a concrete floor.

Bradley stirred. Swiftly, the man unscrewed the silencer, dropped it into his coat pocket then replaced the still-warm Glock in his shoulder holster. He scooped up Bradley, then hurried from the room and into the bedroom where the children were sleeping. He woke them and they stared up at him in wonderment, their fear turning to excitement as he explained to them that he was rescuing them. He shepherded them downstairs then out of the front door, where his Aston Martin DB9 was parked at the pavement. Together, they roared away, out of George Dowty Drive, off the Northway estate and out of Tewkesbury, heading for a new life.

His name was John Hendrickson, and he was how I coped; he got me through it.

John Hendrickson was me, grown up, and he was a mercenary.

He became a mercenary after I saw a film (the title of which I can't remember, but it might have been *The Wild Geese*). He always wore the long coat, although he only started wearing the sunglasses after I saw *The Matrix*. He wasn't just a mercenary; he had other talents as well – at one point he developed an anti-nuclear weapon which would prevent the Armageddon should a nuclear weapon be deployed. Plus, and how he acquired this skill I'm not sure, but he was a dab hand at inventing new fuels for cars, missiles, rockets, anything. Mainly, though, but he would rescue us. Sometimes with, but often without, violence. Just grabbing us, taking us away and putting us in a secure location.

He got his name one day when Bradley and I were playing in the garden. Mother must have been at Safeway because we were both playing in the cars and we were pretending to be policemen, giving ourselves fictional names. He hadn't long seen *Star Wars*, so Bradley called himself 'Jim' Skywalker; me, I was John, after John Wayne because I'd watched a John Wayne film the previous day, and Hendrickson because, well, I'm not quite sure where Hendrickson came from, but that was the name I came up with. He was the person I became.

I'd given him a house, in California, with an underground garage in which he kept all of the best cars known to man: Rolls-Royces, Aston Martins, a Chevrolet Corvette 1978 Stingray. He was super-rich, of course, and here's the weird thing: he used to buy things for Mother. There were times he desperately wanted to please Mother, to make her proud, and often he'd do this on days when she'd been particularly cruel to me. Sometimes, it was as if the more I suffered at her hands, the more John Hendrickson wanted to impress her. He bought her yachts, houses, cars, anything she wanted. He bought her a villa in Florida because she loved Florida so much. Anything to make her happy.

Other times, though, he reached for his Glock 20, put on his sunglasses and paid her a midnight visit.

Spending my day in the fields and gardens at the farmhouse,

John Hendrickson was who I became. When I was away with the fairies I was with John – or rather, I *was* John – speeding through the streets of New York, tooling it along the freeway in LA, assembling firepower, taking on missions, inventing anti-Armageddon devices and working on formulae for new fuels.

John Hendrickson was also the guardian of the Round Yellow Cube.

The Round Yellow Cube was the place in my head where I put all the bad stuff. I'd discovered this place reading the *Encyclopaedia Britannica* one day, reading about depression and how I had the symptoms of it. The article on depression detailed how sufferers coped by locking trauma away so they could get on with their lives, and I decided to do the same. It was a cube, and it was yellow, and at the top of it was a ball, which had a door in it. It floated in space, the Round Yellow Cube, and into it I put the things that most upset me. Weirdly enough, these were rarely the physical things Mother did. Turning George Parker against us, getting him to think that we were no-goods, that went in there. Often when she called me scum I'd put that in the Round Yellow Cube. It was psychological things mainly.

John Hendrickson was the guardian of the cube. It was his job to open the door and put the bad stuff in. Sometimes, late at night, the bad stuff would get out of the box and I'd have to scramble John Hendrickson into action. He'd collect it all back up, put it back into the Round Yellow Cube and, like those people with depression, I could get on with my life.

Chapter Thirty-four

'Children.'

One morning at the farmhouse she called us all upstairs. 'Today we're going to learn about NASA.'

While in Florida we'd visited the NASA Space Centre and she'd collected educational material about space flight. She'd made a board with a poster on it – like a wall chart – all about the development of space travel. We gathered for our lesson, which was being held in the room where Karen and I were starved that time – it was still the emptiest room in the house. As we sat on the floor she addressed us, the wall chart behind her. We had pens on the floor by our feet and I reached for one, but Bradley grabbed it from me. I reached to grab it back and he squealed, and the next thing Mother knocked me flying, punching me on the side of the head.

'Right,' she hissed, 'No food,' and she turned to Bradley to make sure he was OK.

I sat upright, rubbing at my jaw. No food. My heart sank. (This one, it turned out, would run and run.) It was the end of the lesson, too, and she gave us homework – she wanted an essay called 'My Trip To NASA' and she wanted it doing for next week. This was me, Karen and Lulu who had to do homework, not the other two. Next week came around and I had completely forgotten about the homework. I was looking weak by then, swaying on my feet with fatigue and hunger. When I saw myself in the mirror my eyes were sunken, dark rings beneath them, and my trousers hung around my waist.

So Mother called me into the kitchen and told me to sit at the table. I did so, climbing up onto my seat, my head lowered, almost meeting the table. She was cooking lard. I could smell it and, weirdly enough, my stomach did a little gleeful leap at the smell. Maybe it expected the scent of cooking meat to follow the smell of melted lard. Maybe my stomach thought any food was better than no food. I didn't look at her as she stood by the Rayburn. It was my job to keep that cooker lit and now she used it to cook me a lard sandwich. It seemed unfair, somehow.

I heard her slap a piece of bread down, then on went the lard. Another slice of bread went on top. Bread – at least there would be bread. The plate clacked to the table in front of me – contents: one lard sandwich.

'You want something to eat, eat that,' she said. When I looked up at her, towering over me, I saw that her mouth was set, her eyes hard.

'Eat it,' she repeated.

Charlotte came dancing into the room. We didn't know it then but she had less than two years to live. She stopped when she saw me at the kitchen table; saw the sandwich there, too. Mother stared at her. Charlotte had a moment of hanging around, looking uncomfortable, chewing her bottom lip slightly.

'Go on, then,' prompted Mother, pointing towards the door, and Charlotte left, banging up the stairs, back up to her fairy grotto.

'Now eat,' said Mother, and I did. With my mouth oily and sticky with grease, feeling it sit on my stomach, heaving but desperate to keep it down, I ate. She made me eat it all. It was easy, frankly, apart from the heaving. I'd eaten washing-up liquid, bleach, vomit and my own waste, so lard wasn't that much of a problem – at least it was a bona fide foodstuff.

Afterwards, my mouth tasted foul; my lips, teeth and tongue

were coated with a layer of grease that would seem to stay there for days. Mother let me have a glass of water. She was always good like that – always sure to keep us hydrated, especially when we were on starvation.

Not long after that, another day, I was leaning over the Rayburn when she hit me with a piece of lead piping.

Chapter Thirty-five

I don't know why she hit me with the lead piping. I wasn't told then and I wasn't told later. Somebody asked me the other day why I thought she did the things she did, and it's the question that feeds my insomnia. Like I say, to exert or gain control possibly, or because . . . because she could.

Certainly the lead-pipe incident was unprovoked. I was doing my duty, which in that instance was to deal with the Rayburn, my beloved cooker. Cleaning it out, I think.

I was on my knees, my attention focused solely on the Rayburn, unaware of anything else until, behind my back, she swung the lead piping at my head and the lights went out.

Why? I hadn't done anything wrong. I could understand when she hit me for shooing the pig away from the apples, or letting maggots get in the chicken, or upsetting Bradley. They were reasons I could grasp. But for nothing, just to pick up a piece of lead piping (and not many families have lead piping hanging around in their kitchen – just ours) and hit me with it.

It was a solid blow, delivering the same, sickeningly familiar feeling of a sudden detachment from the world, as if everything has been knocked out of kilter, my sight, my hearing, every thought in my head suddenly jarred loose. When you're hit on the head like that, it's almost like you go through a tiny time warp. There you are in one place, then there's an impact which you feel more as a sensation than anything else. Then blackness. Then a moment of complete disorientation, nausea, confusion – and pain. And you come to. And you're somewhere else.

I was out for about a minute and a half, so the girls said later. I came round to find myself face down on the kitchen floor, hearing their voices.

'Chris? Chris, can you hear me?'

I lifted my head from the floor and saw blood, small drips of it that hung from my hair then plopped to the tiles.

Lulu, beside me, put her arms around me, helping me struggle to my knees, where I crouched for a moment or so, my hands going to the back of my head. I found it there, the wound, and it started to bleed. Really bleed. Not just drips of blood now, but torrents of it. Karen was still standing and she reached for the kitchen towel, handing me a bunch that I held to my head. Instantly they were drenched, and we were wadding up more kitchen towel as Lulu helped me to the table, where I sat, all of us trying to stem the deluge from my head.

'It'll stop bleeding,' said Mother, coming into the room. She stood watching us, mouth in a frown, as though disapproving – as though my blood was proof that I was the scum of the earth.

But she was wrong: it didn't stop bleeding. It was still bleeding in the Transit leaving the farmhouse and it kept on bleeding in Safeway car park, where I sat, not joining in the usual messing about, but holding the kitchen towel to my head, feeling nauseous, dizzy, the neckline of my T-shirt soggy with blood. I was as white as a sheet, Lulu told me.

And it kept on bleeding back at home. We went through our usual nightly ritual and all the time I was holding towels to my head, trying to stop the room from spinning, losing blood, going whiter and whiter. Until, at last, Mother stopped saying that it would heal. We were going to go to the hospital.

For the first time she attended to my head herself. From a first-aid kit she took a bandage and some surgical plaster and fashioned some kind of dressing. She sighed as she did it. This is your fault, that sigh seemed to say. If you weren't bleeding we wouldn't have to go to the hospital. Next, she sent Bradley, Karen and Charlotte to bed, told Lulu she was coming with us, and we climbed into the green Volvo.

I sat in the passenger seat, swaying slightly. Mother got in.

'Fasten your seatbelt,' she said. I did. Then she added, 'When we get there, you fell off your bike, is that clear?'

I nodded.

'Say it,' she insisted.

'Yes,' I managed. 'I fell off my bike.'

As she drove, she quoted from the bible: 'Do not withhold discipline from your children; if you beat them with a rod, they will not die.'

It was another of her favourites from Proverbs. We heard it all the time. During beatings, mostly. I often wonder how different my childhood might have been if there wasn't so much stuff about rods in the Bible.

For about two hours we waited in Tewkesbury casualty department. A nurse came to see me and examined the wound.

'And what's happened here, then?' she said.

'He's come off his bike again,' said Mother, looking at me as she said it. For the nurse's benefit, she was wearing a look I hadn't really seen before, certainly not concerning me. It was a look that said, 'Boys will be boys'.

'I thought the bleeding had stopped,' she added, 'but he woke up with blood on his pillow so I thought we'd better bring him.'

'Best to be on the safe side,' agreed the nurse. 'We'll get a doctor to look at him as soon as we can.'

Mother watched her go, smiling. With outsiders, with people from the Social Services, the police, nurses, doctors, dentists, she was one of two Mothers: either hostile and scary, which she passed off as being fiercely protective of us, or soft and concerned. She was that second Mother now. I recognized it from when Lulu had escaped, the way Mother had acted with the police that night.

About an hour and a half later, we were called out of the waiting room and into a treatment room. Lulu waited behind, sitting on a brown plastic chair with her legs pulled up in front of her.

The doctor looked tired. It was about 2.30 a.m., so he had the right to look tired, but there was something distracted about him too. The blinds at the window were open, so it was just black outside. Bright, clean light seemed to wash out Mother's features, or maybe that was just my vision. I got up on a hospital bed as directed, my feet swinging. I still felt out of it. Still dizzy.

The doctor approached, snapping on a pair of surgical gloves. Mother stood behind him and I caught her eye. Concerned Mother was gone. She said nothing, neither did her mouth move, there was just her eyes, dark and drilling a silent warning into mine.

The doctor removed the dressing, parting my hair with his fingers to study the wound.

'Fell off his bike, did he?' he said to Mother, his back to her.

'Yes,' she said.

'Hmm, unusual to get a wound at the back like this. From falling off a bike. What have you been getting up to, eh, Christopher?' He emerged from behind me, looking at me. I glanced briefly at Mother. Nothing there. Just those eyes staring dark messages at me.

I looked back at the doctor.

motherbeatsusandshestarvesusandshemakesusdrinkbleach

'I can't really remember,' I managed, 'I was just riding along and I think I hit a brick or something.'

'You'd come off it forwards, though, wouldn't you? If you hit a brick?' he said. He was smiling slightly.

'I can't really remember.' I looked behind him at Mother again. Her eyes bored into mine.

'I think I know,' he said. 'I think I know exactly what you've been up to.' He stared at me, then said, 'You've been doing wheelies, haven't you, Christopher?'

From behind him there was a sound, Mother making a noise of rebuke to mask what was probably relief.

'Well, have you, young man?' she said.

'Yes,' I said. 'Yes, I was doing a wheelie.'

'Well, that was a bit silly then, wasn't it?' said the doctor. 'Keep it on two wheels in future, eh?'

He checked my reflexes, made sure my senses were all working properly. Then they cleaned me up and the doctor put some butterfly stitches in. We left and drove home, in silence this time.

For two days after that she didn't touch me. Also for those two days the starvation was relaxed and I ate with the rest of the family. The day after that, the starvation began again.

Chapter Thirty-six

*I*t was Lulu who first noticed the two-and-a-quarter-hour rule. What it was, she'd worked out that Mother's visits to Pershore lasted almost exactly two and a quarter hours. If only I'd known that the day Charlotte had decided to show me her trick shot – perhaps I would have avoided being brained by the snooker cue.

Anyway, two and a quarter hours, that was our window. That was how long it took Mother to do her shopping at Pershore market, meet a friend for coffee then return, beeping her horn and expecting children to come running to open the gate – and woe betide us if we didn't. They happened twice a week, her journeys to Pershore.

'Which gives us time to go over the fields,' said Lulu, one day, shortly after Mother had left. She gesticulated with one of Mother's beloved gazebo poles. Lulu had been using it to whack at a thicket of stinging nettles that had grown at the base of my skateboard ramp, but now she was wielding it like a general trying to rally her troops.

Charlotte agreed. 'Yes, come on,' she said, bounding over to where Lulu stood in the yard, joining her there.

Karen and I looked at them, not so sure. Neither of us said anything but I bet she was thinking the same thing I was. Sure, Charlotte, it's OK for you, but you're not expected to open the gate. You won't get beaten if the gate isn't opened. If Mother comes back and we're not here, it's us she'll beat, not you – and she'll do it twice as hard for leading you astray.

'Come on,' insisted Lulu.

She was already turning to go, using her gazebo pole as a walking stick like the great explorer. I looked at Karen and she looked at me. We didn't get to go anywhere. Our life was the farmhouse, Safeway car park, George Dowty Drive, like an interminable loop. Wandering around, lost in fantasies about John Hendrickson, I used to imagine taking him over the fields to see what lay beyond the tree line, but never, ever dared actually do so. Straying away from the farmhouse was a no-no. Mother was always watching out of the window and if she didn't see me she would come looking for me, and I didn't want that.

But now Lulu was striding away, out over the garden, towards the field, and I found myself almost giddy at her daring. She was going – she was going to explore, to see what lay behind the tree line.

Without a word to each other, Karen and I set off, hurrying to join Charlotte and Lulu.

'If we get caught, we're dead,' I said, catching up.

Lulu swiped at some weeds.

'We won't get caught. We have . . . Charlotte, how long do we have?'

Charlotte was the only one of us to own a watch, and she consulted it now, saying, 'Two hours.'

'Which is plenty of time to have a look around, at least to see what's behind there.' Again she gestured towards the trees with her pole. We were reaching the boundary of our land now. I turned and the farmhouse was getting smaller and smaller behind us. Instinctively my eyes went to the upstairs windows, and for a second or so I fancied that I saw a figure there. Mother, glaring out at me: Wait until I see you again.

I turned back, realizing that I'd fallen behind, and jogged to join the group. In my empty belly was an unfamiliar fizzing feeling – fear and excitement. My bladder felt full and I recognized the sensation as nerves.

We entered the trees. I halted once more to stare back at the farmhouse and for a moment it was as though the undergrowth formed a dark corridor, and at the end of it, over a long, flat field, behind an overgrown and untidy yard, lay the farmhouse, which watched me, impassive, as I turned and disappeared from its sight.

I caught Karen's eye. Neither of us said anything but she felt it, too. Lulu, when she called for us to hurry up, smiled as though to say, I told you. I told you we could do it. Only Charlotte seemed immune to the sudden change in atmosphere. But then things were different for her, so she wouldn't have felt the way I felt. At that moment I knew what they meant about having the weight of the world on your shoulders – because I felt it lift.

And then we were running, all four of us. Lulu was whooping and we dashed through the trees, the farmhouse gone, just us kids, running and thrashing at the undergrowth with sticks. Lulu whooped some more and even Karen – who always seemed so serious, so withdrawn – even she was smiling.

We kept on, careful not to lose our direction; careful, also, to keep a check on the time.

'Charlotte, how long have we got?'

Charlotte sighed. She'd got bored of checking her watch a long time ago. Why, her sigh seemed to say. Why do you need to know the time every five minutes?

'We've got just over an hour.'

I stopped. 'We'd better get back,' I said. 'She might be early.'

'OK.' Not even Lulu was going to argue with that.

And then Karen said, 'Look,' and she was pointing with her stick to a gap in the trees through which we could just see . . .

A chimney.

'That's weird,' said Lulu, striding forward to get a better look, 'nobody lives around here.'

We all followed, moving to get a better look at the house, which lay at the bottom of a small valley, just its roof and chimney visible from normal ground level. We stood looking down at it, sticks and gazebo poles dangling from our hands. It was derelict, you could tell. There were no cars, a small garden was overgrown and from our vantage point we could see that windows had been broken. It wore a sad air of neglect.

'Wow, we should go and look,' said Lulu.

'No,' I said, 'No time.'

So, reluctantly, we turned, hurrying back through the trees, across the field and back to the yard. On the way we talked about the derelict house. Mother didn't know about it, we decided. She would have told us if she did; plus, it was so well hidden. It was, we agreed, *our* secret house, and we were going to go back and have a proper look, just as soon as we could.

Shortly after we got to the yard we heard the beep of the Volvo and ran to open the gate, an operation we performed with almost military precision. She drove in, tyres crunching on the concrete, face set in stone, watching us from behind glasses with beady eyes. I noticed Lulu toss aside her gazebo pole, as if it might somehow give her away.

Chapter Thirty-seven

*W*e called it the Cupboard of All Things. I looked at it now. It was a cupboard at George Dowty Drive, and Lulu, Karen and I called it by that name – the Cupboard of All Things – because it was where the food was kept, and I looked at it now because I was very, very hungry.

The door had been left open. Probably Charlotte or Bradley had helped themselves to a treat from the Cupboard of All Things and not closed it after them. So the booty caught my eye as I walked past and I stopped, staring inside at the food products twinkling at me. My stomach shifted and moved.

That morning Mother had realized I'd made a mistake recording *Emmerdale* – I think I'd missed off the beginning or something – and she added three more days. I'd already been on starvation a week, and the only food I'd had had been smuggled to me by Lulu or Karen, and even then it was only scraps.

Inside the Cupboard of All Things were chocolates and biscuits mainly, and they called out to me. But Mother used to count them, so I couldn't risk taking one of those. But then again, how would she know? Maybe Charlotte could have taken one? No. She'd ask Charlotte and Charlotte would tell the truth. She'd know; somehow, Mother would know.

At the side was a tin of tuna. She wouldn't count tins of tuna, she wouldn't bother, surely not. I looked one way and then the other – she was elsewhere, reading one of her women's magazines – then reached and pocketed the tuna, pushing it into my jeans, pulling down the hem of my T-shirt to hide the bulge, and then I darted out of the back door.

The garden at George Dowty Drive was long and thin, and at the end were some trees – the trees we'd shelter beneath when we were made to stay outside as punishments. They gave good cover and I headed towards them now, my prize in my pocket. I went into the trees so I couldn't be seen from the house and placed the tin of tuna at the base of one of them. I emerged, looking up at the house. There was no sign of Mother at any of the windows. I cast my eye around the garden, looking for something to open the tin with – but all I could find was a pitchfork. I cast another surreptitious look at the house, grabbed the pitchfork, then scurried back to my den.

Pitchfork, meet tuna tin. It's no mean feat to open a tin of tuna with a pitchfork, but I managed it. I managed it by jamming the tin between my foot and the tree trunk to hold it still, then driving the outermost prong into the tin. One. Two. Three. I used the fork to prise metal away from the tuna, then – carefully – used my fingers, finally creating a jagged hole big enough to pull tuna from.

I ate.

I pulled tuna from the hole and stuffed it into my mouth with fingers that shone with brine. I sat and ate almost the whole tin until my head was spinning and I had to stop and compose myself on my hands and knees. And then I ate the rest of the tin.

I was sitting there, hidden by the trees, mouth and fingers coated in tuna juice, when Mother caught me.

She'd been calling for me but I hadn't heard her, and I gasped as I looked to see her there, looming over me; she gave a sharp intake of furious breath.

'*What* are you doing?' she roared.

I said nothing. What could I say? She snatched the empty tin from me and with her other reached to the top of my arm, pulling me to my feet then dragging me back down the garden and into the kitchen. She shoved me in, then swung and slammed the kitchen door behind her.

'Hold out your hand,' she screamed.

I did. Palm down. I looked at my hand, seeing it shake slightly, waiting for whatever she would hit me with.

'Other way up,' she ordered.

It turned it over.

She shouted something. What? Scum of the earth, liar, thief, demon child, something like that. And the tuna tin flashed forward, into my hand, the force of it knocking my hand away, so for a moment it was as though she'd practice-punched into my palm and I'd simply absorbed the blow. But then there was the blood, and the pain, which was keen and sharp and immediate and drove me screaming to the floor, clutching at my hand. I looked up at her, tears of pain already flowing down my cheeks, and she was looking down at me with that calm, satisfied expression I knew so well, regarding me from behind her glasses.

Blood pumped from the wound. She'd got me at the base of the palm, the soft mound of skin near the bottom of the thumb, and it was bleeding heavily. Lulu, summoned by the screams, ran into the kitchen, passing Mother who was already on her way out. Blood sluiced the floor. That would need clearing up, I thought, as Lulu came to her knees beside me and took my hand. She looked up into my eyes but said nothing. Fetching some bandage she patched me up as best she could. She'd become really good at first aid, Lulu had.

And it's my favourite scar now, the tuna-tin one. All abuse victims have favourite scars, and this one's mine. I couldn't say why. I couldn't say why I even *have* a favourite scar. I just do. It's a souvenir.

The slash wasn't the end of my punishment for stealing the tuna.

Later that night, she made me stand at the top of the stairs. She got into bed next to Bradley, and opened a magazine, *OK!* or *Chat*, or *Take A Break*. One of those she always got, full of amazing true-life stories about people killing each other.

'Start running,' she ordered, and I knew what to do. I ran down the stairs, then turned around and ran back up.

I was fit and healthy. The leg injury hadn't happened by then. But even so, on about the sixth go it began to be torture, and I slowed.

'Keep on going,' she called from the bedroom. On my return journey up the stairs, I could see her in bed, the magazine in front of her. She didn't watch me; she just read and listened to my ever-slowing footsteps on the stairs. How long was I going? An hour or so. My leg muscles were screaming. At some point I began to whimper with the pain but she told me to shut up. On one of my return journeys up the stairs I saw her lay her magazine to one side and pull herself into the covers.

'Turn the landing light off,' she said, 'and don't let me hear you stop.'

I switched it off. The landing, hallways and stairs were almost dark, just moonlight through the windows, and not much of that. I stumbled slightly as I went, fatigue turning my legs into jelly, tears of pain tumbling down my cheeks.

And then I saw Lulu. She had appeared from our bedroom and she caught my eye, put her finger to her lips. As I reached the top of the stairs, she motioned for me to stop and she took over. To keep the sound of the footsteps going for Mother's benefit, and to give me a rest, Lulu took over the running punishment.

I'm not sure how long she did it for, long enough to let me rest my legs. She got tired herself, though, and with a shrug of 'I hope that helped' she went back to bed herself. I kept on going for a bit, then stopped.

'Did I tell you to stop?' said Mother, her voice sharp in the silence and gloom of the house.

I kept on going. What felt like hours later, she told me to stop and go to bed. I did, looking over at Lulu, who was asleep herself.

Together, we'd got one over on Mother. Another tiny little victory. (And I often wonder whether Mother will read this book in jail. It's at times like this, I really hope she does.)

Even so, it was 2 a.m. by the time I got to bed that night. I had three hours' sleep before waking up to look after Bradley at 5 a.m.

Beatings rarely used to happen at George Dowty Drive, maybe because of the neighbours. A couple of times we were beaten on the landing, but generally speaking the beatings happened at the farmhouse – there, after all, was where she kept her favourite chair leg. So, at George Dowty the punishments were either random punches or the stamina ones, like running or her other favourite, standing.

The standing punishment was another night-time event. Mother would make you stand at the foot of her bed while she went to sleep. The idea was that you had to stand in front of the landing light so that your head obscured the bulb. If you moved, or if exhaustion dropped you to the floor, the landing light would glare on Mother and she'd wake up, then make you stand back up.

I remember doing it one night, standing there until I was certain she was asleep. I'd worked out that if I bent my body while keeping my head still, so I was making a banana shape, then I could reach the light switch on the landing, switch it off and be able to move without the light disturbing Mother.

I reached, banana-shaping my body but keeping my head dead still. My fingers felt for the light switch, three fingers on the switch, not clicking the light off, but rocking it with my fingers so the only sound as the light went off was a tiny, muffled click.

Except it sounded as loud as a mortar attack to my ears, and I stood in the dark of the landing fully expecting Mother to wake up. She didn't. All I could hear around me were the snoring sounds of my family. I exhaled. I reached down and undid the laces of my plimsolls, then stepped out of them. I had a plan. I'd leave the plimsolls there so I knew exactly where I'd been standing. I'd get a couple of hours' sleep then return to the spot and switch the light back on. She'd never even know I'd been away.

It didn't work, that plan. I overslept and she found out what I'd done; she gave me a beating for it at the farmhouse.

There were other little dodges that did work, though. She used to give me lines to do, but I soon learned that she only ever looked at the first page, so I used to do lines on the top sheet then squiggles on the other. She used to give me sums as punishments, too. Who knows, if I'd have done them I might not be so bad at sums now, but Lulu used to help me out with them. She did it not because the old solidarity had returned between us or anything, but because we were growing and finding our feet, and part of that process meant going against Mother, whatever she used to do to us.

Looking back, I think she realized that, Mother did. I think she realized that we were stronger together now, so she did her best to cause rifts between us. Like one day, in the farmhouse, we were all being beaten. It was rare, actually, that just one of us would be beaten on our own – she'd usually do at least two at a time. The crime would be something like locking a chicken in a coop, breaking a plate or (the old stand-by) stealing bread, and instead of finding out who had done it, she'd make us all go and stand in the washroom.

She did that now. It was me; I'd stolen a slice of bread from the side. They'd just had lunch so I didn't think Mother had counted the slices but it turned out I was wrong. Outside in the yard we were working when we heard our names called: 'Christopher, Mary-Beth, Karen.'

It was bad when it was just our three names. If she shouted, 'Children', there was a chance it could be a good thing. But if it was Christopher, Mary-Beth, Karen, then it was bad, always bad.

And so it was. She knew about the bread. For some moments she stood screaming at us then sent us to the washroom. She hadn't asked which of us had stolen the bread, not then. Screaming at us, it was as if we were all guilty. I think she liked to think of us like that, as some kind of single, evil entity. In the washroom, we eyed each other up, only me knowing the full truth.

She didn't make us wait too long. We were told to go into the sitting room, same drill, we thought, and I was already reaching for the laces of my shoes.

'Just Mary-Beth,' said Mother.

I swallowed. Lulu looked at Karen and me, but neither of us returned her look.

Lulu took off her shoes and socks. Mother ordered her to lie down.

She stood with the chair leg dangling at her side. The sheet was up at the window, measly bits of daylight fighting their way into the room. I looked from Lulu, who lay on the floor, her eyes squeezed tightly shut, to Mother, who said, 'Own up. Who took it? Who took the bread?'

Nobody said anything. Mother turned and brought the chair leg down onto the soles of Lulu's bare feet. Lulu screamed, a scream that was more like a moan – a moan of somebody familiar with pain but still unable to bear the anguish silently.

Smack. Another blow. Smack, smack, smack. The blows rained down on her feet, Mother breathing heavily as she continued to beat Lulu, who screamed. Mother stopped beating her and rammed the chair leg into her mouth. Lulu made a strangled, gurgling, spitting sound and stopped. And the beating started again.

'Was it you who took the bread, Karen?' asked Mother, the chair leg rising and falling, the solid slap of it hitting Lulu's feet, like a cricket bat on wet sand. Lulu writhed and the chair leg missed her feet, dug into her side.

'No,' replied Karen.

'Was it you, Christopher?' asked Mother. 'Did you take the bread?'

If I admitted it she would stop beating Lulu. If I admitted it, she would start beating me.

'No,' I said.

The beating continued. Lulu, whimpering, tried to writhe out of the way, struggling now, Mother working hard to keep track of her. 'Own up,' she was screaming and then, when Lulu wouldn't hold still, she turned to us.

'Hold her.'

Dropping to our knees, we did as we were told.

We were made to hold our sister still while Mother beat her. I had one arm and one leg, Karen the other. Lulu thrashed and kicked, more, I think, because we were holding her than from the pain. She was whimpering, I remember that. I remember, too, being grateful that she had her eyes shut. I remember not being able to look at Karen while it happened, and when I did look up I saw that Karen had bent her head like me and was just hanging on, head low, wishing it would end.

Later that night, back at George Dowty Drive, we argued, us three. Lulu hated us for holding her down. She hated us for not owning up to stealing the bread. We didn't know what to say. A victory for Mother that one.

Chapter Thirty-eight

The next day, Lulu ran away again.

We were at George Dowty Drive and there had been a massive row between her and Mother. Lulu was thirteen then, the second-oldest after Charlotte, who never argued with Mother because she had no need to – she got everything she wanted anyway. But Lulu and Mother were always going at it, and at nights Karen and I would tell Lulu to stop. Leading us on trips away from the farmhouse and winning secret little victories was one thing. Actually defying Mother face to face was another.

'Why?' she'd snap, in the darkness.

'Because you're making it worse for us,' I hissed back. 'Just do what you're supposed to do.'

'Why?'

It was her favourite thing to say. She always questioned Mother's treatment of us in a way that Karen and I never did. As I've said before, she had known that little bit of life before Mother, so there must have been some tiny, hidden part of her that instinctively knew we weren't supposed to be treated this way. I wonder now if that knowledge made the abuse worse for her.

Anyway, this argument between them had kicked off. I can't remember the cause, but it ended with Mother locking the doors then shutting Lulu in the kitchen while she took the rest of us into her bedroom for a talk about the Armageddon.

After a while, Mother decided that Lulu should join us and told

Bradley to fetch Lulu. He reappeared moments later saying she'd gone.

She'd climbed out of the kitchen window. She'd taken her duvet with her, too. It was in the kitchen about to be washed so she'd grabbed it on her way out. I guess she just wanted the comfort of it.

As soon as the escape was discovered, we started looking for her. Judith was staying with us at the time, and she joined the search. Assuming that Lulu had probably just gone around the block, we had a walk around the Northway estate and called in at Nanny and Granddad's house. No sign of Lulu there, though. After another hour or so of fruitless searching, Mother gave up and once again, she called the police.

She used to tell us that she could have been a lawyer, so great were her powers of persuasion. Mind games were her thing, too. She loved to think she could pull the wool over people's eyes, whoever they were: us, the police, doctors, whoever. And it wasn't an idle boast, either. After all, she'd managed to outfox my parents and social services; she fooled the world into thinking she was just a normal mum with a big family, coping as best she could. So when the police came she adopted the pose of caring mum, shocked by the sudden turn of events. I don't know how the police felt about not being invited into the house – it must have seemed a bit odd to them. We were told to go inside while Mother spoke to them at the front door, and from the lounge I could hear her telling the police how worried she was and how Mary-Beth had been so moody lately (which was the truth, actually, she had been moody lately and we were all suffering as a result).

We were told to wait, which we did, messing about in the lounge mostly, until, much later that night – maybe one or two o'clock – Lulu came back to us.

She'd been brought home by a lorry driver, and she arrived still clutching her duvet. It turned out she'd walked for about a mile and a half, then fallen asleep by the side of the road. A lorry driver had seen her, picked her up and brought her home, end of story.

That night, things were different with Lulu. I don't know if it was because I saw her with new eyes, or that she had changed in some tiny but profound way, but she seemed bigger somehow, older and more assured. She didn't tell us anything about her adventure, either. When she escaped from the farmhouse we heard about it later, in great detail. Now she seemed to pull away from us. It was as though something inside Lulu had decided she didn't need us; as though she had decided that there was only one person she could rely on, and it was herself.

Whether she was beaten for running away or not, I don't remember. Maybe not. Judith was living with us now – she had a slightly calming effect on Mother – and with work continuing on the farmhouse there were more people in and out. That didn't mean the hurting stopped, of course, it just meant that Mother used to lash out more, rather than beating us on the feet.

She hit out often, sometimes at random. Gazebo poles, knives, sticks, anything she might be holding. She'd shove and push, too. As time wore on, it seemed that her punishments became less . . . well, less *disciplined*. There would be fewer times when we'd wait in the washroom. Or, there were times when we'd be told to wait in the washroom and she'd forget why we were there – a new development, this was. I remember once she told me to remove my shoes and socks and wait in the washroom, then came into the room about two hours later.

'What are you doing in here?' she snapped.

'Nothing,' I said, and scarpered, praying she wouldn't notice that I had bare feet and then remember the punishment.

In exchange, her rages got worse. When she did hit out she would be screaming, spit flying from her mouth. She screamed and screamed at us that we were demon children, scum of the earth. We had been demonized, she shouted. According to her, we were the reason the farmhouse was falling down around our ears.

There was a time we had to do some work on the kitchen floor because the tiles were floating, uneven, moving around as you walked on them. What we did, we got hold of a concrete mixer from somewhere and passed it through the kitchen window. That was an operation in itself. With the mixer inside the kitchen, we mixed up the concrete (brilliant, I loved doing that), then poured it over the kitchen floor. Two days we waited for that concrete to dry, and when it did the kitchen floor was a complete mess. Instead of being a nice, flat surface, it looked as though someone had just spilled concrete onto it. It fell to me to get rid of the concrete mistake and I spent about a week with a sledgehammer, *chuk*, *chuk*, *chuk*, breaking it up, tossing it out into the yard and onto a pile of rubble I called my skateboard ramp. Brilliant fun.

But according to Mother, the reason the kitchen floor was ruined was not because we had no real experience of laying flooring, or mixing concrete, or using a concrete mixer. It was, as she screamed to us at the time, because we had jinxed the house, we demon children. The floor, she shrieked, was the devil's work.

It was the same with the shower. It took us eighteen goes to get it right. Mother had had a special shower made. It could take up to three people at once and it was decorated with Mickey Mouse at the bottom of it. But it just wouldn't go in. The floor wasn't level, so the shower base wasn't stable. We got there in the end, of course – the new shower unit was eventually fixed – but it took *weeks*. The mistakes weren't because we were children and not plumbers, or because the farmhouse was old and the floors not level, and therefore it wasn't practical to try and fit a three-berth shower; it was because we were the devil's work. We had demons inside us.

This was what she used to scream at us. And the starvation continued, and so did the hurting. I spent so much time with bandages around my forearms from the cutting that I forgot what my arms looked like. I didn't sleep, I didn't eat. I worked.

One of the people who visited us at the farmhouse during that period was Lawrence Northam, a friend who was a Jehovah's Witness. He did a lot of plastering around the place, but fell out with Mother, so stopped. We didn't know it then, but Lawrence was to play an important part in our future. It was around that time, I guess, that he first noticed something wasn't quite right in the Spry household.

Chapter Thirty-nine

Karen, Lulu, Charlotte and I stood and watched the Volvo pull out of the gates, Mother behind the wheel, Bradley in the passenger seat beside her.

'Time check,' said Lulu.

Charlotte checked her watch. 'Twelve-fifteen.'

'OK,' said Lulu, 'that gives us until two-thirty. Let's get going.'

We grabbed sticks and poles and set off across the field, much more quickly than we had before, taking the path we now knew. Again, I had that crawly, excited, nervous feeling in my stomach as we stepped away from the watchful gaze of the farmhouse and went into the trees.

We jogged along, reaching the derelict house, taking a path down then creeping up to it, hearts in mouths, making our way through overgrown weeds and stingers. One of the windows had a pallet of some kind beneath it, as though someone had used it to reach the window. We went to it and crouched down, holding our breath as we listened.

Nothing. No sound.

'Hello,' called Lulu. Her voice bounced off walls in the empty house.

'Hello,' she called again. 'Is there anybody there?'

No reply. She looked at us, shrugged, then rose to her feet. We looked up at her like hungry chicks as she peered into the window.

'Bloody hell,' she said.

Four faces appeared at the broken window of the derelict house and we all looked in, mouths agape.

The place was full of stuff. Toys, mainly, in soggy, water-damaged boxes. But also electrical stuff, piles and piles of it. I saw televisions, a keyboard of some sort, even what looked like a computer.

'Hello,' called Lulu again. Still no reply, so she climbed through. The rest of us followed, climbing into what looked like it had once been the lounge of the house, and picking our way over the boxes. Many were in Christmas wrapping and Karen reached to tear the wrapping from one. It had been wet once, but had dried. Beneath the paper was a Barbie doll, and Karen gasped. She loved Barbie dolls.

'Where's it all come from?' said Lulu.

Upstairs we had our answer. Climbing the stairs to explore we peered out of a window and could see the caravan park, studded with mobile homes. Of course. The park had been flooded and there had been outrage in the local paper, lots of stuff about 'sick thieves' who had looted the flood-damaged caravans. They must have brought some of the gear here, leaving behind what they didn't want.

It was forgotten, flood-damaged stuff that was no use to its original owners – no use even to sick thieves. It was our stuff now.

'What's the time, Charlotte?' I asked.

It was 1.30 p.m.

I took an IBM computer that day. Karen, Charlotte and Lulu all took dolls (and there were so many, they didn't even have to fight over who had what). We hurried back to the farmhouse and once there went to the farmer's hut above the chicken shed, the secret place we sometimes hid in after beatings – we were still pretty sure Mother didn't even know about it. Now, not only did we have a den but we had our own stuff in it, too. A whole little life she had no control over.

The next time she went to Pershore we visited the house again.

I came back with a remote-controlled Dodge plus a green screen. I had no idea what had happened to the rest of the computer, but I wanted the screen to try something with my new IBM. Again, the girls returned with dolls, and stuff called My Little Locket, which were little hearts that opened up. As before, we took it up to the secret hut.

Around this time, we were living back at the farmhouse full time. There would be periods when we'd live at George Dowty and other, shorter periods, when we'd stay at the farmhouse. At the time, I didn't know why we would suddenly move from one house to another, especially not when the farmhouse was uninhabitable. I know now, of course: she moved to confuse Social Services, with whom she fought a running battle, flitting between education authorities so neither one could ever get a fix on us.

Living at the farmhouse proved lucky for me, since it meant I could creep out in the evenings and go to the chicken shed. She'd either be watching soaps or reading one of her magazines, so she wasn't paying much attention – she didn't know I was sneaking out of the house and to the farmer's hut.

Once there I examined the IBM. On the back of the unit was a small diagram explaining how to connect the computer to the keyboard and a screen. I had a keyboard, and I reached for the green screen I'd rescued from the derelict house, checking the connections. All compatible.

Hens clucked and moved around in the shed beneath me as I scrabbled around. One of the skills I'd picked up from Judith was electrics – I'd been doing them around the farmhouse and I was getting pretty good. I'd taken a socket from the house and it wasn't too much of a stretch to run power from the chicken-shed light source. I worked quietly, constantly listening out for Mother. If she'd been calling me in the house and found I wasn't inside, she'd come out here looking for me. If I heard her calling I could get down from the hut and come walking out of the chicken shed with a story about a job I had to finish, that I'd heard something out here. I reckoned I could do it without her getting suspicious.

With my gear all plugged together and the electricity hooked up, I reached to switch the computer on.

I wonder now how things might have been different if the computer simply hadn't switched on. If it had sat on the boards of the farmer's hut, amongst all the dust and feathers and hen droppings and stared blankly back at me like, 'No way, I've been in a flood, I've been carried away by sick thieves and now you've given me the wrong screen. I ain't working for you or for anyone,' instead of doing what it actually did, which was to flare up with a white flash of light that I worried for a second might burn out the screen, then flash politely, not at all perturbed by its journey, and ask me something in Japanese. I leaned forward, looking over the keyboard, pressed Enter, and a new screen appeared, this one asking me if I wanted to select English, which I did, and then . . .

Poot.

The computer flicked off.

I sat back on my haunches, feeling nothing – nothing but total and utter elation. The computer had worked. I had got the computer to work.

And it's not as though I then used the computer to go on websites or send emails, or anything, really, that would affect my situation with Mother. I didn't. I didn't, in fact, do anything with it other than take it apart to see if I could get it working again. But opening it up, I found myself fascinated by the gold of the circuit board, tracing connections with my fingers beneath the dim 25-watt bulb of the chicken shed. For me, something, or somebody, was born that moment – a Christopher who had nothing to do with Mother. A Christopher with a secret passion. It was only a computer, only a chicken shed. Still, I remember thinking, You can't hurt me. You can't hurt me in here.

After that, I was taking apart anything I could get my hands on. My next job was a hi-fi that came from a house-clearance sale.

Mother had bought it, then put it in one of the sheds. I split it down and converted the amp from four channels to two. When Mother was out I used to conduct what I liked to call my Maximum Bass Tests on it (bass, and bass tests – one of those fascinations I'd picked up from car magazines).

Next, an Amstrad computer found its way into the house. Mother, who was a huge fan and regular customer of charity shops, had found it in Oxfam and bought it for the grand total of four pounds. I think it was meant for Bradley and she probably thought it had disappeared into the bowels of his playroom. She would have been wrong. One night I sneaked the Amstrad out to the chicken shed, where I set to work taking it apart, comparing the innards of that to the insides of the IBM. Next, Judith's boss gave us an old Apple Macintosh. Again, the Apple Mac first went upstairs into Bradley's playroom before going out to the chicken shed where I attempted my biggest project yet – I cannibalized the two; I merged what I now know is the RAM of the Amstrad with the Apple Mac's motherboard. Why? Because the Apple Macintosh had a black-and-white (or, as I now know, 'greyscale') screen, yet the Amstrad was colour. I wanted to see if I could get the Apple Mac monitor to work in colour. And it did. Crouching in the chicken shed, I switched the computer on and for a few seconds the characters were in – well, 'colour' might be putting it a bit strongly, but not black-and-white anyway, a kind of colour. Again, the machine went *poot* after a few minutes but it didn't matter, I was bouncing with glee.

I am probably the only person in the world who learned how to be a computer geek in a chicken shed. I loved every second I spent in there.

Chapter Forty

I'd made her angry that day, I must have done. She must have been simmering all morning and most of the afternoon to do what she did. Because it was the worst. Of all the punishments Mother ever gave me, that one was the worst.

I was on starvation. What am I saying? Of course I was on starvation. I was always on starvation, which meant it was always a permanent battle between us – between Mother and me. I would constantly be hoping to find scraps of food, or be given them by the girls; or, if I had the opportunity, and I thought I could get away with it, just take them from the kitchen table. She, on the other hand, would be watching me like a hawk; she'd be counting bread and biscuits and chocolate bars. Imagine trying to do that with five children around the place. When food went missing – which it did, of course, *always* – I got the blame, and I would have to be punished.

That day, the weather was gorgeous. I was wearing shorts and a T-shirt because it was so hot. One of my favourite T-shirts. It was afternoon, getting on a bit. I think I must have finished all my jobs because I was playing in the sandpit with Bradley at the time. We were making sandcastles, just generally mucking about, when Mother came out of the house.

She came from the front of the farmhouse, I remember. That was unusual; she would normally come from the back door, but for some reason she'd used the front, walked around the house, then up the drive and into the yard. It wasn't significant that she'd used that door, just unusual. One of those details that sticks in my mind.

I heard her before I saw her – her footsteps on the concrete of the yard – and I looked up to see that on her face was an expression of complete controlled calm. A look I knew only too well. A look that terrified me.

Instinctively I glanced at her hands. With her, you never saw the knife until the last second but both of her hands were empty this time. Thank God, at least there was that.

I stood, sand silting off my clothes as I did so. She was going to hit me, of course, and for some reason I wanted to be standing up when she did it. I don't know why. I just did. Weird, really. Why stand up just to be knocked down again? But there you go.

Bradley, I remember, was looking at her with a half-smile, quizzical, for all the world as if she was bringing us an ice cream each. For him her calm face meant nothing. For him the calm face just meant calm.

She reached the sandpit. I was standing now, empty stomach in a knot and I braced, ready for the blow. My body wanted me to turn and run, or cover myself, but my mind knew better than to do that. My mind ordered my body to stay where it was, to wait for the punch, to take it as I had so many times in the past. Still, I could feel my face half turning away, as though being pulled by wires even as my eyes were fixed on her.

She stopped at the edge of the sandpit, just feet away from me. She looked at Bradley.

'Bradley,' she snapped, and Bradley jumped slightly, not used to being addressed so harshly. 'Inside. Get inside now.'

'But . . .' Bradley looked at me – me, who stood straight like a soldier, almost shaking with the effort of remaining still when every fibre of my body shouted 'Run!' He looked at me as though to say, 'But we were in the middle of playing,' but didn't. Something quietened him.

'Just get inside,' repeated Mother. 'Now.'

Then, to me, she said, 'You. You've taken bread.'

I hadn't. But what was the point of saying so?

'Get over there,' she snapped, and she pointed to where the Transit was parked.

Our yard was always full of cars, that was the thing. We had loads of them over the years. Always breaking down, they were, and we'd often have to move them around. If you go to the farmhouse now you'd see them: cars everywhere. Overgrown, almost invisible thanks to weeds and undergrowth. You look at some undergrowth, squint at it, and you might just see a glimpse of dirty chrome that was once a car. We'd use the Transit to tow them to a corner of the yard and leave them there – and there they'd remain, rusting, rotting. The day before, we'd retired a Nissan Sunny. I'd watched as Mother and Judith hooked it to the back of the Transit and towed it over to the far side of the grounds. They unhooked it, then Mother drove the Transit back to its parking spot and left it there. And, Mother being Mother, she hadn't yet got round to taking off the towrope. She never did. Those towropes always seemed to stay attached to the van for a couple of days. I swear she'd driven off to Pershore with towropes still tied on, scudding along the road behind her. And that day was no different. That day the towrope was still attached.

I did as I was told. I stood by the rear of the Transit van, the towrope coiled at my feet like a lazy snake. She bent to tie it around my leg, my left leg. I stood and let her do it. What she was doing didn't surprise me. I knew exactly what she was doing.

Because it wasn't the first time. It would be the worst, yes, but not the first. It's called calf-roping, I think, where the victim is tied to the back of a car or a van, and the car is then driven. Before – and it had happened maybe twice before – she had tied one of my hands to the towrope, then driven very, very slowly with me following behind, usually at a jog. It was bad, a bit humiliating, tiring when she kept it up for a while, but it wasn't *too* bad. It wasn't the most feared of her punishments.

The leg, though. The leg was new.

As I stood there I was thinking of the times she'd tied me by the hand, and I was thinking – God, how stupid I was – that it would be like those times; the only difference would be that I was tied by the leg and not the hand. I was thinking that I would stay on my feet, that I would walk behind the van as I had before, just that instead of my arm tied it would be my leg, and that I would shuffle, like a manacled slave-convict in a film. That was the picture I formed in my mind.

With the rope fastened, she stood and looked at me, her mouth hard, that same, eerily composed, almost faraway look in her eyes. At times like that it was as if she went into herself somehow; that somewhere deep inside Mother was her doing-hurty place, and she was there now.

She turned and went to the front of the van. I heard the driver's door open, the van settled on its springs as she got into the driver's seat, and the door slammed shut.

Where is everybody else, I wondered? I looked down at my leg, the towrope tied around it, and then towards the farmhouse where the sun reflected off the windows, making them shimmer silver and blank. Were there faces at the windows? Were Karen, Lulu, Bradley and Charlotte staring out of them now, giggling at me as I stood behind the van waiting for my walking punishment? I couldn't tell, not with the sunlight on the windows like that. Were they there, though? I bet I looked daft.

The engine started.

The exhaust coughed a black cloud funnel of smoke against my leg. I looked back at the house and grinned sheepishly, more for the benefit of my invisible audience than for myself.

She blipped the accelerator. I turned to face the rear of the van, ready.

She floored it.

My left leg was whipped out from beneath me and all of a sudden it was pulled straight, sticking out in front of me like it was encased in invisible plaster as I flew backwards, head connecting with the concrete, arms flying outwards. And then my head was bouncing on the ground and I strained my neck to keep it off the floor, to see where we were going, raising my arms, trying to keep them out of harm's way.

Thonk. We hit the back field and the air was knocked out of me. The field had recently been ploughed, was made into furrows, and the force of the impact on the uneven ground sent me twisting around so that for a moment I was face down in the earth, mud slashing at my face, filling my mouth and nostrils, making me cough and splutter as I tried to twist round so I was on my back once more.

My leg. Oh God, my leg hurt. It hurt so much it felt like it might tear away from my body.

My head connected with a clod of ploughed earth and, as if in slow motion, I saw a shower of mud as it disintegrated. I caught another furrow and my elbows made contact with the ground, taking off the skin. And then she steered onto the perimeter track where the mud was packed and hard and dry and moulded into the shape of Land Rover tyres; where the packed-hard mud ripped at my T-shirt, shredding it instantly, tearing at the flesh of my back, making me scream.

I estimate that she drove like that for something like half a mile. That's about the perimeter of the field. I wouldn't like to say how fast she was driving – probably half as fast as it seemed to me, being dragged along behind her – or for how long, although it probably didn't take as long to make the circuit as it felt to me.

When she'd finished, she drove off the field over the ridge that lay between the field and the yard and then onto the yard, where she stopped.

Bumping over the ridge had winded me, and I lay on the ground, writhing, gasping for breath. At least the horrific, unnatural stretching pain in my leg had stopped, replaced by a thumping ache, but my back had flared up; it was on fire. The driver's door of the Transit opened, then slammed shut. I saw her feet below the Transit as she came round to the back of the van, the image split with tears as if viewed through cut glass.

I sensed her at my feet and felt her loosen then untie the towrope. She reached a hand to my shoulder and pulled me onto my back; for a moment or so she regarded me, as if drinking in my agony. Mother's face showed no emotion as she let go of my shoulder, then walked away.

I lay on the ground, catching my breath. Not far away was the mobile home, and when I was able to stand I hobbled over to it, throwing open the door and dragging myself inside like a half-dead animal. The caravan was full of rubbish, of damp cardboard boxes and old suitcases with broken catches that spilled clothes onto the floor. It smelled fusty and wet, and there were rat droppings on the floor. Rat droppings and me, as I lay there, bleeding, catching my breath.

My T-shirt had been ripped almost off my back. Just the neck and shoulders remained. My arms bled, my back – though I couldn't see it – must have been bleeding too. I was covered from head to foot in dirt, dust and blood. I put hands caked in dirt to my face and they came away wet, but I didn't cry. Not from humiliation or hopelessness, I never did. Any tears were tears of pain.

And that, incidentally, was why Mother was never forced to answer the charge of dragging me behind the van during her trial. Both Karen and Lulu told the police what had happened, and Karen mentioned it in court, too. But when it came down to me speaking about it in court, I just couldn't face it and I refused. Whether I was right to do that at the time, I'm not sure. On the one hand, of course, she should have been made to pay for doing that. But on the other, I would have broken down. I would have broken down and cried in court and Mother would have been there to witness it. And I didn't want that. More than anything I didn't want that. There are other incidents, too, that I couldn't face talking about in court – things that I've only now come to terms with. Speaking about them now? Here? Well, at least she can't see the tears.

The yard was quiet when I finally stepped out of the mobile home, testing my leg. At first I thought it must be broken but I was able to walk on it, so probably not, although it hurt like nothing else on God's earth. I looked over to the farmhouse, which stared impassively back at me. So often after punishments we would run to each other, help with first aid, maybe say some brusque words to help things be better, but not today, not for me.

The chicken shed had running water. I used that to clean the worst of the dirt and blood from my body. Hens clucked as I kneeled in the dirt and doused myself in freezing water. When I'd finished I hobbled back to the farmhouse to look for another T-shirt, something to tide me over until we got back to George Dowty Drive and I could have a bath. Bradley was back in the sandpit and he called to me as I limped past, wanting me to join him and play some more. I didn't answer. I couldn't face it.

Chapter Forty-one

J ohn Hendrickson, the computers – that was how I got through it, that was how I say I coped when people ask me.

As for the other things I'm asked: why not run away? Why not fight back? I'm still working on those. The easy answer – the one I guess is most easily digested, is that we didn't realize we were being badly treated; we thought our life and the way we were being treated was 'normal'.

In fact, we never, ever believed we were actually normal – the normal people were the ones who used to shout at us for being weirdo Jehovah's Witnesses. We knew normal mums didn't quote the Bible when they smacked their children, but I guess we always believed that other mothers did smack their children, just that we had it a bit worse because Mother was such a strict disciplinarian. We knew that there were times she had gone too far, but that she knew it, too. Which meant that somewhere there was a line, an invisible line that would be crossed, but only rarely. Because after all, Jehovah's Witnesses are strict disciplinarians; her quoting from the Bible meant that the beatings were given approval from above, and if we didn't think other Jehovah's Witness children were treated like us, well, that was because other Jehovah's Witness parents weren't quite as devout as our mother. They didn't know as much of the Bible as she did. They didn't realize what you were *supposed* to do with children – especially children who had demons in them as we did. So, yes, we knew the way we were being treated was not 'normal' – we just didn't think it was wrong.

When we were released, they did some psychological tests on us – me, Karen and Lulu – and we were diagnosed with Stockholm syndrome. It comes in different types, Stockholm syndrome does. One is where you still love and respect your abuser and no matter what anyone tells you about them you think it's a lie, and another is where you downplay what's been done to you, so much so that you cease to even think of it as maltreatment. That's why we didn't run away or fight back, because we had that. We loved and respected Mother, or at least we thought we did. She was our mother, and you don't hit your mother, you don't want to see bad things happen to her. You want to please her. It was why John Hendrickson used to buy Mother villas and yachts, and why I'd even feel sorry for her sometimes. Like, there was a time she stubbed her toe. It was night-time at George Dowty, I was in my bedroom and I heard her scream in pain – a scream like nothing I'd ever heard from her. I'd seen her in pain before, of course – there would be little accidents, especially around the farmhouse where she might get hurt and yelp – but I'd never heard anything like this from her.

I rushed out onto the landing to find her sitting on the stairs holding onto her foot, her face a picture of agony, and immediately I felt sorry for her. Really, I felt sorry for her, I remember it well. I wanted to help, there was that much blood, and so, the next day, I offered to look at it for her.

I did. I cobbled together some nail clippers and cotton wool, sat on the floor of the lounge and Mother put her foot in my lap while she watched *EastEnders*.

I cleaned up the toe and did my best to trim the toenail, my back to the TV. I remembered Lulu saying that when she was forced to the floor to eat vomit she used to stare at Mother's feet. Lulu had said she thought Mother had ugly feet, and though I'm still not sure if they were actually *ugly* or not, Mother certainly had her fair share of ailments. Sitting there, her foot in my lap, I discovered that in addition to her stubbed toe she had athlete's foot, plus an ingrown toenail.

The athlete's foot was the worst. I studied it. Some of her toe-nail seemed to be hidden by this white crumbly stuff that I later learned was fungus. She had corns and calluses, too. Again, I only learned to identify these much later, when I pored over the *Encyclopaedia Britannica*'s entire entry for feet. At the time, it just looked like Mother had rather mouldy feet.

'Eurgh,' said Bradley, walking into the room and looking at Mother's feet. I shooed him away and looked up at Mother. She said nothing. Her arms were folded across her chest as she watched TV, and on her face was a look that was . . . happy. Well, maybe not happy so much as content, like all was well in the world.

I was eleven or so. Most kids that age are probably thinking about what they'd like to do when they get older. Most want to be a fireman or a tractor driver. Me, I decided there and then that I wanted to be a chiropodist. I was going to start with Mother's feet and the first thing I was going to do was look after her stubbed and bleeding toe.

From then on, I would do Mother's feet at George Dowty Drive. I learned to get rid of the flaps of skin that hung off the big toes. I dealt with calluses and I rubbed cream in to treat the ath-lete's foot. I got good at it, too. The thing with chiropody is that you shouldn't hurt the patient. Obvious, yes, but it's far more dif-ficult than it sounds, especially when you're having to remove dead skin or sand away at calluses with a pumice stone. I only ever hurt her once, and that was when I was removing an ingrown toenail. I did Nanny's feet, too, although she was never as keen on the treatment as Mother. Mainly, I stuck to doing Mother, and it became my aim to train as a chiropodist when I left her care. Of all the things I wanted to do, that was the one that really stuck – that and being a mercenary. Who knows? I could have been a mercen-ary with a sideline in feet, or a mercenary who used chiropody as a commercial front to hide his illegal mercenary dealings. I tin-kered with the idea of becoming a vet at one point, too, and – in common with most other little boys, I guess – I fantasized about becoming a racing driver, driving away, John Hendrickson at the wheel. The times when I was doing her feet, when I used to glow with the pride of pleasing her, Mother was in the passenger seat next to John Hendrickson – and she had that same contented look on her face.

I just wanted to impress her, that was all. And doing her feet was part of that. I wanted to impress her because she was my mother. And of course I would not hit back, or tell the authorities about the way she treated us, not just because I didn't think there was anything wrong with the way she treated us, but because she was my mother.

Chapter Forty-two

*T*hen there's the other question: how could she get away with it for so long? She pulled the same trick with the outside world that she pulled on us. She scared people, kept them guessing; she knew what to say to make them believe her; she flustered them with misdirection.

The Social Services report I was quoting at the beginning of the book mentions twelve occasions when 'concerns about the care of the children were expressed'. I will, in time, want to know what each of those twelve occasions were, but not at the moment. I'm not yet ready to dwell on the missed opportunities there were to rescue me from her. The report says that Social Services did respond to those concerns but that they were never serious enough to warrant further Social Services involvement. It goes on to say: 'Mrs Spry was described as "eccentric" and there was evidence of her being quite controlling and being difficult to engage in professional interventions. Her frequent moves of home added to the difficulty.'

And what that means is: she was clever. She knew the system and knew how to work it.

'Children,' she'd call, summoning us into the lounge at George Dowty.

There she stood brandishing a letter and wearing a tight-lipped scowl. 'We're going to have a visitor.'

Not that this ever meant a great deal. The letters arrived well in advance of the actual visits, giving us plenty of time to tidy up so we could get rid of the animal mess, try and make the rooms as habitable as possible, and giving her enough time to make sure she didn't bruise any visible areas; plus, Social Services appointments were movable feasts to Mother. She'd cancel and rearrange the same appointment several times. When at last a social worker would arrive they'd be let into a nice, tidy house where five presentable children would greet them. Charlotte and Bradley would be the picture of health, of course, and if Karen, Lulu and I maybe looked a little gaunt, well it was obvious Mother wasn't starving us, Charlotte and Bradley were proof of that. We three were just thinner, that was all. The social worker would have a look around the house, then sit and talk to us. Mother would be in the room, of course, and we would be very polite and answer any questions, if they were put to us, although they rarely were.

During one visit I was sporting a set of bruises on my face. Mother hadn't done it deliberately; she wasn't that careless. What it was, she'd been pushing past me on the stairs too roughly, shoved me and I fell – I hit every stair on the way down. The social worker asked her about the bruises. She told him I'd fallen down the stairs, missing out the bit about how I'd only fallen down because she'd pushed me.

'Is that right?' he said to me.

'Yes,' I agreed, nodding and smiling, playing my part to perfection.

And each time the social worker would go, and life would get back to normal.

After the sentencing, the papers were full of outrage about how the warning signs had always been there. According to reports we had been seen by doctors, psychiatrists and dentists and, well, yes, that's true, we were. I went to hospital at least three times. There was the time she hit me with the lead piping; there was another time Bradley accidentally dropped a steel joint onto my head; and a third occasion when I had been called in for a beating, was running to the back door, fell and gashed my head. Did any of the doctors who saw me in A&E express concerns? Were they any of the twelve? I don't know. Did the dentist who treated Lulu for broken teeth – seeing her, according to one report, up to six times – express any concerns? Did friends, family, other Witnesses?

Mostly, we didn't see other people from day to day – not apart from the meetings at the Kingdom Hall. There were the conventions too, of course, plus we used to go shopping with Mother, and sometimes we'd bump into people she knew. But she very rarely let us out of her sight with other people; in fact about the only time I can remember it happening was when we went preaching door to door with the Witnesses that time we got water thrown over us. So she'd always be there, making sure we said the right things and were polite, all the time. We knew if we were anything but supernaturally well mannered we would be beaten, so that's exactly what we were. Supernaturally polite. Which made people nervous, you could tell. They used to smile at us in a slightly lop-sided, forced way and say things like, 'How nice it is to meet children with such good manners,' even though we knew what they actually meant was, 'How weird it is to meet such freakishly polite kids.'

She didn't like us to speak. 'Mrs Spry always spoke for the children,' notes the report, 'and never let them be seen alone.' What she did with other people – whether they were friends, family, healthcare professionals or social workers – was control the meeting. Nobody ever left an encounter with Mother in any doubt about who was in charge. Control. It was always, with her, about control.

Occasionally, of course, she had to let us speak for ourselves. People would ask us questions and we might answer them incorrectly or say something that fell like a stone into the middle of the conversation, something that felt out of place. If that happened to me I could sense Mother bristling beside me, almost as though she gave off a furious electrical charge, a crackle around her body. Her posture would change, her voice would be sharp and she'd end the conversation.

Later, at home, she'd say, 'You got very close to telling them about our lifestyle. Go in and wait for me in the sitting room. Shoes and socks.' And she'd beat me, quoting the Bible: 'Children, obey your parents in the Lord, for this is right! Honour your father and mother!'

The most thorough visits were probably the ones we had for checks on the home schooling. Those Mother took more seriously than the social worker visits, and she used to go to great lengths to prepare, even one time taking us to the Bristol Festival of the Sea, where she stocked up on literature about boats.

The day after we got back, she gathered us in the yard at the farmhouse, all of us, indicating behind her at one of the sheds we had there – the one next to Charlotte's snooker room.

'This is going to be our classroom,' she told us, 'Now get to work.'

We cleaned out the shed, dumping the stuff in the yard, then got to work kitting it out inside. One end would be Mother's teaching end, where she would stand. We painted the walls of the shed and when they were dry put up posters and tacked up literature we'd got from the Festival of the Sea.

Next we moved a picnic-style bench inside, so the finished effect was like a classroom. The night before the visit from the education authority inspector she had us in her bedroom at George Dowty Drive, learning our times tables, and sure enough the next day we were reciting them for his benefit. We passed the inspection, presumably.

We had a visit shortly after our Florida holiday, too, when Mother showed an inspector our NASA material. Afterwards, it was put away again and only came out several months later, when a different inspector saw exactly the same material, only slightly more dusty and dog-eared than it had been before. She used to tell the inspectors that she'd been on the radio with her home teaching, and it was true. Around the same time as the Bristol festival, she invited BBC Worcestershire to the farmhouse as part of a series they were doing on home schooling. Up went the teaching materials. The radio reporter bustled in with a tape machine, microphone in hand. She'd been hearing from Mother how we were learning all about France, she said. Could she ask me a question?

(We had been learning all about France in preparation for the radio visit. Except we hadn't learned about rivers.)

She held the microphone towards me and checked her tape was running. 'Name a river in France,' she said, and fixed me with an encouraging grin, prompting me to answer for the tape. I looked at her. I looked past her to Mother.

There was a long pause.

'The Nile?' I said.

They didn't broadcast that bit.

Even so, it was something Mother proudly used to tell the education people, how she'd been on local radio with her home teaching. It's a tactic I now know is called misdirection. Why would anybody who was withholding home schooling from her children actually invite a radio crew to her home in order to see it in action?

And that was how she created the wall around us – by forcing people to see us as a strange family in order to divert attention away from the truth; by bullying and coercing people using that famous dominant personality of hers. And she kept it up for years. For decades. I remember New Year's Eve in 1999, when we went to the local fireworks display in Eckington. All around us was that palpable sense of change in the air – of hope for the new Millennium. The firework display wasn't that good, and I said so to Lulu, but slightly too loudly so that someone standing nearby heard me, turned and gave me a wink that I returned with a cheeky smile.

When we got home later that night, Mother beat me for that. My first beating of the new Millennium.

And it wasn't going to get any better. The year 2000 would turn out to be a devastating year for our family.

List of the five worst punishments given to me by my evil foster mother Eunice Spry

1. The calf-roping punishment, when Mother dragged me across the field behind her Transit van
2. The hypodermic needle punishment
3. The cricket bat punishment
4. The punishment for eating the tin of tuna, when Mother slashed me across the hand with a tuna tin, which gave me my favourite scar
5. The punishment for nearly taking a slice of bread, when Mother held my hand on the hob

Chapter Forty-three

We were in convoy. How many of us? Well, first there was the big Transit van, and in that were Mother, Karen, Lulu, Nanny and Granddad, Eunice's brother Tom, plus Granddad's wheelchair and all of our stuff.

Behind that was a car, an Audi 100 driven by Mary Jackson, Mother's friend from Safeway. With her were her husband Tony, their grandson Josh, and Bradley, who was best friends with Josh. Behind them was another car, a Renault 19 driven by Mary and Tony Jackson's daughter Samantha, with Charlotte and me as passengers.

And we were all going on a summer holiday. A long weekend, from Thursday to Monday, at the Pontin's holiday camp in Brean in Somerset. The Pontin's Brean Sands Holiday Centre, to be exact.

'You're only coming because I can't get anybody to look after you,' Mother had hissed that morning.

I honestly can't remember what it was we'd done, but it had happened the previous day. Something involving all three of us it was, and we'd been beaten for it, the chair leg on our feet. Whatever the crime it must have been bad because we each had around a hundred strokes. Afterwards, Mother, exhausted, told us we wouldn't be coming to Brean; we were going to stay with Nanny and Granddad while she took Bradley and Charlotte to the holiday camp. Lying there, crying with pain, we didn't much care. I know I didn't. I held my feet and squeezed tears from my eyes and wished for nothing more than Mother to leave the room so I could bear my pain in peace.

The next morning, though, the reality of it sunk in as our family prepared for their trip without Karen, Lulu and me. Mother informed us that she'd spoken to Nanny and Granddad, and that we'd be staying with them.

Any holiday involving our family involved a superhuman amount of preparation and we used to leave all the packing until the last minute, so the scene at George Dowty Drive was utter chaos. Except it was utter chaos that didn't include us. We, the demon children, slunk around, feeling sorry for ourselves. I didn't want to miss a holiday. Florida was still fresh in my mind and I remembered how we had been like a proper family. Those hugs and kisses from Mother. As we were going with other people I knew she wouldn't hurt us while we were there, and I so wanted to go to the seaside, play on the go-karts, visit the theme park that was next door; I'd heard Mother telling Bradley all about it – there were sand buggies and fairground rides, and I'd been imagining myself as John Hendrickson speeding along the beach at Brean on my sand buggy. Karen, Lulu and I gave each other glares, each silently blaming the other for the fact that we weren't going to Brean.

Until there was a phone call. Nanny and Granddad had decided they would like to come to Brean, could they join us? Perhaps it was the prospect of looking after us for four nights, but either way they'd decided they wanted to come and could they squeeze in? A phone call later and yes, they could. Once again, Lulu, Karen and I were sharing sidelong glances, except this time our eyes were dancing, and on our lips were suppressed smiles. We were going after all.

Mother caught us staring at one another, read the victory in those glances, and let it be known that we were only allowed on the trip because there was no other option.

'And don't think you'll be going on any of the rides, either,' she snapped.

I stared, feeling my eyes go wide with disbelief.

'There'll be no go-kart, no rides . . .' she looked right at me, as though she could somehow see inside my head where John Hendrickson sped along the beach, '. . . and no sand buggies.'

My heart sank as I got to work helping with the packing. As I passed the lounge I looked in at where Bradley and Charlotte were sitting, playing, virtually oblivious to everything that went on around them.

Much later that day, we finally drew into the main gates at Pontin's in Brean, and already it didn't look good. There were very few people around. Worse, much of the place seemed shut. Driving through the complex, it was like something out of a Western – one where the heroes come riding into a deserted town, get off their horses and say, 'What happened here?'

'Because of the fuel crisis, probably,' guessed Samantha as we found a space, gawping at the lack of holiday spirit around us. She was right. Trust us to go on holiday slap-bang in the middle of a fuel crisis, but that's exactly what we had done. An alliance of farmers, lorry drivers and taxi drivers had been blockading oil refineries in protest at rising fuel taxes, and now the stuff was in short supply – in some places more than others, it had turned out. Because of the crisis, Pontin's had closed almost all of its attractions. Or, as far as we were concerned anyway, all of the good ones. In a short while we were to discover that because of the crisis there were no go-karts, no fairground rides and no sand buggies.

Still, we found our chalets and settled in. I was sharing with Mother's brother, Tom. Bradley was in with her, some of the girls in another, and Nanny and Granddad and the Jackson family were in chalets further along the row. We had almost a whole section of Pontin's to ourselves. Later, we did some exploring, and we wandered on the beach where my feet hurt on the sand – still throbbing from the beating we'd had the previous evening.

The next day, this was Friday, Judith turned up. Work commit-
ments meant she couldn't join us the previous day but she'd
managed to get away for Friday afternoon. Looking back now, it's
horribly ironic really – originally she hadn't been planning on
coming to Brean at all – too much work on, so she said. She'd only
decided to join us at the eleventh hour. Now she appeared, driving
the little blue Suzuki Carry that she used as a runaround.

I never particularly liked it, that van. Not because it was always
'Charlotte's car', the one she would be given when she was old
enough to drive. Just *because*, really. Or, maybe it was for that
reason. Maybe I didn't like the Suzuki because it *was* Charlotte's
car. She who had never, to my knowledge, expressed any interest
in cars, who got everything she ever wanted, and even, in this case,
something she didn't.

Pontin's in Brean is a labyrinth. What feels like thousands of
chalets are arranged in rows, and more or less in the centre are all
the attractions, the rides, the sports facilities, shops and restaurants. That night we all ventured out, the whole lot of us, to eat.
Mother kept reminding Karen, Lulu and me that we were on dis-
ciplinary, so we hung back slightly as we made our way past
chalets and to the heart of the complex. By the time we'd eaten,
though, Mother had relaxed slightly and on the way back we
were more like a proper family, walking and talking together. For
a while I even spoke to Judith, who I hardly ever talked to. Normally she was a bit cold and distant and we didn't really get on.
I was wary of her and I used to remember things, like her words
at the dinner table that time – *You should have left them in there* – or
the time she'd held me down while Mother emptied the washing-
up liquid into my mouth. But, for now at least, we chatted. Up
ahead of me, Lulu and Bradley were walking along together,
guiding the party home. There was laughter, I recall. We were
happy.

As we reached our chalets, Lulu and Bradley were still talking
so he went into the girls' chalet. I went into the one I was sharing

with Mother's brother and sat on the bed to read. And then I heard a scream. Not that loud, not too agonized, but a scream all the same. I got off the bed, went to the door of the chalet and stepped outside.

There were two rows of chalets, their doors facing one another, separated by a strip of grass and paths that led to the front doors. Mother and Tony Jackson were standing on one of the paths now and, as I came out to investigate, Mr Jackson was shouting at Mother.

'You should learn to control your children,' he roared. 'Children need to be disciplined, not spoilt.'

Mother took a step back. I felt my own mouth drop open. I had never seen anyone speak to her like that before. I had never seen her – even if it was for only a split second – look the way she did now. Uncertain. Cowed, even.

But it was only for a split second. (Enough to make an impact on me, though; enough for maybe another brick to drop out of that wall she had built around us.) Then she had regained her composure, and her reaction was volcanic.

Mr Jackson recoiled as she roared back at him. A comment about his own children that I didn't quite understand but could tell from the look on his face was below the belt, because his face seemed to register shock – at what she'd said, but also at the ferocity of her attack. This was not the Eunice Spry he knew, the one who spent so much time with his wife in the coffee shop at Safeway; this was a different woman.

He recovered and began shouting back at her. Across the strip of grass I could see curtains twitching as other holidaymakers peeked out at the commotion, and with Mother and Tony Jackson still shouting at each other, I dashed to the chalet next door.

The scream had been Lulu. A few minutes ago she and Bradley had seemed like the perfect brother and sister, but somehow a fight had broken out. Who started it I never found out, but Bradley had finished it. He'd finished it by throwing a full tin of baked beans at her head. She sat on the sofa nursing it while Bradley skulked around the edges of the room looking defiant and like he didn't care that his sister's head was already growing an egg-sized bruise.

Outside, the shouting abruptly stopped and Mother and Tony Jackson came into the chalet, peace apparently having broken out. Immediately, Mother went to Bradley to cuddle him. She was already starting to lay into Lulu for provoking Bradley into throwing the beans at her head.

'You. What do you think you are doing?' she snapped at Lulu; then, to Bradley, 'Are you all right, little one?'

Warm in her embrace, Bradley nodded, looking up at her with puppy-dog eyes and pushing out his bottom lip.

From the door Tony Jackson watched, mouth agape, as though he was unable to believe what he was seeing.

'Why are you cuddling *him*?' he asked Mother. His voice was more measured than before. Instead he sounded incredulous as he added, 'It's your *daughter* who needs you now.'

We all looked at Tony Jackson: Go to Lulu? Are you insane?

Chapter Forty-four

*T*he next day it threw it down. Absolutely poured. Rain that burst in little watery explosions from the concrete of the holiday camp; saturated the strip of grass outside our chalets; forced us to pull our clothes over our heads to run, stamping water, from one chalet to another. It rained so hard that the chalet I was staying in flooded. Bradley and I spent a happy hour or so running through the lakes of water on the carpet, jumping up and down in them and kicking water at each other, joyous with the novelty of inside puddles.

But we were the only ones having fun. A strained, taut atmosphere had settled on the group, waves of resentment coming off Tony Jackson and Mother, who didn't speak to each other but seemed to circle one another like combat aircraft. Our one group became two, with Mr Jackson shepherding his family, Mother seeing to ours. All that linked us were Bradley and Josh, the two friends who played together regardless, in blissful ignorance of the ice-cold atmosphere.

Tony Jackson had wanted to go home, Karen told me. Because of the argument, because of what Mother had said to him, because he obviously disagreed with her parenting style. And whether that was because he thought she was too lenient with Bradley or too strict with Lulu we would never find out. Either way, Samantha had persuaded Tony to stay, and so they would.

Not that it was easy. With hardly anything open to do and the two families at loggerheads we did a lot of nothing much, barely talking even amongst ourselves apart from the constant whines of Bradley and Josh that they wanted to go on the go-karts, they had been promised go-karts, *please* could they go on the go-karts, for two more days and nights. The next day we went to the beach again and Charlotte wanted to swim in the sea. Mother said she could, until Charlotte insisted that we come in, too.

'Bradley can swim,' said Mother, firmly.

'Everybody,' insisted Charlotte, and because it was Charlotte insisting, we all had a chance to go in the sea, Bradley, Charlotte, the demon children, all of us.

Until at last it was Monday morning, and we all woke up thanking God the holiday was over, even us three demon children who knew that going back meant more beatings. Even us.

(Somewhere else a lorry driver, who would that day be returning from a delivery to a warehouse in South Devon, woke up too, not knowing that today he would cause the death of two people, and seriously injure two others.)

'Please can we go on the go-karts,' whined Bradley for what felt like the billionth time.

And at last Mother snapped.

As the rest of us packed our stuff – hurriedly, dying to get on the road – Mother went off. Where she went we weren't sure, but we kept on packing. The plan had been that we'd get on the road as soon as possible in order to miss the traffic. We didn't want to be stranded in huge tailbacks, massive lorries jostling our exhaust pipe on the M5.

The Jackson family got their stuff together and gathered outside their chalets. Still no sign of Mother, and there was a moment of awkwardness between our lot and theirs as we said goodbye. Then they turned and left, walking off down the strip to the car park, Josh giving one last wave to Bradley, and we returned to getting our own stuff ready to leave.

'Bradley, you're going go-karting.'

Mother had returned. And wherever she'd been she seemed to think she'd organized a go-karting expedition for Bradley. He threw a look down the line of chalets as though Josh might still be there, but Josh had left ages ago. In the meantime, me, Karen and Lulu had packed our things, made sure the chalets were left tidy, and done all the stuff that you're supposed to do when you're packing up after a holiday – all the stuff we knew from experience that Mother would want us to do. Now, we picked up our cases and carried them to the go-karting track where what seemed like a team of Pontin's Bluecoats were waiting for us.

We stood by the track, suitcases at our feet, Mother's arms folded and lips pursed as Pontin's Bluecoats hurried around us. Bradley bounced on his heels expectantly. There, on the still-wet go-kart track, were go-karts under plastic covers. Go-karts. So near.

'Are we going on the go-karts?' Bradley asked me. I shrugged.

'Yes, you are going on the go-karts,' said Mother, then to me, '*You* can only watch.'

The Bluecoats had spoken to the gardening team apparently, and from them they'd got some petrol so Bradley could ride on the go-karts. With a flourish a young Bluecoat took a damp cover from a kart, filled it up and ushered Bradley in, all the time stealing glances at Mother, who watched him like a hawk, eyes round and piercing behind her glasses. I looked at her. She was in her mid-fifties then. I was eleven and would be twelve in just over two months' time. I remember looking at her and thinking that she looked old all of a sudden. There was some grey in her hair, which was pulled back into a fierce bun; her face bore frown lines. Still, though, the intensity never left her, and it was with that same familiar stare that she watched the Bluecoat now, seeing to it that Bradley got his go-kart ride.

Which he did. We stood, the whole family (apart from Granddad, who sat in his wheelchair, grumbling every now and then about the weather), and we watched Bradley do circuit after circuit of the go-kart track. At first he waved to us as he went past, and we all waved back. Then, after a while, I was the only one waving. Then even I stopped.

The go-kart ride meant we didn't leave as early as we planned that Monday morning, which meant we wouldn't miss the traffic jams. We piled into our vehicles. In the Transit was Mother, driving, Nanny, Granddad, Tom, me and Lulu. In the car park of Pontin's we said goodbye to the others, who got into the blue Suzuki Carry. Judith was driving, Charlotte next to her – she always insisted on being next to Judith in the front. Karen was in the back seat behind Judith, with Bradley strapped into his booster chair behind Charlotte.

We left first in the Transit. The Transit was more powerful and, anyway, Charlotte and Judith wanted to stop off at Cribbs Causeway and the Mall, which is the huge shopping centre they have there.

So off we went, a pretty straightforward journey back. Arriving in Tewkesbury at about midday, we dropped off Nanny and Granddad at their house and drove round to George Dowty Drive to leave the Transit. That done, the three of us walked back to Nanny and Granddad's house, where Nanny had started some dinner for us all.

By 4 p.m. there was still no sign of the Suzuki. Mother tried Charlotte and Judith's mobile phones but there was no answer. Both of them just rang and rang.

And then Judy appeared, Nanny's next-door neighbour. Her face was white. She'd seen something on the news, she said. The van. She was sure it was the little blue Suzuki. And then everything seemed to happen at once.

Chapter Forty-five

The crash happened on the M5 just outside Weston-super-Mare. An earlier accident had caused a tailback after police closed one lane of the motorway and imposed speed restrictions.

The driver of the 24-ton lorry was returning from his delivery at the Devon warehouse. Later he told police that he didn't see the stationary traffic or the speed restrictions because he had been adjusting his radio. That was why his lorry ploughed into the stopped traffic, hitting first a Citroen, at the rear of the queue. The Citroen, luckily for its occupants, had pulled out slightly, and was pointing into the hard shoulder as though the driver was about to do a sneaky overtake or simply wanted a better look down the line of traffic. Because it was at this angle it was shoved off the road by the oncoming lorry, and as far as I know, nobody in the Citroen was seriously hurt. The lorry continued forward, however, and hit the Suzuki Carry, which ploughed into the back of a 38-ton lorry in front.

The Suzuki was crushed to a third of its original length in the collision, from 3.23 metres long to 1.13 metres. The front of the van disappeared under the 38-ton lorry, the rear of the Suzuki concertinaed forward and those in the front of the van didn't stand a chance. Judith was decapitated; her severed head landed in Karen's lap and Karen still has nightmares about it. Charlotte also died instantly.

In the back, Karen was seriously injured. Her spine was broken, her legs were crushed. She was airlifted to hospital where she would spend a month in intensive care. That she's alive now is a miracle, an absolute miracle. Bradley fared slightly better. The child seat protected him. It was one of those models with high sides and it prevented him from being crushed the way Karen had been. His legs were broken, though, and I think he broke a shoulder from being thrown around.

The police told us later that Judith and Charlotte's phones had been ringing when they reached the car. The police aren't allowed to answer them, apparently. They have to let them ring, so they rang as rescue teams cut open the car and pulled Karen and Bradley out, both of them covered in blood. Karen told a medic that she couldn't be given blood, because she was a Jehovah's Witness. Ranting about it, she was, so much that they tried to give her morphine, at which point she thought they were trying to give her blood and punched the medic, before they bundled her into a helicopter which took her to hospital.

Back at home, there was a phone call from the hospital.

The phone rang moments after Judy had appeared, standing in the doorway at Nanny and Granddad's, saying that she'd seen a motorway pile-up on the news, footage of it, and she was sure – she put a hand to her mouth – sure that the wreckage had been of our little Suzuki Carry. And the phone rang.

Nanny reached for it, listened for a moment then handed it to Mother, saying nothing.

We watched Mother, her face draining of colour. 'Oh my God,' she said into the phone, then, 'Thank you,' and she put the phone down.

For a moment or so she looked around the room. What she was looking for I don't know. Nothing, probably. Just a nervous reaction to the news. Her hand went to her chest.

'I've got to . . .' she started, still looking around the room, still searching. 'I've got to get to the hospital, there's been an accident.'

Judy gasped, her hand going to her mouth again. I felt myself freeze.

'What's happened?' asked Lulu.

'I don't know, I don't know,' snapped Mother, flustering. 'I've got to call Mary Jackson.'

For a mad second I thought she meant to arrange a coffee at Safeway, but of course she didn't, and not long later, the two of them left in Mary's car for the hospital.

Lulu and I sat on the pavement and watched them draw away, Mary Jackson worried and pale at the wheel, Mother staring straight ahead, neck rigid.

For some time, the two of us sat on the kerb, knees drawn up, resting our chins on them. Something terrible had happened. Nobody would tell us what was going on, but something terrible had happened. I felt as though in the house behind me people were talking about things that concerned me, but I wasn't allowed to know. I sighed and agreed when Lulu said, 'I just want to know what's going on.'

Some time later Nanny came out. She'd been crying and we looked at her hoping that she might tell us what was happening. But she didn't. We asked and she still wouldn't.

'Not yet, not yet,' she said. Instead, we were told we were going to stay with Ted and Sarah Benson, friends from the Kingdom Hall.

Once there, we were ushered upstairs, our queries ignored, and it was so comfortable, so tidy, so warm and hospitable that we almost forgot about what was happening. Almost. But stuff was happening beneath us.

In the guest bedroom of the Bensons' house we moved a small rug to one side and pressed our ears to the floorboards, listening to what was happening below us. Jehovah's Witnesses were arriving in the house. Word had got round. They were having a crisis meeting to decide who should go to the hospital. They were concerned an intervention was needed to prevent Karen or Bradley being given blood. All night the phone was going and Lulu and I overheard snippets of conversation. From what we heard – things about giving 'them' blood – we decided that everybody was still alive. In bad shape, but alive. Perhaps we slept a little easier that night.

It turned out that the Jehovah's Witnesses were too late. Karen had needed blood but because she was under eighteen the hospital had given it to her anyway. It saved her life.

The next morning, Rebekah arrived to pick us up. I'm not sure whether she knew all the details, but if she did she didn't say anything. The journey passed almost in silence. I remember staring out of the window, trying to think about my computers, watching the landscape zip past, attempting to keep my mind from wandering. The thing was, we still hadn't been told anything. What we thought we knew we'd gleaned from conversations that had drifted up through floorboards, from looks passed between adults. In my imagination I saw the motorway strewn with bits of the blue Suzuki. I saw blood. But whose? Were they all alive? Were they all dead? Rebekah would only shake her head when Lulu asked her questions, and in the end Lulu gave up and, like me, looked out of the window. I wonder what she was thinking about as we drove. Escape, knowing her.

The Sega took my mind off it for a while. When we arrived at the hospital they plonked us in a games room in what I guess was the children's ward. For some reason, being in the children's ward, I began to relax slightly. I had decided Judith was all right. In my mind's eye, I saw bits of the blue Suzuki across the motorway, but there, on the hard shoulder, stood Judith, and she was OK, and that was why we were in the children's ward, because Charlotte, Karen and Bradley were here. So I sat and played on the Sega for a bit, hoping that no other children would come in wanting a go on it. But they didn't. And Lulu sat on an easy chair not far away, her arms folded, watching me but not really watching me.

Then Mother walked in.

She closed the door behind her, checking first there was nobody around. She looked at me and I paused the Sega, placed the joypad to the carpet tiles and turned in my chair to face her. Lulu, too, drew herself up straighter as Mother took a seat at the end of a table in the middle of the room.

She placed her hands in her lap, and seemed to straighten as though trying to shake off the tiredness that showed on her face. She was wearing fawn-coloured trousers, I remember. A blue fleece, too.

She said, 'I'm sorry to tell you, children, that Judith and Charlotte didn't make it.'

The words seemed to numb me. In my head I heard static that drowned out all other thought but the words . . .

Bradley? Karen?

'Karen is in intensive care,' she continued, 'she may not make it.' Mother took a deep breath.

Bradley?

'Bradley will be OK.'

I felt relief. Then guilt that I felt relief. Then I became aware that beside me Lulu was sobbing, and I too began to cry, great walloping sobs. Sobs like punches; that felt as though they began deep in the pit of my stomach then rose up through my entire body.

It was, I realized, the first time I'd ever cried. Properly cried. Not the first time tears had ever sprung from my eyes. That had happened hundreds, thousands of times – almost daily – from the pain of being beaten. But it was the first time I'd ever cried from shock or sadness, from loss or emotion. The first time my feelings had ever been born as tears. It was as though something inside of me which had been buried was at that moment free. As though my emotions had been kept in check by a dam that was now crumbling.

This was her. This was her fault. My life with Mother was years of keeping my emotions hidden, of pushing them so deep I ceased to care about myself, about anybody else. I had to – to survive. Even now, Karen, Lulu and I talk about our 'emotional cries'. We discussed it one day and we found that each of us had kept a tally. I was on three, the lowest of us all. I think Lulu had cried the most, which surprised me at the time – I'd always thought she was the strongest of us all.

For some time we sat and cried. Mother didn't try to comfort us, not with a hug or a kiss. Nor did she say anything to help us get over the shock. She simply sat on the edge of the table with her hands in her lap, staring straight ahead. Cold, almost. She had lost Judith, her eldest daughter. And Charlotte, too. She'd looked after Charlotte since birth, she'd doted on her, bought her anything she wanted. At home in the farmhouse Charlotte's pink princess grotto would remain unfinished, caught in a state of cold storage, only half of a mural completed, furniture still in its plastic wrapping. Like the pictures of boy bands on the walls of her disused snooker room, things would get old, suspended in time. And now Mother mourned Charlotte in her own way, straight-backed and staring into the distance. I looked at her, wanting there to be emotion there. When there was none, I got up and left the room.

Rebekah found me outside, came to me and gave me a hug – the first time anybody had hugged me since Florida. It felt good.

'He's been asking for you,' she said, drawing away to look me in the face. 'Bradley has been asking for you.'

A short while later I was led into the room where Bradley lay in a hospital bed. I stopped, and my mouth dropped open. He was covered in blood. Something to do with his injuries, not wanting to cause more damage, but they hadn't washed the blood off him and he was covered in it, head to foot, as though he'd been painted in blood. Hardly any of it was his own. The blood belonged to Judith, to Charlotte, to Karen. His eyes were open but he didn't say anything – and that was a first – just watched me as I gawped at him.

Then I turned and vomited into a basin at the side of the room. I vomited again. And again. And in the end I had to leave the room.

A short while later, having composed myself, I sat by the side of his bed. He was staring at me still. The whole time he hadn't said

a word. A nurse had told me he was coming out from under anaes-
thetic and that he would be speaking soon, but even so, it was a
surprise when he finally did.

'Which do you think is the best 2CV?' he slurred, groggily.

I sat forward. 'Bradley?'

He smiled dreamily. His eyelids flicked shut then opened.
'Which do you think is the best 2CV,' he repeated, 'the Dolly or the
Classic?'

I leaned forward. Madly I thought I should press a button and
call the nurses, the way you see people do on TV, but I stopped
myself.

'Which do you think, mate?' I whispered.

'The Classic,' he said.

I looked at him, my eyes misting up. He was OK. My little
brother was OK. I leaned forward some more.

'No way,' I said, 'the Dolly's miles better. That extra horsepower
makes all the difference.'

Chapter Forty-six

I looked at Mother. She wore a brown suit. She was standing very still at the front of the congregation in the Kingdom Hall, an air about her, as if she was there, but not really there.

The place was packed: a mix of Jehovah's Witnesses – hundreds of us, all smartly dressed – and Judith's folky friends, who had tried their best, but . . . well, you could tell who were friends from the folk scene and who were friends from the Kingdom Hall. Never have two sets of mourners been so clearly defined.

All through the service I kept stealing glances at her. Every time, I saw the same. The same blank stare, the same composure. I was looking at her to see if she would cry. I studied her eyes behind her glasses to see if they shone with tears for Charlotte and Judith and their joint funeral. But no. Around her, people grieved. Women clutched hankies to their noses, men stood with inclined heads. I saw our neighbour a few rows down and he was crying, his thumb and forefinger pressed to the bridge of his nose like he was trying to squeeze the tears back into himself. Everywhere in the hall, people openly mourned.

Only Mother, it seemed, did not.

Those in the congregation were careful not to be overheard, not when the children were around, but I knew what they thought. They thought that Mother was a trooper, that she was bearing up well by putting on a brave face for the children, shielding us from the worst of it, protecting us. But all I could see was control, and I wanted to see it slip; I wanted there to be a person beneath that brave face. There was no one. She caught people's eye and greeted them with a tight-lipped smile and down-tipping eyes, an incline of the head. She stood with a straight back, looking ahead of her, the Kingdom Hall vibrating with suppressed grief around her. The grief she felt – and she must have done because Judith was her eldest daughter and Charlotte was her little princess, so she *must* have done – was all kept locked up inside, where maybe that grief would fester and rot and become something else. Become rage.

I had seen her cry, once. It was at the hospital. Bradley had been in and out of consciousness. I had stayed with him and so had she. He'd come round, we'd trade a few insults or swap car facts, and then he'd drift off again. It was a tense, horrible time. Not far away, in her own room, Karen was unconscious. She had a broken spine in three places. Her neck was broken, so was her arm, and her leg was fractured in many places. She also suffered massive internal injuries. It was touch and go at that point. Nobody thought she would live. When I stood by the side of her bed I felt small and useless and didn't know what to do with myself. At least with Bradley I could do something.

Mother was there, too. Bradley was lying in bed, his eyelids fluttering, and he started to come round. She moved forward in her chair, the legs of it scraping on the tiles with a harsh sound.

'Bradley,' she said, and he opened his eyes and looked at her.

She started crying. From the other side of the bed I watched her, staring at her over Bradley-shaped hillocks in the sheet, hardly able to believe my eyes. She put a hand to her eyes, wiping away tears as they escaped from beneath the frames of her glasses. With her other hand she held Bradley. She snuffled slightly, more tears falling from her eyes, rolling down her cheeks, and, looking at her, I felt – I don't know – odd, I suppose. As though the world had stopped turning. As though the grass had turned blue and the sky green. Because Mother was crying.

What I didn't feel was pity. Or sympathy. Not then, and not at the funeral. Like Mother, I didn't cry at the funeral. I looked down the row of mourners at where Lulu stood. She wasn't crying either. Karen was still in hospital, but they allowed Bradley out for the day. They'd wheeled him in on a hospital bed, a blanket over him. Afterwards, we all filed out and into the car park, one of those crisp autumnal days when the sun is shining but there's a chill in the air. I pulled my suit jacket closed and returned a smile from one of the Witnesses, blinking in the afternoon light and seeing, for the first time, the cars. They were everywhere, clogging up what was normally a quiet Tewkesbury street, and not just cars either, but caravans, Gypsy-style caravans, giving the street a carnival, surreal look. Folk friends with bent heads returned to them, getting into the caravans, helping each other up. I recognized some of them. There was the guy with the wonky van, of course, the one who'd driven me to the farmhouse that day. He was there, but I didn't see the van, long since retired, probably. There were other people I recognized, too. Judith had run a clog-dancing team called Hopping Mad. I remember one outing where we'd danced in the grounds of Eastnor Castle, years ago. Another time we'd been on a float at an event in Pershore. There were happy times.

So why did I feel nothing?

Because of the ADHD medication, perhaps? Because I was never close to Judith and Charlotte – because Charlotte had been spoilt while I was tortured and Judith had held me down for Mother to pour washing-up liquid down my throat. *You should have left them in there.*

Or because she had taught me well, Mother had. Taught me to be a blank so that I felt now the same way I felt when I was being starved or beaten: empty. As though all this was happening to someone else – someone I didn't particularly care for. I shed no tears for Judith or Charlotte, felt no sympathy for Mother. I shed no tears for myself. Me, Lulu and Mother – sun or not, we were the coldest people there.

Standing there in the car park I looked at Bradley, who was

being Bradley. Lying on his bed he was chatting to one of the Witnesses and, quite without warning, he lifted up the blanket that was covering him. Typical Bradley, he had nothing on underneath. We were killing ourselves laughing about it.

Mother stayed at the hospital the whole time Bradley and Karen were there, which was a month in all. After her initial scare, Karen was out of the woods. Well, out of the woods in the sense that she wouldn't die, at least, though she'd had to have a series of operations: on her spine, on her neck, to rebuild her stomach, even. They repaired her broken neck with metal rods; shattered and splintered bone in her legs was replaced, also with rods. These days she jokes that she's more metal than bone, and she probably is.

Meanwhile, Lulu and I returned to stay with the Bensons while Mother remained at the hospital. She stayed there for that whole month, mounting a vigil by the side of Bradley's bed, and then she discharged the pair of them.

Staying at the Bensons' house was great. I loved them and I loved the month we spent there. Sarah and Ted even bought us little presents. I don't recall what Lulu was given but they bought me a mother-of-pearl and gold tiepin. Smart, it was. I wore it to Witness meetings, and we went to loads of meetings with them. Other times, Nanny, Lulu and I used to go round to George Dowty Drive to feed the animals out the back, while Ken the Wonder Mechanic took care of the animals at the farm. Or we'd scoot round to Nanny and Granddad's or go to the hospital to see Bradley and Karen, where I'd spend my time on the Sega and watch Bradley and Karen's card collection grow. And it really did grow. You wouldn't believe the strength of the Jehovah's Witness network. Bradley and Karen were getting cards and presents from all over the world. There were hundreds of them – so many that nurses literally ran out of places to put them. Lulu and I spent hours reading them.

And then Karen and Bradley came home.

We knew it was going to happen – there'd been talk of it. We knew also that Mother was having problems with the doctors at the hospital. It would be a good few years before I'd discover the full implication of those problems she'd been having, because at the time it was just normal. Mother and people in positions of authority simply didn't get on, doctors included. And they'd had plenty of time to rub up against each other. She'd been sleeping in the car park of the hospital at first, in the Transit van. But then they'd found her somewhere to sleep in quarters above the children's ward, where, thinking about it, she must have been the nurses' worst nightmare – the ultimate interfering relative. And that's before you consider the ulterior motives that would only become clear years later. So, even though she sprung Bradley and Karen out of hospital over a week before they were scheduled to leave, I bet the hospital were glad to see the back of her.

The day they returned we said goodbye to Sarah and Ted with mixed emotions. On the one hand I was desperate for Bradley and Karen to be back home, I so wanted to see them; on the other, I was sad to leave the comfort of the Bensons' house, where the beatings had become a distant memory and the only reminder of my normal life had been going back to George Dowty to feed the animals. During that time, nobody had hit me, nobody had told me I was the scum of the earth or said I was a demon child and I had eaten every single day. For a while there, I'd allowed myself to believe that this was how things would be from now on. And then . . .

'You,' she snapped. 'What are you doing here? Get back to the house right now.'

One of Nanny and Granddad's neighbours had bought a new Golf and I'd gone along the road to have a look at it. Me and the neighbour were standing on his drive, with him no doubt wishing this kid would stop staring at his new car and let him get on with his day, when the Transit van drew up, driver's window down, Mother glaring at me from the driver's seat.

She ignored the neighbour, just snapped at me to get back home, *now*. I looked at him, stole a smile of thanks and registered the look of shock on his face, then ran, as fast as I could, back to Nanny and Granddad's.

I arrived there just as they were getting out of the van. Bradley came down on a pair of crutches, Karen in her wheelchair. I looked from her to Granddad – wow, we were a two-wheelchair family now – and then at Bradley, hobbling along the pavement towards me, a huge, cheeky grin on his face and plaster-casted legs swinging out from under him.

'Guess what I've got, Chris?' he said.

'Go on,' I said. Mother was already starting to unload things from the Transit. Out came suitcases and Safeway carrier bags bulging with cards taken from the hospital, a whole set of Furbies bought for Bradley and . . .

'A PlayStation,' announced Bradley.

'And it's not for you to play on,' snapped Mother, to me.

Still, it was a happy day. I was overjoyed to see Bradley and Karen again, even though they'd both been in the wars. They were alive, that was the main thing. Mother seemed closer to Karen, too, which was encouraging – as though they'd somehow become closer during the hospital stay.

The way she'd spoken to me on the neighbour's drive, though. The daggers she gave me when my eyes lit up at the mention of the word PlayStation. Something told me that, for me, things were soon going to get back to normal.

Chapter Forty-seven

*A*ctually, things didn't get back to normal for a while. For six weeks after Karen and Bradley got back from the hospital, we lived with Nanny and Granddad in their tiny bungalow. Lulu and I slept in the hall; Karen, Mother and Bradley in the living room; Nanny and Granddad in the bedroom. Why we did this, I'm still not quite sure, but possibly because George Dowty and the farm-house simply weren't fit places for Karen and Bradley to recuperate, being virtually uninhabitable. The other possibility – and the one that seems more likely the more I think about it – is that Mother was trying to avoid someone. Given that she'd just discharged Bradley and Lulu, and bearing in mind what I now know, she was probably trying to avoid contact with the hospital. She wanted to keep any outpatient care to such a minimum it was virtually nonexistent.

Then, we moved out of Nanny and Granddad's house. We moved back to George Dowty Drive, and the day after that, Mother, Lulu and I drove to the farmhouse for the first time in over three months.

'Oh no,' said Lulu, even as I was diving out of the Transit to open the gate, which I wrenched open and swung back, letting it clunk to the stopper and seeing the almost total devastation around us. Mother eased the Transit through the gate and into the yard, tight-lipped. Stepping down from the van, she shielded her eyes with a hand and swept her gaze across the expanse of the farmhouse, the yard, the garden, the fields. It had been immaculate once, George Parker's pride and joy. Now it was derelict. Like the house Lulu and I had discovered, it looked abandoned, unloved, unkempt.

'Oh God,' repeated Lulu. No wonder. She and I would have to clear this up. She and I would have to cut down the weeds and stingers that ganged up on the yard; the brambles, like barbed wire, turning the orchard into a no-man's-land.

The hens were OK, at least. So were the pigs. Ken had been popping over to take care of them. Unfortunately, nobody had told him about the fish we had in a container by the back door, so they were dead. It also meant Ken hadn't approached the house, which was probably why he didn't notice that the kitchen window was smashed. And since he reached the farmhouse by popping across the fields from the back, he hadn't noticed that the front door had been kicked in, either.

I felt a tickling at the base of my stomach when we came around the front of the house to see the door hanging slightly open, splintered wood along the doorjamb. We looked at one another. Mother pushed on the door. It creaked open, all of a sudden feeling not like our front door, but like the front door in a Freddy film.

'Hello,' called Mother. The hallway yawned back at us. I came from behind Mother to look down it. Empty. Empty apart from our usual clutter; the mess, the boxes, the old familiar pile of sticks propped in a corner near the kitchen door. Bits of bamboo, the chair leg with its bitten, splintered end, rust-red with blood.

'Hello,' repeated Mother.

When there was no answer, when we were certain there was nobody in our house, we walked in, into the hallway, craning to look into the sitting room with the sheet at the window. The TV and video were still there, at least. Then, through to the kitchen where we noticed that the toaster had been moved, but that nothing had been taken. We went upstairs, and again nothing had been taken, though Karen's dolls had been attacked. She'd be devastated, I thought.

Back outside and we discovered that one of our older Transits had been trashed. Bradley kept toys in it, and all the windows had been smashed. Inside, his toys had been wrecked, one of his favourite jeeps trampled. We'd been ransacked. Not quite burgled, not quite vandalized, just sort of attacked. My theory then was that someone had lived there for a while but Mother decided it was a burglary, which is what she told the police when she called, and what she told the local newspaper when she called them, too. The paper even did a story on it – 'Tragic Family Hit by Heartless Thieves', that kind of thing – while a local policeman arranged for the police community fund to make a donation to us. Local firms got in touch with the paper to donate things.

And every day I kept an eye on Mother. I wondered if any minute now, she was going to break down. I expected her to start grieving; I thought something would give. When it did, I didn't want to be anywhere near her, but for the time being at least she behaved as though nothing had changed. Charlotte and Judith were mentioned, but never with any particular emotion or emphasis. We simply carried on. We were two people missing, that's all.

The driver of the lorry was charged, and a court date set (Mother's back straightened slightly and her eyes hardened when she told us the news). He appeared and pleaded guilty to causing death by dangerous driving (a righteous tone to her voice when she told us). We would go to Bristol Crown Court to see him sentenced.

Meantime, there was no starvation. For weeks I waited for her to turn around and snarl, 'No food,' at me, but she didn't. Same with the beatings. 'Into the washroom,' I kept expecting to hear. It got so that I almost *wanted* to hear it, just to get it over with. But the order never came. It never came.

'Where is Bradley?' she said to me, one day.

I was at the bottom of the stairs, she was a few steps up, and she wanted to see Bradley for some reason. She'd got very touchy-feely with him, clingy almost. She needed to know where he was all of the time, and was always taking him on little outings from which they'd return bearing even more toys.

'They're not for you,' she'd warn me, and the toys would be squirrelled away upstairs, up the ladder we'd built especially for Bradley and into his playroom. He was into cars and stuff mostly. Occasionally, something cool and electrical would appear and I'd try and have a play with it. If she came back with something from a charity shop and I thought it wouldn't be missed I'd smuggle it out to the chicken shed late at night. Only if I was sure it wouldn't be missed, though. The last thing I wanted to do was upset Bradley. If she found out . . .

'Where is Bradley?' she repeated.

'I'm really not sure,' I said and I looked around the side of the banisters down towards the kitchen then back at her, just as she smashed me in the face. Maybe I'd looked insolent to her? I don't know, but the punch caught me on the chin, knocking me backwards into the stairwell, where I dislodged plastic toy cars and a cardboard box full of jigsaw puzzles.

'Don't backchat me,' she said. I watched her legs go past me. 'And find Bradley now.'

I lay there in the stairwell, staring up the stairs piled high with boxes and boxes of games and toys. There was a little cubbyhole up there where Mother used to put me for punishments. If I craned my head I could see it from where I lay. To get to it she made me crawl over a pole laid from a shelf to the cubbyhole, and once there I had to squeeze into it, bringing my knees right up to my chin. And stay there.

The thing with that cubbyhole was that you couldn't fall asleep, not safely anyway. There was always the danger that you might fall out – and if that happened there was a drop to the ground floor below, down to where I lay now. Other than that, though, it wasn't too bad – the cubbyhole was one of her better punishments. It got cold; I don't know why, but the wind really whistled around those stairs. But it wasn't as cold as when she made us stand outside in the garden at George Dowty Drive. Or the times she made us stand in the snow at the farmhouse. Five or six hours in the cubbyhole wasn't too bad in comparison, even the whole day was bearable. I remember that I missed a full solar eclipse thanks to a cubbyhole punishment. But that was in 1999 and I hadn't been in the cubbyhole for a while. Perhaps she knew that it was the soft option. Anyway, after the accident, her punishments became more random, more sudden – sometimes terrifyingly so.

The day after the punch, I was in the yard, and I was just standing, staring at nothing in particular. I shouldn't have been doing that, of course, I should have been getting on with my jobs, but it would happen every now and then. I'd just drift off, lose myself with John Hendrickson, stowing a still-hot Glock in the glove compartment of his Aston Martin after another successful 'black ops' mission. Just away, as usual – away with the fairies. Mostly I'd catch myself and give myself a little shake, throwing a look at the farmhouse, always thinking I'd see that face at a window. Today I did the same, thanking whatever god watched over dreamers that she hadn't caught me.

Except, she had. She'd seen me from a window, motionless and with a faraway look on my face. Through the kitchen she'd come, out into the yard, approaching me from behind – I wonder how quietly she crept – and not saying, 'Hey, wake up, sleepyhead,' or, 'Earth to Chris, earth to Chris,' but picking up one of her beloved gazebo poles, an evil aluminium totem of hers, raising it and bringing it swishing down with a sound that cut the air, using it to whip the back of my legs so that I fell forward to the dirt of the yard, screaming with shock and pain, hearing the discarded gazebo pole clatter to the concrete by my head.

'Get on with your work,' she said, and I listened to the sound of her feet, crunching away from me and back to the farmhouse.

*

To help us after the yobs had smashed our things, a local firm donated a doll to Karen, plus a toy guitar to Bradley, and we were also given tickets for a day trip to a safari park. In the paper, Mother was quoted as saying, 'I can't believe how caring people have been.'

Chapter Forty-eight

'Right,' I said, 'I'm going to feed the dogs.'

Bradley had just had his lunch. The girls had prepared it for him – Karen, still in her wheelchair. Now it was the turn of the animals. I reached up to the Cupboard of All Things for the tins of dog food, brought a couple down to the worktop, hunted around for the can opener. The kitchen was empty apart from Mother and me, and she was behind me somewhere.

Poor old Karen was on a million different kinds of medication then. At one point she was taking something like thirty-two pills a day, painkillers mainly, plus she had daily injections. I'm not 100 per cent sure what all the tablets and injections were doing, but I'm pretty sure they were keeping her alive for a time. She'd been rebuilt, like the Bionic Woman, and the pills were there to help the process along. Meanwhile the injections were to give her nutrients, something to do with the fact that she'd had an operation on her stomach.

When she'd been in the hospital and Mother mounted her vigil it had felt like the two of them had grown closer, bonded somehow. But that hadn't lasted. Perhaps a normal mother might have helped Karen with her daily injections, but not ours. Karen had to inject herself, taking needles from a pot of them on top of the microwave. When she'd done her injection she replaced the used needle in a second pot, which we called the sin bin.

Now, where was that tin opener? I shifted junk around on the worktop, yanked open a drawer, found the tin opener at last and opened up the cans. From the lounge came the sound of the TV. The theme tune to *Neighbours*. 'Everybody needs . . .'

Holding the two tins I walked over to the back door. Mother was facing away from me, her back to me, doing something at the kitchen table.

(I wonder what she was thinking at that moment. I wonder if she was thinking about Judith and Charlotte. Or maybe she was thinking about nothing. Thinking nothing. Gone blank and into her doing-hurty place.)

I put the two tins on the worktop and reached to open the door. Behind me, Mother moved away from the table and to the corner of the kitchen where the microwave sat.

I opened the back door and went to pick up the tins. My arm was across the worktop, reaching for them, when Mother brought her fist down onto it.

I yelped, more in shock than anything else, then looked at my forearm, where her fist remained, then into her face.

(I'm taller now, I thought, abstractedly, we're almost the same height, me and you. At the same time I heard the *Neighbours* theme tune from the lounge. '. . . good neighbours'. Heard Bradley chatting.)

'It should have been you,' said Mother. Her mouth was set tight, hollowing her cheeks into stony valleys, her eyes blazing.

I must have looked confused. Should have been me?

'It should have been you,' she repeated, spitting the words like poison sucked from a snakebite. '*You* who died in the accident. Not them. It should have been you.'

The words hit me, knocking the wind from me. For a second I could only stare at her, part of me unable to believe she could say such a thing, part of me thinking she was right: it should have been me in the Suzuki Carry because that was the original plan. I was to go in the Suzuki and Charlotte in the Transit, but Charlotte had wanted to sit with Judith. She wanted to sit with Judith in the front of the van, which was where I would have been sitting when it went under the truck. Mother was right. It should have been me.

'. . . that's when good . . .'

At that moment the pain in my arm suddenly bloomed, going from dull bruise-pain to sharp, an explosion of agony that made me yank my arm away from beneath her fist.

There was a snapping sound. Something clattered to the floor, and looking down I saw what it was. The syringe part of a hypodermic needle.

Just the syringe part. No actual needle.

Slowly, it dawned on me what had happened. The snapping sound, the plastic plunger on the kitchen floor, the pain in my arm.

The blood.

I sank to my knees, shouting and cradling my arm, hardly able to believe my eyes, hardly able to believe the tiny bit of needle that protruded from the flesh of my forearm, the teardrop of blood at its base.

She'd driven it almost all of the way in. Yanking my arm away had snapped the needle from the syringe, and it was now embedded, just that tiny quivering tip visible, in my arm. I was making strange, strangulated gurgling sounds, my fingers reaching to the needle but somehow unable to touch it, almost as though it were on fire.

She walked out leaving me to it, and I crouched there. Again, my fingers went towards the needle, which I so badly wanted out of my arm. But somehow I couldn't bring myself to touch it.

At my back the door nudged open and Jet was there, probably drawn by the scent of the open tins of dog food, wanting his lunch.

'Are you all right?'

Lulu was standing in the doorway of the kitchen, drawn by my screams.

'I . . .' I began, 'my arm. Can you help?'

'Mary-Beth,' snapped Mother from the lounge. 'Get back in here now.'

Jet was snuffling at the kitchen unit, paws scrabbling, shoving me out of the way to get to the dog food.

'I need help,' I managed, 'I've got to get this out.' Sitting on the floor I raised my arm so she could see the wound, my face screwed up with the pain, Jet still shoving me as he tried to reach the dog food. My arm hurt. It hurt so much.

'Mary-Beth!'

Lulu's head swivelled to look back into the lounge. 'He's hurt,' she said to Mother.

'Let him deal with it.' Mother's voice was disembodied, drifting into the kitchen. She would be in the lounge, sitting on the sofa, cuddling Bradley, watching Aussie soaps. 'Mary-Beth, get back in here now,' she insisted. 'It's started.'

Lulu looked back at me, pulling a face, a what-choice-do-I-have face. She was right, of course; she had none.

Jet shoved me and I nearly keeled over. 'The dog needs feeding,' I said through clenched teeth.

'The dog needs feeding,' relayed Lulu to Mother.

'Karen can feed the dog,' came the disembodied reply, 'get back in here.'

Lulu flashed me a look that said she was so sorry, and left. A moment or so later, Karen wheeled herself into the kitchen, coming over to the unit where I still crouched on the floor clutching my arm.

She looked down at me, saw the syringe on the floor, the needle sticking from my arm. She winced in sympathy, although not because she was sensitive: Karen had seen too much pain – her own and other people's – too much blood and too much hurt to be squeamish about it. She watched as my fingers danced around the needle. I could feel the shaft of it in my arm, this foreign object in my flesh.

'You need a pair of tweezers,' she whispered, reaching to the counter for the dog food, shooing Jet out of the back door at the same time. 'Go to the bathroom and get yourself a pair of tweezers. It'll be fine if you get the needle out. It'll be sterile.'

She fed the dogs and wheeled herself back out to the lounge while I gathered myself on the floor of the kitchen. The pain had been joined by nausea and I was retching, bile collecting in my mouth as I swallowed vomit, desperate not to puke on the kitchen tiles. At last I pulled myself together, stood up, still holding my arm, and walked through the lounge.

My family sat there, watching *Neighbours*. I glanced at the screen where two characters were arguing in a coffee shop. Mother and Bradley were glued to it, Bradley wearing his riding hat for some reason. That was his new thing. Mother was taking him horse riding once a week now. We used to go with them sometimes, but not to join in.

Karen and Lulu both watched me but I couldn't look at them as I walked through the lounge, into the hall, up the stairs and into the bathroom. Finding the tweezers, I sat on the toilet lid and rested my forearm along my lap. It was my left arm that she'd stabbed, so at least I could hold the tweezers properly with my right. I used them to grip the tiny bit of protruding needle, held my breath, then pulled.

It slid out, trailing a strand of blood. Did it grind against the bone in my arm or did I imagine it? Either way, I dropped tweezers and needle to the bathroom floor, slid off the toilet to my knees, raised the toilet lid and vomited into the bowl, all in one fluid motion.

Much later that evening, Mother asked me if I'd managed to get the needle out. I told her yes. Had I disposed of it safely, she wanted to know. Yes, I said, it was in the sin bin with the other used needles. Good, she said.

My fear of needles began that day. Very common, apparently, a fear of needles; something like 10 per cent of the population suffer from it. I've looked it up: trypanophobia is its proper name. Mine started then, and maybe it wouldn't be such a painful legacy if I didn't need constant medical attention as a result of other injuries she gave me. At the time of writing, barely a month passes without a visit to the hospital for any one of a variety of reasons, so I get to confront my fear a lot.

Sometimes I dream about it, too. I dream of the thump, and then the needle sticking out of the skin, and I wake up already massaging a phantom wound, the place where the needle went in.

Then I reach for the PlayStation joypad and try to ignore the voice in my head that says, 'It should have been you.'

Chapter Forty-nine

We all went to Bristol Crown Court for the sentencing. We wheeled Karen in, took our seats and, not far away from us in the gallery, was another woman in a wheelchair. This one was the defendant's wife. The wife of the lorry driver. At a previous hearing he had pleaded guilty to two counts of causing death by dangerous driving in the accident that had killed Charlotte and Judith, left Karen in a wheelchair and Bradley with a limp. Now, to see what penalty he would receive, we had attended court, dressed as we would be for church: smart, Mother with her customary straight-backed pose.

From the prosecution we heard that Judith and Charlotte had both died. We were reminded that the Suzuki Carry had been reduced in length from 3.23 metres to 1.13 metres, such was the force of impact. We heard that Karen, now fifteen (and described as 'autistic'), had not been expected to survive and had been in intensive care for a month following the accident, and that Bradley, now eight, had also been severely injured; that they'd been pulled out of the mangled van and flown to hospital.

The defence told us that the lorry driver had been so traumatized by what had happened that he could no longer bear to be around lorries, and that his wife, who was herself in a wheelchair after breaking her spine in three places, had attempted suicide twice since the accident.

Then the judge, summing up, said how difficult it was to deal with a case like this. The lorry driver had shown great remorse and was of previous good character, he said, plus a prison sentence would cause great hardship to his wife.

I could see Mother tensing slightly, a tautening of the lips I recognized.

However, said the judge, the lorry driver's driving had caused the death of people and serious injury to two others. He had no choice but to jail him for eighteen months.

I sat back in my seat, a wooden bench, looking at the driver as his head dropped. He'd caused the death of Charlotte and Judith. He'd got eighteen months. I checked myself – checked my feelings the way you check for blood after you've been punched. But there was nothing. No feelings for Judith and Charlotte, none for the lorry driver or his wife in a wheelchair. None for Karen, Bradley, Lulu. None for Mother. None for myself. I felt nothing.

And I still felt nothing as we left the court, filing out behind Mother to the outside of the courthouse, where she was approached by a reporter.

'Mrs Spry,' he said, introducing himself and his paper, 'I was wondering what you thought of the sentence?'

She drew herself up, fixing him with a glare that he didn't notice because he was too busy writing shorthand notes as she spoke.

'I'm not a vindictive woman,' she began, and then went on to say how she was grieving very much for her daughters, and how she had also thought of the lorry driver and his family. She would have liked more than nine months . . .

(But he'd got eighteen months, I thought.)

. . . which is what he was realistically going to serve, she added, and she implied that she wasn't sure whether nine months was enough jail time for having devastated a family, although she felt it was right that he had received a custodial sentence. Prompted by the reporter, she added that she was disappointed with the judge's summing up. She was careful to choose her words, never letting herself slip into bitter-vindictive mode, always maintaining the brave, grieving-mother face. The summing up disappointed her, she said, because so much attention had been given to the effect that jail would have on the lorry driver's family, and so little to the fact that his actions had decimated her family.

'We cannot put the pieces back together because there are two pieces missing,' she said, looking meaningfully across at us, her children, standing obediently by her side.

After I was released from Mother I had a counsellor, Jane, who I saw when I was being 'reintegrated', which is what they call it when you've had no contact with the outside world and they need to get you back in it.

Jane was great. *Is* great. Warmth and understanding in human form, a wicked laugh and forthright opinion never far away. One of the best, a hero, alongside Graeme, another counsellor whom I became close to. And together they saw me through depression, drinking, suicide attempts, the guilt I felt about giving evidence against Mother at the trial and the desire I had to see her again. Jane helped me to see Mother not as Mother, but as Eunice, the woman who abused me for over a decade. And I can't thank her enough for that.

One of the things we established during our sessions was that I didn't feel love, not for people anyway. It was as though my emotions were in cold storage. At that time I felt affection only for things. For cars, for a leather jacket I had at the time. For computers, for mobile phones and games consoles. For the Chevy that Mother bought, and the narrow boat.

The Chevy we ended up buying because Mother had decided she wanted us to have a Dodge Ram. The Dodge Ram was the van we'd hired in Florida. She'd loved it – we all had – and I guess there was an element there of trying to recapture some of that holiday, a happy time for the whole family. So we visited a dealership in Birmingham – one that specialized in American cars – where there was a Dodge Ram for sale. We had a look at the vehicle, and I don't know if everybody else felt it, too, but looking round it I was struck by a keen sense of it not being right somehow. Like it was a Dodge Ram, the same as we'd had in Florida, but it wasn't *the* Dodge Ram, just a poor facsimile of it. At that moment, on another part of the forecourt, one of the salesmen needed to move a Chevy. A Chevrolet Sherrod to be exact, which meant it was a van in limo form. It had an all-leather interior, lighted step wells, air conditioning and a flat-screen TV that came with wireless headphones. No joke. But what really caught our eye, or our ears, I should say, was the engine, a V8 that cleared its throat, barked an order and started up.

That was Mother sold. We all looked over to the source of this awesome sound and, before we knew it, Mother was striding over. Not long after that, we left, Mother having bought the van.

Before it was delivered, she told us she had cancelled the sale, and our faces dropped. But then one day at the farmhouse I was working outside when I heard it. The engine. The unmistakable sound of that V8, and I stopped working, cocking an ear, grinning as I rushed to the gate, hearing it come closer, into Eckington and along the road towards us, where I opened the gate and stood by as it glided in, filling the yard with the rumble of the V8 engine, which brought the others running.

I was in love with the Chevy, but even that took second place to our narrow boat. I'd fallen head over heels for it the first time I clapped eyes on it, which would have been, oh, 2002, one of those days when we were coming back from horse riding with Bradley.

We'd often stop by the marina at Upton-upon-Severn on our way back home. A Transit van-load of us would get out and admire the narrow boats moored there, the canal slapping peacefully at the bows. Some of the boats moored there overnight would have holidaymakers aboard, who would wave at us from the deck and say, 'Hello!' as they wrung out clothes into the canal or emptied pots of tea, going about a daily business that seemed so relaxing, so calm, and so attractive. Though Mother had never shown any particular interest in canals or canal boats before then, we could tell she was drawn to the whole lifestyle, so it was no great surprise when we went along there one day to discover that she'd bought one. Something like £45,000-worth of narrow boat, she'd bought. Apparently, she paid by cheque.

The boat was 72 feet long, which is big for a narrow boat; one of the longest you're allowed to use on UK waterways. It was big because it was an ex-charity boat adapted for wheelchair use. Wheelchair users reached it via a lift at the rear, and it had been fitted so that a wheelchair user could steer it, too.

We lived on it for a while – I think around six months all told. The mooring was close to the farmhouse, so it was easy to live there and still keep up with the animals and jobs on the farm. We lived on the boat either because things were too much of a mess at both the farmhouse and George Dowty, or because Mother wanted to pull a disappearing act to confuse the education and medical authorities. It's not like we were ever consulted or asked why we were living on a boat – we just lived where we were told to live.

The best time on the boat, though, was the holiday. A big holiday where we spent six weeks on it. It was only meant to be a fortnight, but then we got up to Worcestershire and decided to take a left and go along the Llangollen canal, one of the busiest in the country, with a strong current that takes you twisting through jaw-droppingly beautiful Welsh countryside, then across the Dee Valley on the Pontcysyllte Aqueduct – the longest and highest aqueduct in the UK.

That whole holiday was great. Nanny and Granddad were with us, plus we'd brought a load of animals along for the trip. As well as Jet we had ducklings that were too small to leave at home, plus some fish and guinea pigs. So we had a whole boatful, a Noah's Ark of us. But out of all the people on board, I was the only one who could use the locks. I'd had to learn as I went along, but I'd done it, and now they all depended on me to keep us going. I had a small folding bicycle that I used for racing ahead along the towpath so I could open the locks as well as warn other canal users that there was a massive 72-footer on its way – one with nutters driving it. I spent so much time on that bike I reckon I must have cycled most of the way from Upton-upon-Severn to Wales.

Some days, if there was a long gap between locks, or if the canal wasn't too busy, I'd sit on the front of the boat, making sure we didn't hit anything or run aground, trading insults with Bradley or talking to Karen. I remember once, sitting there and catching sight of Lulu, who was perched on the edge of the boat, staring out at the landscape as we passed it by. Or perhaps she was staring at nothing. Dreaming. She didn't say much these days. Nothing much apart from arguing with Mother.

But then there'd be a lock coming up. We'd stop. I'd get off, unfold the bike and pedal off along the towpath, going fast, fast, *fast*, standing up on the pedals, the bike swinging beneath me. I'd get to the gates and operate them for the boat – water levels rising, falling – and it was always with a sense of pride that I watched our boat pass through the lock. It was an imposing boat, it really was. People used to compliment us on it all of the time. Once – maybe on that holiday, maybe another time – we had someone paint it, and the painting hung for a while on a wall in the farmhouse. A painting of our narrow boat, which was called *Charlotte*.

Chapter Fifty

We were at George Dowty Drive one day when Mother asked me a question. It was something to do with one of the ducklings, but I honestly can't recall exactly what it was. We were outside, that I do remember, just outside the back door on the little bit of patio we had there. The same back door and patio familiar to millions of homes on similar estates all around the country. Back door, bit of patio, strip of garden. At the end of our garden were the trees we'd shelter beneath when we were made to stay outside overnight; where I'd hidden to eat the stolen tuna that day. It was just like any other garden in the country, really. A bit messier, perhaps, in keeping with the rest of the house. With the farmhouse. With our lives.

Which was why there was a cricket bat on the patio. A full-size, adult cricket bat that belonged to Bradley. And whatever it was that I'd said, it annoyed her — it would have been something like 'I'm not sure' in answer to her question, something as insignificant as that — because she picked up the cricket bat and smashed it into the back of my leg.

Not that it did me much good, but some kind of inner survival instinct registered that she'd picked it up. I had my back to her, trying to scoop up a tiny furry duckling, but I hadn't got him. My fingers had brushed him and he'd lost balance a little before skittering off across the patio, quacking as he went. And behind me there was that sound, of wood scraping from concrete. And I had a second to think, Oh no, and was about to straighten and turn when it hit me.

It hit the back of my kneecap with a sound that wasn't good. Really not good. I was thinking how un-good that noise was even as my legs buckled and I keeled forward to the patio, face making contact with the concrete, suddenly at eye level with the duckling, which scooted away to the safety of an upturned cardboard box. My feet kicked on the paving slabs, plimsolls scrabbling, shoelaces flapping, and for a moment the pain was so great that I opened my mouth to scream and nothing came out. For a second I was mute, shouting agony up at a sky that looked indifferently back at me, and then the shout came: a yell of pain, anger and frustration as pain bloomed behind my knee and somehow, instinctively, I knew that she'd really done it this time, she'd done permanent damage.

And then, with the same vicious inevitability that marked almost all of the hurt she gave me over the years, Mother dropped the cricket bat to the patio and stepped inside the kitchen, away, off to read *Hello*, or the *Watchtower*, or catch up on the afternoon soaps.

The noise. It had been a grating noise, like the noise you get when you're slicing into a joint of meat and you hit the bone. The blow was to the back of my left leg, but I fell to my right knee, then forward. It's lucky I fell to the right knee. If I'd fallen on the bad knee . . . I don't know, I probably wouldn't be walking now. As it is I walk with a limp.

Once the pain had subsided I placed my hands to the slabs and tried to pull myself upright, testing my left leg, which wouldn't support my weight. When I finally got to my feet it was only by dragging myself over to the house and pulling myself up by grabbing hold of the wall, using just my right leg. Sweat running off me with the pain, I took myself into the kitchen, found a stool and sat down, my injured leg straight out in front of me.

Karen came into the room. Whether she knew something was up or not I don't know, but there she was, chair in front of me – she knew a thing or two about not walking – staring at my leg with concern.

'How does it feel?' she asked.

'Hurts,' I gasped. 'It's gone floppy.'

The whole of the bottom half of my left leg felt as though it had somehow become detached, like it was held on by bits of ropey sinew and nothing else. Since I've left Mother I've had scans down there and they show bits of bone sort of floating around under the skin. I should have gone to hospital then, obviously, but I didn't. Karen, Lulu and I were tough. We were well-trained little soldiers. We'd had to put up with so much pain over the years we ended up just getting on with things – even when 'things' meant not being able to walk properly.

For a couple of days after that, I borrowed Bradley's crutches and got around on those. After a while I was able to walk, albeit with a limp, and it's been that way ever since. It turns out it's a cartilage injury. You have your kneecap, and behind that you've got cartilage that holds the knee in place. When she hit me with the bat bits of the cartilage were smashed off, so now they just float around and keep touching the kneecap, which causes pain. If I sit down for any length of time it hurts. It happened when I was on *This Morning*, after Eunice was sentenced. Because there was so much sitting around, my leg just completely seized up. If I go cycling it has a tendency to lock up, and it's bad when that happens. I have to sort of flop onto my right knee and hope that it sorts itself out.

There's an operation they say has an OK chance of fixing it. They drill into the kneecap, have a look round and see if there are any sizable pieces they can grab and pull out. Who knows? Maybe they'll sort it, maybe they won't. It's just one more thing to add to the list of stuff she left me to cope with. There's that; my fear of needles; a fear of heights (for some reason I haven't worked out); nervousness, just general nervousness; and the sleeplessness, of course.

Sometimes I try and picture her face when I'm trying to sleep, and it's funny because I can't. What comes to me is the police mug-shot picture they showed on TV and in the newspapers, the one on all the websites. It's her, but it's not really her. To me she always looked like a mother. She looked like Mother.

Not long after that, Lulu escaped again.

Except, this time, she really did escape. It was 2003, and she was old enough, so she exercised her right to leave home. One day, Mother drove her to a hostel in Bristol and dropped her off.

And that was that. Lulu left home. It really was as quick and as unemotional as that. I'm not sure she even told me her plans beforehand. One moment she was there, the next she was gone. Bradley continued his horse riding. Karen was becoming more interested in her faith and was spending time with the Jehovah's Witnesses.

Me, I had a new job. Life carried on as normal. I felt the same when Lulu left as I did when Charlotte and Judith died. Which was next to nothing. She'd trained me well, Mother had.

Chapter Fifty-one

The last time Mother ever tried anything, I'd just returned from Nanny and Granddad's house, and she came at me with some sandpaper, one of her favourite weapons.

It was summertime, one of those warm evenings where it feels as though everybody is out; walking across the estate you can smell the burning charcoal of a hundred barbecues, hear the distant *thump-thump* of music from cars and from teenage bedroom windows, hear footballs being kicked and hopeful shouts of kids playing. All of those sounds were wafting across the estate as I made the short journey from Nanny and Granddad's back to ours.

I was fifteen. As I made my way back, limping slightly, I listened to the sounds of the cars from the main road, the one we'd use to get to the farmhouse, and I tried to guess the makes of the cars just from the noises their engines made. By my side, John Hendrickson walked with me.

My new job was looking after Granddad, so I was spending a lot of time there. Well, it was looking after both of them, really. Nanny had become ill. Really ill. She had cancer and was having treatment for it so she couldn't look after Granddad at the same time. Luckily, we lived nearby so it was no problem for me to go over and do the jobs that needed doing, and I was going over more and more. Granddad needed a lot of help; the Parkinson's and arthritis were both advanced, plus he'd gained weight – he was huge, around twenty stone – and the Parkinson's gave him the shakes so badly he needed a can of Stella first thing in the morning just so he could read the paper. I guess he had a right to moan. The same with Nanny, also chronically ill, who was never slow to tell me if she thought I was slacking.

Limping home, exhausted, I was still smarting from the other day, when Mother, Karen, Bradley and I had been in the living room at the farmhouse and Bradley had been pushing Karen into the kitchen. Bradley really did have the demon in him that day and he was messing about, pretending to tip Karen out of her chair. I gave him a push to stop. I was close to Karen; in many ways, I was closer to her than I was to anyone, and I didn't like to see her being treated like that. So I gave Bradley a shove. It wasn't a hard or a violent shove. It was no different to the kind of shove any older brother gives his sibling, and Bradley was definitely in the wrong. But suddenly the atmosphere in the room changed and Mother, without saying anything, stormed out. Moments later she returned, and hit me so hard around the face that I staggered. I staggered backwards.

But I didn't fall.

I stood my ground and rubbed the side of my face, dismayed that I'd been punched for helping Karen. For giving Bradley such a tiny little shove, that's all it was. And when he was in the wrong, too. After all, if he'd pushed her, Karen could have gone sprawling forward.

Walking home from Nanny and Granddad's a few days later, I was still upset. It didn't seem fair.

But I wasn't hurt. Not physically. Mother spat something at me after the punch. Something about being a demon child, or being possessed, something like that. The usual kind of stuff.

And that hadn't hurt, either. In fact I'd thought, What a load of rubbish. And after that I realized that I'd taken the punch, deflected the pain and absorbed the demon words – and none of it had hurt me.

I arrived home at George Dowty, stepping out of the balmy

evening and into the house, with its mess and animal droppings and still (weirdly) its welcome feeling of home, to find Mother doing something with the banisters, sanding them down. Sanding the banisters was one of those long-term projects that had been on the go for a while, so there was often sandpaper hanging around. Like I say, it was one of her favourite weapons. Not in the top five, perhaps, but top ten, occasionally climbing the charts if it was close at hand.

Which it was now, of course. I stopped in the kitchen, looking around. Earlier that day, Mother had come over to Nanny and Granddad's to see how I was getting on, and she'd been nice to me, she'd even ruffled my hair – she did that, sometimes, in front of other people – and she'd said something about having a meal ready for me when I got home. At times like that it was obvious why Nanny and Granddad never suspected anything; at times like that I almost believed myself that nothing was wrong, that things were different.

'What are you doing in there?' I heard from the hallway as I stood looking around the kitchen, half in a daze, as usual.

'I was going to make a sandwich,' I replied, hunting about for the bread.

All of a sudden she was there beside me – in my face – and I recoiled slightly. But only slightly. We were the same height now and when our eyes met they were level. I looked into hers. I looked into them and I knew things were different. I'm not saying there was a blinding flash of light, or I had a moment of revelation. I didn't suddenly think: things between us have changed. But things had.

Too late I saw the sandpaper. It caught me on the side of the face, shearing a layer of skin off. I jerked my head away, saw the sandpaper coming again for a second strike, and this time I caught her arm.

And shoved.

She fell, tumbling backwards against the kitchen cabinets and to the floor, landing in a messy tangle of arms and legs and pure shock, and for a moment or so there was a dreadful silence in the kitchen during which I stared down at Mother on the floor – where *I'd* shoved her – and she stared back at me, one leg tucked awkwardly beneath herself, glasses lopsided and skew-whiff on her face, her mouth a mute zero of surprise.

The planet seemed to tilt out of alignment. Mother, hurt on the floor. Me, standing over her. Suddenly dizzy, I reached and grabbed the worktop, disturbing an empty cereal box that span on the surface, flakes skidding on Formica, the sound like an aerial assault in the stunned silence of the room.

And then it was me who left the room. Left the room like she had so many times before, leaving her hurt on the kitchen floor.

I went upstairs. Perhaps I should have felt triumph, or freedom. Maybe I should have been empowered and done high-fives with John Hendrickson. But actually what I felt was that I had done wrong. It was wrong to lose control of my temper, and so, so wrong to push my mother to the floor. It's not right to push a lady over, even one who's caused you so much pain. It's not right to push your mother down.

It left its mark, the sandpaper. An angry patch of hurting skin pinpricked with blood, the same as those she'd inflicted on the girls previously, Karen in particular. A while before that day she'd attacked Karen with the sandpaper, taking the skin off her face and hands, with Karen almost defenceless in her wheelchair. At the time, one of the breakfast cereals had been giving away disposable cameras, and the next day I was fooling about with it, taking pictures of Karen. One of the photographs – of Karen's grazed, injured face – was used in court and made its way into the papers afterwards. It's still on the Internet now: Karen, or 'Child A', a black band across her eyes to protect her identity, grinning beneath her injuries. It looks weird, her grinning like that, it's so at odds with the marks you can see. But the thing is, I wasn't deliberately trying to take injury pictures. It's not like we were gathering evidence or anything. We were just kids messing about with a disposable camera.

Later, Karen gave the pictures to DC Victoria Martell. They were used in court to help prove Mother's guilt, and now they're all over the Internet. All that from a free camera given away with breakfast cereal. Golden Grahams, I think they were.

Chapter Fifty-two

On 26 December 2004, Detective Constable Victoria Martell of Gloucestershire CID – who must have drawn the short straw to be working on Boxing Day – took a call from a girl who didn't celebrate Christmas; who told her that she'd been abused by her foster mother for most of her life.

It was Karen, the girl on the phone. I didn't know it then, but she'd left home. One day while Mother was out horse riding with Bradley, Lawrence Northam and his wife Vicky had arrived at the farmhouse and they'd helped Karen escape. She'd been spending time in their company. With Mother's full approval she'd become more involved at the Kingdom Hall, more devout. And also more aware. She'd confided in Lawrence and Vicky. Together, they'd hatched a plan for escape, then Karen had called the police. DC Martell was on duty that day.

She first arranged to meet with Karen, then invited her to the station for a formal interview, which took place early in January 2005. Having spoken to her, the police contacted Lulu, and DC Martell spoke to her, too. Though Karen and Lulu had not seen each other for almost two years, their stories were almost identical. Mother had been systematically abusing the children, and Bradley and I were still in her care. The police began to prepare an operation to get us out of there.

But I knew none of this then. Because in August 2004, I had gone to live with Nanny and Granddad, as their live-in carer. It was my job to lift them up, put them in and out of bed, prepare food, and help clear up. And other stuff. Granddad had problems with his bowels, so it could get unpleasant at times. He had a huge hoist to get him out of bed but we couldn't keep taking it through the house each day, so we'd converted the living room into a bedroom and the kitchen became like a living room. Meanwhile I slept in the hall rather than the bedroom. I needed to be as close to them as possible in case there was an accident or something. Besides, I was used to sleeping in a hall.

While I was there, of course, there was no hurting. If I'm honest, I'm not sure there would have been abuse even if I'd been at home. Since the day I'd pushed Mother she'd hardly touched me. The odd slap, that was all. Instead, the violence of living with Mother was replaced with the difficulty of caring for Nanny and Granddad. I didn't mind – I loved them. But it was hard doing everything by myself. It was physically and mentally demanding, and it was unrelenting. I missed Bradley and Karen, even though, as I found out later, Karen had escaped. Still, I did as I was told. And as 2004 ended (and in December that year I turned sixteen – yet another birthday I didn't celebrate) and 2005 began, there were all kinds of things happening – stuff I had no idea about.

Like what happened the day I ran away. Mid-January, this was. I'd had an argument with Nanny, the two of us shouting at each other.

'I'll phone Olive,' she screeched. Olive was what Nanny and Granddad called Mother. Nanny had been shouting at me. She'd been shouting at me to wake up, and saying that I needed to show her more respect. I'm ashamed to say that I swore at her.

'I'll phone Olive,' she screeched again, so I walked out – well, limped out. It was 6.30 a.m. Behind me, Nanny must have phoned Mother, who in turn phoned friends at the Jehovah's Witnesses. One of them was Lawrence.

I walked to the road that led to Eckington, where I knew there was an abandoned bike in a hedge. I'd seen it once before, and on that occasion I'd fantasized about using it to make an escape. Not quite John Hendrickson and his custom-built Aston Martin, but still, I got on it and started making my way towards Cheltenham, burning with shame for having sworn at Nanny, and with resentment at having been called half-awake.

An ancient thing, it was, the bike, it even had a basket on the front. Plus, not only was it old but it had a wobbly saddle. So it wasn't the easiest cycle in the world to ride. Even so, I'd got as far as Homebase in Cheltenham before I came off.

What happened was, my bad knee locked. It locked, the leg froze and whatever human-mechanical action had got me this far suddenly ground to a halt, pitching me to the road, where I landed on the bad knee. I was sitting on the kerb in agony when a Land Rover drew up, containing Lawrence and another guy, who helped me up, chucked the rusty old bike into the back of the Land Rover, and bundled me into the cab. Lawrence took me to a café for breakfast, and looking back, he didn't grill me for all kinds of details, even though he was working with the police by then. Certainly, he called them afterwards, telling them I'd had a fall off my bike, because later that night – after a day at the hospital where Nanny was having chemotherapy treatment – I had a visit from two lady police officers. They called ahead and spoke to Nanny, who then phoned Mother, who told her not to let the police in until she had arrived. But what do you do with a couple of policewomen on the doorstep? It's not like you can keep them waiting. So they came in, where they inspected my leg. At the time I thought it was odd having my leg looked at like that. They checked over the rest of my body, too. It all makes sense now, of course.

Mother arrived literally moments after the two police officers left, and she was furious. 'Why didn't you wait for me?' she wanted to know, directing her anger at me. Karen had left by then, done her daytime flit. I wonder if Mother knew. I wonder if she knew that forces were massing against her.

*

It all culminated in the operation on the day of 5 February 2005, when my life with Mother ended; when there was a knock on the door of Nanny and Granddad's house at 7.30 a.m.

The house was in virtual darkness. All the curtains closed, and quiet, too: just the hiss of the shower from the bathroom, Nanny in there, Granddad snoozing in the lounge, the hoist parked by the side of his bed like a gallows in the gloom.

I went to the front door and opened it. I was wearing pyjamas, baggy, sky-blue pyjamas, and my hair was big and frizzy in a huge Afro. Mother never liked me to have my hair cut for some reason. About twice a year it would simply get too big and she'd trim it in the kitchen. The rest of the time it just grew. And it was big that day, the day I answered the door, me a kid just turned sixteen, pyjamas and an Afro, the hall of the bungalow hazy with shower steam at my back.

At the door stood a policeman and a woman in plain clothes. She was a social worker, I'd learn, and I remember being suddenly struck by how pretty she was, even as it dawned on me: there's a policeman standing on the doorstep.

I froze, staring at them, thoughts speeding through my head, such as, Has there been an accident, is everybody OK? I felt a sudden flash of guilt like I might have done something wrong; I felt fear, suspicion; I remembered Mother telling us that the outside world doesn't like Jehovah's Witnesses. 'They' don't approve of us.

Behind the policeman and the social worker the estate was grey, quiet and still sleepy, roads and pavements dark with damp from an overnight rainfall. The social worker looked at me. The policeman, I noticed, didn't. His hand was on his belt and he craned his head to look down the hall behind me. Looking for Mother, I guess.

'Your mother, Eunice Spry,' said the woman, 'has been arrested.'

The information hit me. The beatings, I thought. It's for the beatings. 'They' don't approve of Mother's ways.

From the bathroom, Nanny called, 'Chris? Who is it?'

'It's the police,' I called back over my shoulder, a tremble in my voice.

'Can you come with us, please?' said the woman, and she stepped to one side, gesturing with her arm. What? Now? I thought. Dressed like this?

'Well tell them to go away,' called Nanny.

'No, sorry,' I told the woman, and shut the door.

I walked into the lounge and around by the bed, where Granddad was still snoring. There was another knock at the door, and I opened it, ready to tell them to go away again.

'Can you come with us, please? Your mother's been arrested,' she said.

It's for the beatings.

'Chris? Who is it?' called Nanny, her voice muffled.

'Can I get some trousers?' I asked the social worker, and without waiting for a reply, I moved back into the house, leaving the door open. My visitors stepped over the threshold and into the bungalow.

'Who is it?' repeated Nanny.

'It's the police,' I called back. I'd found a coat. For some reason I also grabbed the torch that I kept in the lounge. It was always so dark in the lounge – we had those blackout curtains so Granddad could sleep – and I often used to creep around the place by torchlight. 'Mother's been arrested,' I said, pulling on my coat, keeping my eyes on the policeman and the pretty woman, who had now made their way into the lounge.

'What? Why?' called Nanny.

Wordlessly, the social worker gestured to me, her eyes meaningful. I glanced behind at Granddad, who slept on, unaware of the whole thing.

'Chris? What's happened?' called Nanny as I walked out of the lounge, into the hall and then over the doorstep, breath steaming in the February chill, the social worker walking behind. As we walked, she placed a hand on my shoulder.

Parked at the kerb was a Toyota Rav 4, and at the window was a face I recognized. Bradley. He was sitting in the back of the car, grinning, waving at me. Despite the shock, the cold, I felt my heart leap, grinning back at him as I was ushered in at his side.

For a second we sat and beamed at each other, him bouncing slightly on the seat. I glanced back at Nanny and Granddad's bungalow where the uniformed policeman stood in the doorway, maybe speaking to Nanny, maybe gallantly remaining outside while she got herself together. At the wheel of the car was another woman. She was Claire, she told us, a social worker, explaining, 'Your mother has been arrested and we're going to take you to a safe place to ask you some questions, is that all right?' The other woman, the pretty one – she was introduced as Juliette – had a notepad out and was scribbling something.

But I wasn't really paying attention.

'It's a Rav 4,' said Bradley. Like me, he was in pyjamas and a coat.

'I hate Rav 4s,' I said. 'There's no legroom in the back.'

The engine started, and the car pulled away from the kerb, up to the junction, indicator click-clicking as we pulled out and away from the Northway estate.

I saw Juliette's eyes in the rear-view mirror looking at us. Giving Bradley a meaningful look, I said, 'So, how is the big car at home?'

'Oh,' he said, 'that's gone.'

'How big was the payload?' I said.

'Quite a few big,' he replied.

Thinking about it now, who on earth did we think we were fooling with our little code?

'OK,' I replied, 'Well stick to the chassis plan.'

'OK,' he said.

The plan. I was thinking about it as we drove along. Not that there *was* a plan as such. But we'd heard it enough times in lectures about how 'they' didn't like Jehovah's Witnesses, and what to say if we were ever asked about our lifestyle. To say that we were occasionally smacked on the bottom, that the house wasn't a mess. I knew that I had to stick to what we were always told to say. I was urging Bradley to do the same thing.

We drove to Tesco. Eight o'clock in the morning at Tesco: two kids in pyjamas and two official-looking women, walking in and going to the clothes section where we picked out something to wear. I chose a pair of tracksuit bottoms and a T-shirt with a caption that said 'I'm It!'. Bradley chose jeans and a T-shirt with a picture of a car on it and, as we pulled away from Tesco, he and I were discussing what sort of car it was on the T-shirt. We never really decided. I don't know – it probably wasn't even a specific make, just some design they'd put on the shirt.

They drove us to the house. Just a house, it looks like any other house along the street, but it's a child-protection house. It's where they take people like Bradley and me. Vulnerable kids.

For a while, I was upstairs in the protection house while they took Bradley off somewhere, just one not-very-talkative plain-clothes policeman for company. I didn't want to speak anyway; I was still gathering my thoughts. I'd gone into stealth mode.

After what felt like hours, Bradley returned and it was my turn. I accompanied Claire and Juliette to the camera room.

'Are these cameras going?' I asked.

No, was the reply.

Good, I thought, even though I was prepared if they were. One of the things Mother had always told us was that they have lie detectors inside the cameras. So what we had to do was tell, not the whole truth, but a heavily censored version of it. I'd had it drummed into me so much that when the questions began, I was rattling off answers with no difficulty at all.

Did your mother ever punish you?

Yes, I said, equably, we were sometimes made to go to our rooms.

What if you were really bad? What would she do if you were really bad?

Oh, sometimes she smacked me on the backside.

Claire and Juliette shared a look. I felt a surge of pride.

Were you ever forced to go without food?

Yes, sometimes we were made to miss a meal. Just the one, though.

Your room is a mess. Why is your room such a mess?

I haven't seen my room for six months, I'm staying with Nanny and Granddad.

The kitchen is a mess. Why is the kitchen a mess?

I don't know. Perhaps because we're doing some work to the house.

I gave them nothing. I gave them nothing more than she'd ever told me to say. Nothing that meant they could take Bradley and me away from her.

There must have been some frantic phone calls made from the child-protection house that morning. Certainly they contacted Karen, who was in hospital at the time awaiting an operation – something to fix an internal injury sustained during the accident. Who knows what was said, but not long later we were back in the Rav 4, all of us, and not long after that Bradley and I sauntered into Cheltenham hospital, me feeling pretty pleased with myself that I'd managed to outwit the social workers, already anticipating the victory I'd share with Karen when I saw her – the pride at how we hadn't let Mother down, how we hadn't folded under questioning. In the car Bradley and I had done a bit more of our rubbish code and I'd worked out that he hadn't said anything either. All was going to plan.

But when we got to the ward, then into the room where Karen was staying, there was something about the atmosphere that I hadn't expected. Karen was familiar with the social workers, which was weird. They said hello and smiled to one another. The two social workers looked meaningfully from Karen to Bradley and me, as though to say, 'Karen, you know what you have to do.'

What had I expected, coming into the room? Us and them, I

suppose. Shared looks between me and Karen. Triumphant smiles, taunts mumbled under our breath. Not this.

Not Karen getting up from the edge of the bed where she sat and walking across the room towards me.

It took what felt like hours for me to process the information standing there, gawping at Karen, until, eventually, 'You can walk?' I said, weakly, as she stood before me.

'Yes, I can walk,' she said, 'I should have been walking years ago.'

Lucky for me there was a basin in the room. Somewhere I could be sick.

Chapter Fifty-three

*I*t took a while for it to sink in that Karen could walk – it would take weeks, in fact – but for the moment I gawped, dropping stunned to a seat in her room as I watched her walk around. No crutches, no stick, nothing.

It had required some physiotherapy, she told me, to get her legs back in working order. They were weak, obviously, from almost half a decade of disuse. But as for there being anything fundamentally wrong with Karen's lower half – anything that should have kept her confined to a wheelchair – there was nothing.

It all made sense. Mother discharging Karen and Bradley early, then the cramped six weeks we spent at Nanny and Granddad's bungalow. The constant moving between the farmhouse and George Dowty and the month and a half we spent living on the narrow boat. All of it part of Mother's usual strategy to cloud and confuse. Of course, she couldn't avoid all contact with medical professionals. Karen required a number of operations for years after the accident but she was always ordered to insist that, yes, she was exercising her legs but, no, they didn't seem to be getting better – even though the real reason they weren't getting better was because Mother wouldn't allow Karen to exercise. Mother used to tell Karen, sounding concerned, 'If you exercise you'll do more damage. There's more to life than that, and you should have it.'

Whatever she meant by that, I don't know, but it sounded convincing. Meanwhile, the doctors would be saying that Karen needed physio, but Mother would start shouting; she'd claim she needed a second opinion and demand to see another doctor. And nobody ever won an argument with Mother. Oh no. It was like arguing with steel. She would get into your head. She could get in there and mess with it. Mother vs Doctor. It was no competition. She always stayed one step ahead. And the disability benefit kept dropping through the letterbox.

All of this, going through my mind as I sat in the hospital room, head in my hands, fighting nausea and confusion.

'You've got to tell them,' said Karen.

Without looking at her, my eyes on the floor tiles, I violently shook my head. I pictured glances being exchanged above me.

'You must tell them the truth, Chris,' insisted Karen.

Still I said nothing, shaking my head, but thinking: Why is she saying this? Why is she saying this in front of them – these outsiders?

'She beat us.' Karen had this way of speaking in tiny, bite-sized facts. From her they always sounded like little chunks of calm. 'She locked me and you in the room. She dragged you behind the van . . .'

I flinched, head still in hands.

'. . . she stabbed you with the needle. She hurt my face. She made me stay in the wheelchair . . .'

No, I was thinking, my fingers clawing at my temples, shaking my head at the same time. No, this isn't right. No, no, no.

'What she did was wrong. She beat us.'

I interrupted, straightening and addressing Juliette, who stood by the door. 'Can I speak to Karen alone?'

'No.' Juliette shook her head, shooting a look at Karen. 'Sorry, Chris. We can't allow that.'

I stood. 'OK, then . . . let me get a glass of water.'

And I left the room, heading for the nurses' station and the water cooler there. Only, instead of pausing by the water cooler I scooted straight on, crashed through the double doors at the end of the ward and took the stairs which led to the floor above, wanting to take them at a run but unable to, suddenly feeling the pain in my leg which brought me to a dead stop on the stairs. I was there, breathing heavily, absorbing the pain, when below me the double doors opened and Claire appeared, glancing around then seeing me stranded halfway up the stairs.

'Chris,' she said, 'are you all right?'

I nodded, already moving to join her. Yes, I was all right.

Not long later I was back in Karen's room. This time she said, 'Do you want to speak to me alone, Chris?' and even though it was obvious it was something they'd cooked up while I was away, I agreed, waiting for Juliette, Claire and Bradley to file out and looking around the room as though there might be a hidden social worker somewhere before snapping, 'What are you doing?'

'It's wrong what she did,' said Karen in reply. 'I've told them the truth. I want you to tell them the truth.'

'We can't.' I dropped down into a chair. 'We can't desert Mother.'

'Why?'

'"Why?" Because . . .' I searched for the words. 'Because she's our mother.'

'She's not my mother. She's not your mother.'

'No.' She *is*, I was thinking. She is my mother.

Instead I said, 'Lulu . . .'

'Mary-Beth's told them everything,' said Karen. She always called Lulu Mary-Beth for some reason. Probably still does. Even though Lulu hates it.

'Really?' I said. 'You've spoken to Lulu?'

'Yes.'

I shot her a look. 'You have? You've spoken to Lulu? How is she?'

'I've seen her, Chris. I've met with her.'

I looked at Karen aghast as she told me about Lulu. How, shortly after Mother dropped her off at the Bristol hostel, Lulu had got herself a job in a kitchen, then a boyfriend and then . . .

'Look,' said Karen. She was searching about for something in the room, then found it. Her phone. She handed it to me. 'It's probably best that you speak to her.'

I dialled. I don't know if Lulu had been expecting the call, but she picked up quickly.

'Hello,' she said, and it was her. It was Lulu. I had a sudden keen sense of loss, as though it had been dormant before.

'Hello,' I said, my voice dropping almost to a whisper, nearly hoarse with what would have been an emotional cry if I'd let it come out.

There was a pause. Opposite me, Karen took a seat on the edge of her bed, chewing her lip. I still couldn't get over that she was walking.

'How are you?' said Lulu in my ear. I could hear a baby crying from her end.

'I don't know . . . I'm . . .' I couldn't find the words. Distantly, I wondered why I could hear a baby in the background, then said, 'Lulu, what have you told them?'

'I've told them everything.'

'Oh no,' I said, shaking my head. 'Oh no, I don't believe this. What about Mother? What will happen to Mother?'

'She's not our mother, Chris. She never was. Not our real mother. And she was never a mother to us. I know that now – now that I'm a mother myself.'

'What?' I said, sharply. On the bed, Karen lowered her eyes. She'd known all along, of course.

'Her name is Sofie,' said Lulu, 'that's her you can hear now. She'll be one this year. You're a sort of uncle, Chris.'

I gripped the phone. Squeezed my eyes shut. Still I denied that emotional cry.

Bradley and I stayed at the hospital until about 5 p.m. that day. When we went home it wasn't back into the care of Mother. We went to a new set of carers under the terms of a hastily arranged care order.

I had agreed. I had agreed that 'things' had happened; that Mother had done things to us. And I had agreed to speak to the police about those things. The following day I met DC Victoria Martell for the first time, and she interviewed me. She was then as she was throughout the whole time I knew her: tough, determined, professional – and wearing a pink cardy. I wouldn't say I was the most accommodating interviewee in the history of police investigation – that drilled-in distrust of authority wasn't about to abandon me in a hurry – but she seemed pleased enough at the end of it.

Mother was released on police bail. Later she was charged and released on bail again the conditions of which were that she didn't contact any of us. Of course, she never was one with much respect for stuff like that.

Chapter Fifty-four

*A*ll Bradley and I knew of our real Mum and Dad were the barest details. They were devil worshippers and they lived in a certain street in Cheltenham. Any contact with them throughout the years had been limited to cards they sent to George Dowty Drive, even though they couldn't be sure we still lived there. Mother's campaign of misinformation had extended to convincing them we were living a happier, better-off life in America, but they still sent cards, more in hope, I suppose, than any expectation we might actually get them. When we did, Mother let us look at them, just a glance really, and then we were made to destroy them or throw them away. If there was a fire going in the yard we'd be forced to burn them. They were infected by demons.

For me, they were evil right up until the day we were reunited. I rarely thought of them when I lived with Mother for that very reason. I was, I suppose, scared of them. Brainwashed into being scared of them. Bradley was the same. And then, when Social Services made them aware of the change in our circumstances, my real Mum and Dad asked in return: could they visit their children?

Claire, the social worker, asked us if we'd like to meet our real parents. They'd requested a meeting with us, said Claire, did we want to? Bradley was up for it, of course. Bradley was pretty much in denial about everything that had happened with Mother. For a start, he was never hurt. But he was also so much younger, so he just seemed to bounce from one situation to the other without anything seeming to affect him. I'm sure it did, of course. I'm sure it's left permanent scars, but I wouldn't like to speculate how, and it wasn't visible to the naked eye at that time. He just carried on being Bradley, and meeting our real Mum and Dad was simply one more adventure. When he was told that Dad used to be a Hell's Angel, that was it. He was looking forward to that visit the way most kids look forward to Christmas.

Me, I had mixed feelings about it. I had been brought up to believe that my Mum and Dad were devil worshippers, that they were evil. Even so, I reluctantly agreed, and the meeting was arranged for four o'clock one Wednesday afternoon, early 2005.

It wasn't the first time I'd ever met them, of course, but in a weird way it felt like it was. Beforehand, in Claire's car, I was fidgety and nervous – so much so that I bickered with her for about ten minutes when she told me she was going to take notes at the meeting. No, I said, I didn't want her taking notes. She had to, she argued back. No notes, no meeting. Fine by me, I said. 'But Chris,' whined Bradley from the back seat, 'we've got to meet Dad. He used to be a Hell's Angel.'

I gave in, of course. But still, by the time we walked into the room to find Mum and Dad sitting there, I had added defiance to my original mix of nerves and trepidation.

The building was a Social Services property. They showed us into a large room which contained a low, black coffee table, some plastic school-type chairs, some toys and our Mum and Dad, who sat on the plastic chairs at the opposite end of the room, looking uncomfortable.

I glanced briefly at Mum, who looked as nervous as I was, then at Dad, the same. Then, from behind me, Bradley bounded up to them, taking them both by surprise, giving each of them a hug in turn. There was laughter, slightly forced, halting laughter, neither of them quite sure how to react as Bradley took them in then started looking around for toys to play with. More reserved, I stepped forward and shook them by the hand, almost wanting to play up the formality of the occasion for some reason, I don't know why. Another weird thing: I was finding it difficult to look at Mum, found that I was focusing all my attention on Dad as Bradley took a seat next to him and the two of them started talking – talking about farts.

Looking back, I don't think poor old Dad knew what to do with Bradley apart from join in. So join in he did and, before long, the pair of them were giving each other impressions of their own personal top trumps, me, Mum and Claire staring at them, none of us quite knowing what to say.

I'm not sure if Claire bothered taking notes of that meeting in the end. I wouldn't mind seeing them if she did. Forty-five minutes of a child and a grown man doing fart noises. Now they're the sort of meeting notes I'd love to see.

As we stood to leave, I guess I wasn't the only person in the room glad the ordeal was over. Still, we'd got on sufficiently well to want to meet again, and we did. And again. And again. And I found that I liked my real parents, and they liked me.

Very slowly and gradually, over the course of the next two years, I got to know them, so that now I see them every week, at least. And very slowly I've confided in them just exactly what happened when I lived with Mother. However, it took a while for me to relax enough to do that. And before all that could happen I had stuff to deal with: the guilt, the court case.

Much, much later – when I was, in effect, a different person – I spoke to DC Martell in preparation for this book. She was one of the officers who attended George Dowty Drive on the morning of the raid, and she described Mother as being very cool, calm and collected that day, saying that it was surprising. Anyone would have thought that with all those policemen in her house she would have been shouting and screaming, registering some shock at least. But there was nothing. According to DC Martell, Mother showed no emotion at all.

That morning, the day of the raid, DC Martell had walked

through our house at George Dowty and been shocked at what she saw there. One of the distinguishing features of the whole investigation was that she completely believed in us, the kids, and I'd put money on it being that moment when any doubts she had faded – the moment when the smell hit her as she walked through the house, the boxes and toys and clothes everywhere, the geese living in a cardboard box in the kitchen.

During her interviews, Mother was cold. She was talkative and trying it on with DC Martell the same way she had with everybody else over the years – the social workers, education inspectors, doctors and nurses – providing them with long, plausible answers, bombarding them with information, trying to confuse them, misdirect them. Certain things she admitted in those interviews (perhaps she really did believe there were lie detectors in the cameras), agreeing that she had disciplined us on occasion. She even admitted using the chair torture, although she claimed it was an 'exercise' aimed at improving our weak leg muscles, and that we'd never been forced to endure it for any length of time. She denied ever using sticks during our punishments, of course, because that wouldn't fit with the defence she clung to from the day she was arrested: that the harshest discipline she ever used was a smack on the bottom. A smack on the bottom – that was what she said. Yet the sticks she collected in the farmhouse hadn't been used to smack our bottoms. She'd used them to thrash our feet and for shoving down our throats. And during the investigation DC Martell showed Karen, Lulu and me sticks seized from the house, and we each identified the same sticks: that one was used to beat my feet, that one was shoved down my throat.

Those same sticks were eventually shown in court, as were the photographs – the ones taken on the breakfast-cereal camera. Mainly, though, the prosecution case rested on the evidence given by me, Karen and Lulu. I would have to appear in court.

To understand the impact this had on me at the time means understanding who I was when I was released from Mother. I was . . . different. Put it this way, the person writing this today is a million miles away from the sixteen-year-old of 4 February 2005. I had no education, no social skills. All I knew of life was with Mother. The idea of testifying against her – I can't begin to describe how I felt. Guilt. Blank fear. I remember at the time feeling that things were moving faster than I had a chance to process. Perhaps Mother's whole obsession with control had rubbed off on me because there were moments when I felt like I was losing it, starting with that first police interview when I sat there, DC Martell in the room, her putting events to me, and me thinking, 'God, they know so much. Karen and Lulu have told them so much.' And dismayed because I hadn't wanted to give them as much detail. The sixteen-year-old me wanted them to dance to my tune. But of course that wasn't going to happen. I was young and naïve to ever think it. I was too much Mother's son.

There would be times, between then and the court case, that I'd want to see her. When it seemed that everything was too much for me. There were doctors studying my body for actual scars, other doctors trying to examine my head for psychological ones (the diagnosis was that I had post-traumatic stress disorder, Stockholm syndrome, depression and low self-esteem – we all did), there were police interviews, interviews with social workers. I was coming off the ADHD drugs. It was all too much, and sometimes, God help me, I just wanted to see Mother. And not just see her, either, but go back to her, back to our life together. I felt as though I'd happily return to an existence of beatings and abuse rather than appear in court against her. Anything other than that.

Chapter Fifty-five

A nd why should I, anyway?

Why should I go to court and testify against Mother. Why should I help them when it was they who got me in this situation in the first place? Why the hell should I?

I thought that as I drove in my foster carers' Renault Clio. No licence, no insurance, not a clue. Just one very messed-up kid in a Clio, driving illegally and dangerously on a Tuesday night.

At that time I was going to regular counselling sessions with Jane, and she was helping me to understand that Mother was not a mother, but a Eunice. An evil woman who had locked me up, starved and beaten me, kept me in squalor, denied me of love. She was the opposite of a mother.

But even though I used to hear what Jane said, and at some level, of course, I agreed with her, I still didn't hate Mother, I still thought what I was doing to her was wrong, an act of treachery. A betrayal.

And that was why I was in my new carers' Clio, doing stupid speeds, taking roundabouts recklessly. Dumb, mixed-up kid in a car. I'd told DC Martell I wasn't going to appear. She'd said, Tough, you have to do it. But they couldn't make me do it, could they? Not if I was dead.

There's a road in the area, the Golden Valley, the dual car-riageway that connects Cheltenham and Gloucester, and over it is a cattle bridge that I drove to now.

I'd taken the car before, and I'm sorry to admit to my carers if they ever read this book: I know you found out I took the car once – but actually I'd taken it a few times. At first I just took it because – oh, I'm not sure, really – out of anger, I suppose, resentment and frustration, because I could. Those times I'd taken it because I'd decided I wanted to die. I'd decided that I was going to die a John Hendrickson death, speeding into a central reservation, taking out the Clio and myself with it. I got it up to 75mph, which isn't bad, really, for a Clio, and I was going to smash it into something. But I stopped myself, got my head together and went back home.

And this night, thinking that same thing: Why the hell should I? Why should I testify? I once again crept out and took my foster carers' car, this time driving it to a narrow cattle bridge that crosses the Golden Valley road. And I got out and walked along the bridge, got halfway across, four lanes below me, the traffic sparse because it was so late at night, or early in the morning – I'd lost track of the time – and I stood at the edge and looked down. There was a railing, about waist high. I let it press into my stomach – the feeling of it almost comforting – as I leaned forward and peered over.

Below me was the road, headlights painting it phosphorescent white as cars passed.

They can't make me give evidence, I thought. They can't make me if I climb over the railings then take a step forward, one foot forward, then down to the road below. I'd need to time it, of course, make sure that I got my leap just right so that I'd land in front of a car. But I'd put in enough hours on the PlayStation. I reckoned if anybody could time a leap properly then it'd be a gamer; I'd steered Lara Croft to enough pinpoint landings in my time. (And, no, I wasn't thinking straight. I was a kid on a bridge in the middle of the night. A kid suffering from post-traumatic stress disorder, Stockholm syndrome, depression, and low self-esteem, coming off medication.)

OK, just a case of timing the leap properly.

There were no tears. No howls of frustration into a black and unforgiving night. Like Mother I was cold, no emotion. I stepped over the railing, onto a tiny concrete ledge, which was now all there was between me and the road below.

How far was it? How long would it take me to fall?

(And would I go head first or feet first? Would I scream? If it were possible to somehow take a photograph of me as I fell, what would my expression be like? Would I regret it as soon as I took that final step? Would I twist and try to grab the concrete cattle bridge but miss, and fall anyway?)

Have to time it, that's the thing.

A car beeped. A car directly below me. The shock almost jerked me off the bridge and I had to grab the railing to stop from falling. Another car, I saw, slowed, was flashing its lights either to attract my attention or warn oncoming traffic. A second horn sounded. Oh God, the traffic – especially the oncoming carriageway directly below me – was slowing. Nobody stopped – at least there was that – but they were aware of me. They were beeping, flashing their lights, shifting into the other lane.

Dazzled by yet another set of full beams, I stepped back and swung my right leg over the railings, thinking I'd try again when the traffic had got back to its normal speed. This time, though, there'd be no hanging around. I'd have to time my jump quickly, perhaps even before I got over the railings . . .

I felt the pain in my left leg as I pulled it back over the railings, heard Jane's voice in my head telling me that Eunice was not my mother, that what she had done to me was wrong.

No, I decided, making my way back to the car. Tonight was not the night. And I got back in, drove home, parked it and went to my room, where I timed leaps with Lara Croft on the PlayStation. I didn't attempt suicide after that. Not because I immediately stopped wanting to die. Just that it seemed – I don't know – so *uncertain.*

*

The year passed. I passed it by playing PlayStation, with the occasional secret binges on alcohol to dull my daily pain (until my carers caught on and started hiding the drink in the house), and also by going to reintegration school, where I began catching up on the things I had missed. I caught on quickly. They found me work experience in retail sales and there I did well, managing to impress my employees despite the fact I didn't have the necessary qualifications – well, *any* qualifications – and that led to the job I still have now. I can't say where or what it is, obviously, but it's working for a large retailer you would have heard of. I loved it. I threw myself into it.

Always, though, the threat of the trial hung over me. And still I seemed hard-wired to believe I was betraying Mother. I was helping 'them' against her. And at nights I'd be visited not only by the memories of things that had happened, but by feelings of guilt, buffeting me, gnawing away at me.

Chapter Fifty-six

'Hello, Christopher.'

I didn't hear it, but I saw her lips move. I stopped, stared at her. In my ears, my iPod blared 'The Final Countdown' by Europe. That song, or something just as cheesy. I was really into big, epic, inspirational songs at the time. All part of my recovery.

Which, in one fell swoop, took a massive step backwards as I stood looking at Mother, who had been waiting for me on the petrol station forecourt, my stomach instantly tightening into a knot so I thought that I might be sick (oh, please no, not again), feeling all of a sudden at a loss and disconnected, forgetting where I was, what I was doing there. Everything at that moment compressed. To just me. And her.

She wasn't supposed to be anywhere near me, of course. She wasn't supposed to contact me, talk to me, anything, but here she was, her trial due to begin at the end of the year.

It was 2006 then, and I hadn't seen her for almost two years. I'd done nothing but think about her, of course, but I had not seen her, not until now. I'd been coming out of work, popping across to the garage to get some lunch, not really paying a great deal of attention to the Volvo parked under the canopy, my headphones blaring out feel-good cheese. It wasn't a car I recognized anyway. She'd changed it. A Volvo 850T. As I drew close, the door had opened and she'd stepped out, the sight of her stopping me in my tracks.

'Hello, Christopher,' she mouthed again, and I reached to flick the earphones out of my ears.

'Hello . . .' I started, realizing I didn't know how to address her, instinct wanting me to say 'Mother', the influence of my counselling preventing me, so instead I just said, 'Hello . . .' letting it tail off.

If the stilted greeting bothered her she didn't show it. She looked the same, I noticed. Older, perhaps. A little more drawn. It didn't make her any less terrifying.

'How are you?' she asked. Somehow she made it sound like a threat.

We stood a few feet apart. Not far away, drivers manned petrol pumps and squinted up at whizzing numbers on meters. Inside the garage shop, customers queued up to pay.

'I'm OK,' I said, trying to keep my voice steady.

'Good, good.' She didn't smile. 'And how's Bradley?'

'He's fine,' I managed, trying a smile. 'Same old Bradley.'

'Is he at school?'

'Yes.'

'Where are they teaching him?'

'Oh . . .' Thank God I had the presence of mind to lie. 'I'm not sure actually.'

'Right.' A twitching at the corner of the lips, like she knew I was lying. Like she wanted to stride forward and slap me across the face the way she had done hundreds of times before.

'How is Granddad?' I asked.

'He's very ill, I'm afraid. Very ill. But hanging in there.'

'Right, right,' I nodded.

There was a silence. On the road beside us, cars passed.

'I've got to go, I only have fifteen minutes,' I lied.

'OK,' she said, that same tightening of the lips.

'OK,' I said, 'Goodbye,' and I ran, as though scooting quickly back to work. I didn't bother about the sandwich, I just ran. How did she know? I wondered, as I darted back to the safety of the shop. How did she know to wait for me here? Had she been to the shop before? Hung around? Had she seen what time I usually came for lunch, the fact that I always came across the road and to the garage?

Yes, was the answer. And it awoke sleeping fear in the pit of my stomach. Of course she had. Coming here was her way of saying, 'I know where you are. I know what you do. *I can reach you.*'

The second time she came, she had backup. A big guy, a friend of the family, who said nothing but hung back, a huge intimidating presence behind her.

They'd been waiting just outside the foyer of the shop, and it was later this time, about 7.30 p.m., when I came out, saw them there, felt that same space-closing-in shock as we once more came face to face.

Over the way, one of my mates from the shop was collecting trolleys and saw us there. Later, he'd testify in court against her, when she faced a charge of perverting the course of justice, for which she was found guilty. I don't know where he is now, that guy, but I owe him one.

She was more abrupt this time, as though she'd decided to get down to business, and I'd hardly had time to process the surprise of her being there before she was firing questions at me.

'How's Bradley?' her voice sharp and hard.

'He's OK,' I stammered, eyes flitting to the big guy behind her. He wasn't just there to give her a bit of company, I was certain of that.

'Why are you doing this?' she snapped.

'What?' I said.

Flinty eyes said: Don't mess me about. 'Taking me to court,' she spat.

'I've got no choice,' I replied, 'it's the police doing it now, not me.'

Which was the truth. When things had been bad I'd told DC Martell I wanted to withdraw my statements, but she was having none of it. It didn't matter, she said. The trial was going ahead with me as a witness whether I liked it or not.

'Drop the charges,' said Mother now, 'and you can have the narrow boat. You can have the *Charlotte*, all to yourself. Your mother's in a wheelchair, you can take her on holidays.'

No reference to my mother worshipping the devil – perhaps for the first time ever.

Then, without saying another word, or even waiting for my answer, she turned, and she and the big guy returned to their car. Another different car, I noticed. A Golf.

I didn't give it a second thought, her offer, by the way. Well, maybe a second thought, but not a third or a fourth. Turned out she'd sold the narrow boat anyway.

DC Martell got wind of the visits via my carers, who had worked out something was wrong. At first I denied they'd happened, but as with every other aspect of the case, DC Martell was tenacious and she used to come into the shop to speak to me. In the end I gave in and told her what had happened, and they added that charge to what was already a pretty hefty list: page after page of assault, cruelty, wounding, indecent assault and, now, perverting the course of justice. There were thirty-eight counts in all.

Those indecent-assault charges, incidentally. She was found not guilty of those charges and therefore I can't discuss them. What I will say is that there are things that happened during my life with Mother that I can never talk about. There are things I have never told anyone, and never will. Likewise, during the course of this book I haven't spoken much about the abuse endured by Karen and Lulu, though it was as regular and as harsh as that given to me. The reason for this is because what happened to them is their story. It belongs to them and it's up to them to tell it, if and when they want to. I can only tell mine.

Chapter Fifty-seven

The date of the trial was moved – for administrative reasons, I think – so a new date was set, this time for November 2006.

I was seventeen then, so I'd be giving my evidence via video link, which was the only saving grace of the whole process as far as I was concerned. Then, Mother sacked her defence team. Apparently the judge was livid, but it's her right to do that, so the trial had to be postponed. A new date was set, this one for March 2007, by which time I would be eighteen and I would have to give my evidence live in court.

The day I heard that news, I got drunk. I got drunk a lot around that time. Jane helped me get over that.

About a month before the trial, DC Martell set up a visit to Bristol Crown Court, when Karen, Lulu and I got to see the actual courtroom.

It was empty. I remember Karen went and sat on the judge's seat, grinning at us all, pretending to bang a gavel. Every now and then it would dawn on me: she can walk. The way she scampered about the courtroom that day, it was like she was still captivated by the novelty of the idea herself.

And then it came round; the month passed. We three children would all give evidence. Only Bradley was excused. We would each be at court only for the time we were needed; the rest of the time, Bristol Crown Court was out of bounds.

It was a Thursday, the morning I appeared. DC Martell arranged a car for me, my foster carer Ray, plus my guardian social worker for the trip, Phil. There was already press interest, with photographers outside the court, so I was asked to duck down as we approached the court – luckily it was a Ford Mondeo. Black. Plenty of legroom.

From the car, we took a lift down to the witness-protection room, where I sat with a cup of coffee, making small talk with Ray and Phil, waiting to be called. I looked at my watch. It was 9 a.m.

'Are you nervous?' asked Phil.

'No,' I lied, but I was. Or was I? I don't know, everything was so unreal: the Black Mondeo; me, with my entourage of social workers and police, being bundled down in the back of the car; then this place, the courthouse and witness-protection room.

In the last year or so I'd had a crash course in real life, I'd seen enough interview suites, consulting rooms and hospitals to last me forever, but even so, all this was so new. What I felt sitting there wasn't so much nerves as a kind of wonder.

And then she came to get me, a girl from the Crown Prosecution Service. Ten o'clock it was, almost on the dot. She led me up a set of stairs to the ground floor, paused a moment as she reached the door, looked at me, gave me a reassuring smile, opened the door and ushered me through.

Immediately I glanced at the box where Mother sat. Or, where she would have sat, I should say, if she'd been there. But she wasn't. One of the things they'd told me in preparation for the day was that she would be led out of the courtroom before I entered. The idea was I wouldn't see her, and I didn't, not that day at least. The witness box had a curtain drawn around it and I stepped up into the box, took a seat, got my bearings. From behind the curtain I could see the judge, the jury, the barristers, but not where the accused sat, nor the press or public gallery.

They swore me in. Then the prosecution barrister began asking me questions and it was immediately weird because I'd been expecting an easier ride than I actually got. After all, he was the prosecution; he was on my side, right? At times it felt like he wasn't – almost as though he was trying to trip me up. Before my appearance, he and DC Martell had both briefed me on what to expect and either it was a deliberate tactic so I would look as genuine and natural as possible, or they just hadn't done a very good job, because I immediately felt under attack. He wanted me to go into so much more detail than I had expected to. He'd constantly ask me if I was sure, as though he didn't want to take my word for things. I asked for a fifteen-minute break, to calm down and collect my thoughts, and they took me back down to the witness-protection room. Then it was lunch and I wanted to leave the courthouse but wasn't allowed, I had Ray and Phil following me around and, believe me, the novelty of having my own entourage was beginning to wear off by then – I just wanted to be left alone. I just wanted to be left alone and for the questions to stop.

Except they didn't. After lunch they resumed, and along similar lines as before, until 3 p.m., when the prosecution finished and I asked for a break before the defence began their questioning. Exhausted, I went back to the witness-protection room, where I sat for fifteen minutes, then twenty, then thirty, then forty, and by now I was beginning to wonder what on earth was going on when Ray went to find out what the hold-up was all about. He came back and told me that court had been suspended for the day because Eunice's father had died.

I'm not sure if Ray knew how close I was to Granddad; that during the last months of my time with Mother I'd been his carer.

Sitting there in the witness-protection room I let the news settle around me. It wasn't unexpected, I suppose. That day at the garage Mother had said he was only just hanging on, and he'd been chronically ill when I last saw him. But still. Nothing really prepares you. I pictured him in Florida, pretending to be asleep, moaning about the TV channels. I pictured him reading the newspaper in the bungalow, saying, 'Morning, little man.'

I wondered how Mother had taken the news.

*

The next day was Friday, when I was supposed to be questioned by the defence. But as a mark of respect for Granddad proceedings were adjourned until Monday. I guess the jurors must have loved that, a day off. But for me it meant a nervous and uncomfortable weekend mulling over the ordeal to come.

Which, in the end, wasn't that much of an ordeal, funnily enough. It was so not-much-of-an-ordeal that I became overconfident, which, I was later told, could have worked against us. The main thrust of the defence seemed to be that I was inventing details of the abuse having read about them in the book *A Child Called "It"*, which, given all the physical evidence, seemed ludicrous.

Later in the proceedings, which went on for five weeks, press interest growing by the day, the prosecution presented other, expert, witnesses. Out came a paediatrician, a psychiatrist and a forensic medical examiner, each of whom explained to the court what damage had been inflicted by our mother, the forensic medical examiner telling how many layers of skin needed to be flayed away before a scar would form, and how the marks that showed up all over my body were fully consistent with an extended period of abuse. DC Martell told me all of this, later. I also heard that Mother smiled when the jury came back with the verdict, finding her guilty on twenty-six of the thirty-eight charges. And not just a little smile, either, but a broad grin.

I wonder why? I wonder why Mother grinned like that. Who knows, perhaps she was smiling at the not-guilty verdicts on the indecent assault charges. Perhaps the cruelty and assault and wounding were one thing in her mind, the indecent assault quite another. Perhaps she was also pleased about another count for which she was also found not guilty, where she was charged with unlawfully and maliciously wounding me by cutting my penis with a knife. And just to clarify, she was found not guilty of that. Yet I have a wound that doctors say means I can never have children.

*

OK, deep breath.

I was at work the day of the sentencing. It was weird, because all through the trial there was never a single doubt in my mind that she would be found guilty, so when the verdict was announced I hardly turned a hair. The sentencing, though. I think we'd expected something like eight years, but the judge really threw the book at her, one of the worst cases he'd seen in forty years, he said. And Mother's demeanour during the trial had shocked him, too, he said, adding, 'It's difficult for anyone to understand how any human being could have even contemplated what you did, let alone with the regularity and premeditation you employed.'

He gave her fourteen years.

DC Martell, who the judge commended for being meticulous and scrupulous, said that Mother showed no emotion during the sentencing. I wonder if that was why the judge was so harsh with the jail sentence. All though the trial she had been cold, showing no emotion, even smiling sometimes. I wonder if the judge saw the same smile that I saw, that day of my appearance at court, when the defence had finished his questioning and I was allowed to step down.

It had all seemed over quite quickly, the defence bit. Mother's barrister accused me of cribbing my life from a book, and I told him flatly that wasn't the case, end of conversation, or that's what it felt like. Then, when it was over, the judge had motioned for Mother to leave the courtroom, then indicated to me that I should leave, too. But she wasn't quite out of the door, and I was so desperate to get out of the witness box that I took off the second he gave me the go-ahead.

And as I descended the two steps to the floor of the courtroom I glanced over, catching sight of Mother, who was looking behind her, and our eyes met.

That same compressed moment. She smiled at me. A thin, tight-lipped smile that was close to a smirk. Above that, nothing.

Her eyes were dead.

List of five life-changingly cool things I've done since being released from my evil foster mother Eunice Spry

1. Test-driven an E60 BMW M5
2. Got to know my real Mum and Dad
3. Appeared on *This Morning* and Sky TV
4. Written this book
5. Started my new life without her

Epilogue

And now I'm sitting in the green room in the ITV studios in London, the room where they put the guests before the show, just me and Jane in there at present, though other people are always in and out: other guests, production assistants wearing headsets and carrying clipboards.

In the room there is coffee and pastries laid out on a table, fruit juice, too, but neither Jane nor I are peckish. I don't know about her, but I'm too nervous to eat. Or, not nervous so much, but filled with that same sense of weird, spaced-out wonder I had when I appeared in court. Jane and I are making small talk, but I'm also running through my head what they might ask me. I've done the Sky interview, and I've done a press briefing – both in front of the cameras – but the Sky interview was quite short and the press briefing was scripted. This is different. This is *This Morning* with Philip Schofield and Fern Britton; plus the agony aunt, Denise Robertson, is sitting in, too, so the chances are it'll be more in-depth than anything I've done before. They'll want to know how I feel about Mother now, which is something I haven't yet worked out – something I'm still getting to grips with even now. Maybe they'll want to know what I think of the sentence, and if they do I'll tell them I think it seems fair, because it's almost as though she has a year for every year of abuse inflicted on us, which I think has a nice symmetry. Of course, I'm hoping they won't want to know too much about the actual abuse, and it's an early-morning programme so I'm assuming they won't want me to go too in-depth about the time I had my face pushed into faecal matter, or the time I was made to lick up vomit from the floor, or was dragged behind a van. I don't suppose they'll ask much about my plans for the future, either, but if they do I'll tell them that they include hopefully getting my leg and other injuries mended, passing my driving test, getting a car and moving into my own place. Also, one day, I'd like to join the police force, and not, as you might think, so I can pose around in fast cars, but for another reason. So I can do what DC Martell did. So I can believe in children.

Like to start a family one day, Chris? Well, no, I can't do that. But even if I could, would I? Would I want to? They say there's a circle of abuse where the victim becomes the abuser. Is that me? Could it ever be me? I don't think so, no, but it's something to keep an eye on, I suppose. Something I'll have to work through. Put it on the list, along with everything else.

Along with the guilt, of course. The guilt I feel. An unwanted guest in my head that still won't go. The guilt I feel at putting her in jail. Because you shouldn't, should you? You shouldn't help put your own mother behind bars.

Except she's not your mother, is she, Chris? I'd heard it from Jane and Graeme. From Karen and Lulu, and from DC Martell. From all of the people I'd met in the outside world who had helped me to understand that I am not a demon child, not the scum of the earth. That I am worthy of this life. And that life is worth living.

The door to the green room opens and a production assistant enters, headset round her neck, clipboard held like a shield. She looks at Jane and me, then at her clipboard, running a pen down it as she speaks.

'You're . . .' she says, checking down, 'Christopher, are you?'

I agree I am.

'OK, great . . . and you're here for the item about . . .'

She pauses.

I lean forward, about to help her out, finish her sentence for her by saying, 'That's right, about my mother,' then stop myself, catching sight of Jane and hearing all those voices in my head, saying instead, 'That's right. About Eunice Spry.'